THE AD-FREE BRAND

Secrets to Building Successful Brands in a Digital World

Chris Grams

800 East 96th Street
Indianapolis, Indiana 46240 USA

The Ad-Free Brand: Secrets to Building Successful Brands in a Digital World

Copyright © 2012 by Christopher Grams

ISBN-13: 978-0-7897-4802-7 ISBN-10: 0-7897-4802-9

Library of Congress Cataloging-in-Publication Data:

Printed in the United States of America

First Printing: August 2011

Trademarks

Warning and Disclaimer

Bulk Sales

Que Publishing offers excellent discounts on this book when ordered in quantity for bulk purchases or special sales. For more information, please contact

U.S. Corporate and Government Sales
1-800-382-3419
corpsales@pearsontechgroup.com

For sales outside of the U.S., please contact

International Sales
international@pearson.com

Associate Publisher
Greg Wiegand

Acquisitions Editor
Rick Kughen

Development Editor
Rick Kughen

Managing Editor
Sandra Schroeder

Project Editor
Seth Kerney

Copy Editor
Megan Wade

Indexer
Cheryl Lenser

Proofreader
Leslie Joseph

Technical Editor
Jonathan Opp

Publishing Coordinator
Cindy Teeters

Interior Designer
Anne Jones

Cover Designer
Anne Jones

Compositor
Bronkella Publishing, Inc.

CONTENTS AT A GLANCE

what is Teqqa in
their minds?
a
[the market]

TABLE OF CONTENTS

About the Author

 Chris Grams is president and partner at New Kind, where he builds sustainable brands, cultures, and communities in and around organizations. The open source way—including themes like openness, collaboration, transparency, community, and meritocracy—is a key influence in his work.

Previously, Chris spent 10 years at Red Hat, the world's leading supplier of open source solutions, where he played a key role in building the Red Hat brand and culture, most recently in the role of senior director, Brand Communications + Design.

Chris blogs about the "dark matter" of organizations—brand, community, and culture—at Dark Matter Matters (www.darkmattermatters.com) and about the intersection of the open source way and business at opensource.com. He is also the Community Guide on Gary Hamel's Management Innovation Exchange (www.hackmanagement.com), where he often writes about how to enable communities of passion in and around organizations.

We Want to Hear from You!

As the reader of this book, *you* are our most important critic and commentator. We value your opinion and want to know what we're doing right, what we could do better, what areas you'd like to see us publish in, and any other words of wisdom you're willing to pass our way.

As an editor-in-chief for Que Publishing, I welcome your comments. You can email or write me directly to let me know what you did or didn't like about this book—as well as what we can do to make our books better.

Please note that I cannot help you with technical problems related to the topic of this book. We do have a User Services group, however, where I will forward specific technical questions related to the book.

When you write, please be sure to include this book's title and author as well as your name, email address, and phone number. I will carefully review your comments and share them with the author and editors who worked on the book.

Email: feedback@quepublishing.com

Mail: Greg Wiegand
         Editor-in-Chief
         Que Publishing
         800 East 96th Street
         Indianapolis, IN 46240 USA

Reader Services

Visit our website and register this book at informit.com/register for convenient access to any updates, downloads, or errata that might be available for this book.

Introduction

Do you dream of building a world-class brand? If so, your time has come.

In the past, great brands were only within the reach of the organizations with the biggest marketing budgets.

Today you can build a powerful, enduring brand at an amazingly low cost—without expensive ad campaigns, huge budgets, self-interested outside agencies, or deep specialized expertise.

So if you lack the money for an expensive advertising campaign, if you question the value of your current marketing and advertising strategies, or you'd like to move beyond superficial applications of the latest digital media tools, you've come to the right place.

The Ad-Free Brand is a complete, step-by-step guide to building a brand from the inside out, using the energy and passion of the community of people who care about it most, both inside and around the organization.

Why an Ad-Free Brand?

Every day advertising appears somewhere new—on an airplane tray table, on the sidewalk, in our schools, written in the sky, printed on our clothes, embedded in our favorite TV shows.

In fact, it may be quicker for you to name the places where you *do not* see advertising today than to name the places you do (if you can think of any at all). Yet traditional advertising has never been less effective than it is today. It has become background noise filtered out by our brains before most of it can even register.

I reject the notion that adding to the clutter of advertising is a necessary element of building a great brand.

ad-free brand: A brand built from the inside out using the energy and passion of the community of people who care about it most, both inside and around the organization.

I believe money and time can be much better spent investing in meaningful, productive relationships with the community of people in and around the organization who care deeply about a brand. These people are an energy source waiting to be activated. Properly engaged, they can help your brand succeed in ways that advertising never will. And a new breed of digital media tools and strategies has made it easier and cheaper to identify, organize, and motivate your brand community than ever before.

The Ad-Free Brand marries the classic positioning principles used to develop many of the great brands of the twentieth century to the new community-building strategies and tools now available for twenty-first-century brands.

The best of the old world meets the best of the new.

Who Can Use This Book

You don't need a marketing background or previous marketing experience to build a great brand. Some of the best new brands are being built by people who wouldn't consider themselves marketing experts at all.

I've written this book to be useful to anyone who is interested in building a world-class brand. So, whether you have 25 years of brand experience or no experience, whether you are in an organization of 10,000 employees or CEO in a company of 1, you can use the concepts you'll find in these pages to build a more valuable, enduring brand.

Do any of the following statements describe you?

- I'm interested in reducing or eliminating advertising, marketing, or PR expenses where I am receiving little value in return.

- I'm competing against organizations I'll never be able to outspend.

- I'd like to develop more valuable, sustainable relationships with customers, employees, or other communities.

- I see the benefit of building a more resilient, enduring brand that can weather crises that might destroy other brands.

- I'd like to nurture a community of people that will be open to—and even prefer—new products, services, and ideas from my organization.

- I'd like to innovate faster and incorporate the ideas of the people in the communities surrounding my brand.

- I'd like to ensure my organization is successful at recruiting and retaining the best and most passionate workforce available.

By the time we are done here, you'll have the knowledge you need to create a great brand of your own that can do all these things—at a lower cost than was ever possible before.

What's in This Book

The Ad-Free Brand is a step-by-step guide to building a brand using a collaborative, community-based approach I learned during my 10 years helping build a $1 billion brand at Red Hat, the world's leading open source software company.

In this book, you'll learn how to conduct simple, inexpensive research to uncover what your brand stands for today and what people might value in it in the future. You'll learn how to develop brand positioning that is desirable to your community, deliverable by the brand, and differentiated from the competition by collaborating with trusted members of your brand community. Finally, I'll share techniques and strategies for rolling out this positioning internally and externally in meaningful ways without resorting to advertising.

Once you've finished, you'll know how to:

- Sidestep the clutter, cost, and ineffectiveness of traditional advertising

- Identify "points of difference" your customers will really value

- Develop brand positioning that feels true because it *is* true
- Dramatically reduce the cost of brand research
- Build your brand by guiding, influencing, and *being*—not *telling*
- Quickly prototype your brand positioning and apply what you learn
- Empower the brand advocates who know and love you best
- Communicate brand positioning with low-cost social and web tools
- Adapt classic positioning techniques for today's new world
- Consistently focus first on low-cost, high-value strategies
- Evolve your brand for changing markets, customers, products, and services

Sound interesting? Then keep reading—it's time to build an ad-free brand of your own.

1

Genesis

It must have been fun to be in charge of a big twentieth-century brand. Things were a lot simpler then. You could easily control the direction of your brand image because there were only a few vehicles, in particular advertising and PR, through which the brand story could be told.

Great brands were built on the back of great advertising campaigns. Advertising was heroic. Great advertising could build a brand from nothing. Or it could be the savior of a troubled brand.

Many of the classic heroic advertising campaigns were born in the post-World War II era, as mass consumerism started to really hit its stride in America. Famous examples like the Volkswagen campaign to "Think Small" (named by Advertising Age as the top advertising campaign of the twentieth century[1]) were even able to create a market for a product where one didn't exist before.

But during the 1960s, while great advertising minds at the big agencies like DDB, Young and Rubicam, and Ogilvy and Mather were doing some of their best work, deep within the United States Department of Defense, the seeds of the future of branding were being sown.

---

1. You can find the full list of *Advertising Age*'s 1999 list of the best advertising campaigns of the twentieth 20th century at http://adage.com/century/campaigns.html.

The Internet Revolution

I doubt there was much talk about the future of branding in October 1969 when the folks at the Department of Defense Advanced Research Projects Agency connected the first two nodes of what would later become the Internet.

But the Internet, which has dramatically changed the landscape of our whole world in so many ways over the past 20 years, has had an equally explosive impact on the way brands are built.

The Internet is a great equalizer, and while we don't often stop to analyze its broad-reaching impacts (that would cut into our Facebook and Twitter time!), it probably makes sense to take a few minutes to highlight the differences between the pre-Internet and post-Internet branding world that paved the way for the emergence of what I call the *ad-free brand*.

To Be, Rather Than to Seem to Be

In the pre-Internet world, great brands were built by *telling*. An organization told the story of its brand, primarily through advertising and PR, and the story was consumed by an audience. Organizations talked, people listened (or didn't).

Great twenty-first-century brands won't be built by telling; they will be built by *being*.

Today, organizations must *live their brands* through everything they say and do. In large part due to the power the Internet gives to the consumers of brands, it is no longer enough for brands to simply tell their story through advertising and PR. In fact, for many twenty-first-century organizations, advertising and PR are neither the most efficient nor cost-effective ways to build a brand.

> Great twenty-first-century brands won't be built by telling; they will be built by *being*.

My home state of North Carolina has a motto: *Esse quam videri*, which translates as "To be, rather than to seem to be."

The roots of the phrase can be traced back to the works of Aeschylus, Plato, and Cicero,[2] but it was also famously flipped around by Machiavelli in *The Prince* to read *videri quam esse*: "To seem rather than to be" (Machiavelli used this phrase to describe how he thought a ruler should act).

Maybe *seeming* rather than *being* worked in the 1500s during Machiavelli's time, or even in the 1950s. But, in the age of the Internet, the organizations that spend their energy seeming rather than being do so at their own risk.

---

2. http://en.wikipedia.org/wiki/Esse_quam_videri

Ask BP, whose "Beyond Petroleum" advertising campaign will likely go down as the most devastating, expensive brand positioning disaster in history.

BEYOND PETROLEUM: A CASE OF *VIDERI QUAM ESSE?*

In 2000, British Petroleum hired one of the top advertising and PR agencies in the world, Ogilvy and Mather, to help them attempt a global brand transformation following the acquisition of Amoco and a few other small organizations.

Their goal was to reposition BP "as transcending the oil sector, delivering top-line growth while remaining innovative, progressive, environmentally responsible and performance-driven." This quote came directly from an Ogilvy and Mather success story about BP (since removed from their website). The success story stated that the launch of the new "Beyond Petroleum" brand positioning "far exceeded expectations" and resulted in high brand credibility and favorability scores and two *PR Week* Campaign of the Year awards.

A job well done? Perhaps, according to advertising standards.

But BP's new brand promise wasn't in alignment with the actual BP brand experience. In fact, during the first quarter of 2009, 98% of BP's revenues still came from oil and gas.[3]

Disaster struck in April 2010, when the Deepwater Horizon drilling rig exploded in the Gulf of Mexico. The explosion killed 11 people, injured 17, and created an underwater gusher that could not be stopped for almost 90 days. By the time the well was capped, over 200 million gallons of crude oil had spilled into the Gulf, creating one of the worst environmental disasters in American history.

The Deepwater Horizon incident led to an enormous backlash against the company, and the facade of the "Beyond Petroleum" brand positioning quickly came down.

By building a brand position based on seeming rather than being, and getting caught in the act by an angry public, BP created a branding nightmare from which the organization will be hard-pressed to recover.

Losing Control

Pre-Internet brands were Machiavellian in more ways than one. Before the Internet, organizations had complete control over almost every aspect of their brand images.

---

3. http://www.walletpop.com/2010/06/11/bp-before-the-oil-spill-an-environmentally-friendly-company/

When the brand could be built through advertising and PR, the marketing folks controlled the brand.

Today, organizations no longer *control* their brand so much as they attempt to *curate* it. Brands are no longer built inside the walls of corporations, but instead they are built together by organizations and the communities of customers, contributors, partners, advocates, and detractors surrounding them. In the best cases, this relationship becomes a beautiful friendship, but in the worst cases, brands can actually be hijacked by their communities.

Scott Bedbury, the branding legend who helped build both the Nike and Starbucks brands in the '80s and '90s, uses the metaphor of the brand as a sponge. I've always remembered this quote of his, which I believe is an exceptionally good way to describe a modern brand.

> "Brands are sponges for content, for images, for fleeting feelings. They become psychological concepts held in the minds of the public, where they may stay forever. As such, you can't entirely control a brand. At best you can only guide and influence it."[4]

If a brand is a sponge that soaks up everything it comes into contact with, branding can no longer be viewed as the job of the marketing department or advertising agency alone. In the twenty-first century, branding becomes a cultural function and the job of every person inside an organization. And if you are lucky, many people outside the organization will view branding as their job as well.

The Second Internet Revolution

If the rise of the Internet was the first great disruption to the brand-building status quo, a second Internet revolution began even more suddenly in the first few years of the twenty-first century with the mass popularization of user-generated content and social media tools.

It wasn't so long ago that the only people with websites and blogs were those with the technical savvy to build them. But as we entered the twenty-first century, services like Blogger, MySpace, and later WordPress, Facebook, LinkedIn, and YouTube made it possible for anyone to have a presence on the Web. These tools flooded the world with new content and new voices.

For advertising and PR, this democratization of content represented a huge threat. The airwaves were no longer controlled solely by those who could afford to buy advertising, airtime, or influence with the news media. Instead, anyone could publish his own content whenever he wanted, and many did. The signal-to-noise ratio

---

4. This quote is from page 46 of Scott Bedbury's book *A New Brand World*.

went up, and advertising and PR began to lose their monopoly on the messages and stories reaching consumers.

What's more, we consumers gained the ability to amplify our own voices to compete with advertisers. If we didn't like what an organization was saying, had an issue with a product or service, or believed advertising to be inauthentic to the true experience of a brand, we could say so on our blogs, on our Facebook pages, on discussion boards, and in many cases even on the organization's own website.

If enough people agreed and spoke up together, the combined impact of all of these individual voices could even exceed the impact of advertising. Social media tools amplified the power of the individual even more because they made it much easier for people to instantaneously share thoughts and ideas, likes and dislikes.

Today, the traditional brand monologue is becoming instead a lively conversation engaging brands and the members of communities that surround them. People who are interested in the brand are now as much in control of the brand as any branding expert within an organization. In fact, what the organization says about its own brand has become less and less relevant as brand communities begin to drown out advertising and marketing.

What's the bottom line?

Where before the Internet, companies controlled nearly all of the stories relating to their brands, twenty-first-century brands control only a small percentage of the stories related to their brands.

For the vast majority of organizations, advertising and PR are no longer the most significant drivers of the success or failure of brand efforts.

...advertising and PR are no longer the most significant drivers of the success or failure of brand efforts.

All Is Not Yet Lost

If you are reading this book, you are probably interested in building and positioning a brand successfully. Right now you may feel very depressed about your prospects of doing this well, given the loss of control and the increasing uselessness of some of branding's most powerful traditional tools.

Sorry about that.

I once received a fortune cookie with a fortune that read "all is not yet lost." It struck me as a poetic combination of depression and hope.

Remember the last two lines of the Scott Bedbury quote: *"You can't entirely control a brand. At best you can only guide and influence it."*

I first read these words almost 10 years ago, when I was working for a small, growing technology company that didn't really advertise—not because it didn't want to, but because it couldn't afford to. We learned how to build an ad-free brand by guiding and influencing, by being rather than telling, because we had no other choice.

As I write this book in 2011, this ad-free technology brand is on the verge of becoming 1 of only about 20 software firms in history to surpass $1 billion in annual revenues.[5]

My Experience at Red Hat

When I joined the Red Hat marketing department in July of 1999, the company had just over 100 employees, almost all of whom worked in a small, one-story building hidden at the back of a nondescript office park in Durham, North Carolina.

I think I was the eighth person to join the marketing department, led at the time by Lisa Sullivan, who had been hired as co-founder Bob Young's first employee back in 1994. We were a young, eager, but relatively inexperienced group.

I'd spent the two previous years in a marketing role at IBM, but prior to that virtually my entire career had been spent in book publishing as an editor and a literary agent. I considered myself a writer, an editor, and a communicator, but I never for a second thought of myself as a marketing person.

The single biggest branding event in the history of the company (perhaps even to this day) came about a month after I joined, when the company went public at the height of the Internet bubble in one of the most explosive initial public offerings (IPOs) ever.

Figure 1.1 *On August 11, 1999, Red Hat's IPO day, staff members watch the stock rise on CNBC. (Photo by Chris Grams)*

---

5. This was first reported in an article in *Forbes* magazine on November 30, 2010, entitled "Red Hat at $1 Billion." You can read it here: http://blogs.forbes.com/ciocentral/2010/11/30/red-hat-at-1-billion/

Red Hat stock opened at $14 a share and ended its first day of trading at $52 a share, raising almost $84 million and setting the stage for a series of other record-breaking open source software company IPOs.

In one day, what had been a relatively obscure technology brand known only to a small fringe group of open source enthusiasts became a mainstream brand with a $3 billion market cap being mentioned in the same sentence with industry titans like Microsoft and Sun.

By the time I left Red Hat in early 2010, the company had grown to over 3,000 employees in 50+ offices in 28 countries around the world.

Most people who have heard of Red Hat now think of it as a Linux or open-source company. Certainly the company did well because it was one of the first to success-fully employ a unique business and innovation model based on open source soft-ware. But fewer people realize that Red Hat also built a unique brand, culture, and community model deeply inspired by the open source way, as well.

I believe this model was a critical element in Red Hat's success. My partners and I at New Kind founded our business on the idea that the same brand, culture, and com-munity model we employed at Red Hat could be used to build great brands in any organization of any size in any industry without the need for the expensive adver-tising campaigns of the past.

Powerful, enduring brands, built at a lower cost than was ever possible before?

Absolutely. All is certainly not yet lost.

The Ad-Free Brand: Built from the Inside Out

So how do you create an ad-free brand? You build it *from the inside out*, using the timeless brand positioning principles found in the core of the greatest brands of the twentieth century, but applying them in a new kind of way for a new kind of world.

Where twentieth-century brands were built through strong positioning repeated over and over in advertising and PR campaigns, ad-free brands are built by empow-ering the people who know and love the brand the most to *be* the brand: your employees, customers, and others citizens of the communities that surround your organization.

Esse quam videri, in all its ad-free glory.

What Is Brand Positioning?

Like many of you, I'd been familiar with the concept of brand positioning for as long as I could remember, and I had even participated in several positioning proj-ects over the years.

But when Red Hat CEO Matthew Szulik walked up to my desk one day in 2001 with a copy of the Jack Trout and Al Ries book *Positioning: The Battle for Your Mind* and a simple instruction ("Read this."), it was the beginning of a new chapter for me.

AD-FREE BRAND HEROES

Throughout this book, you'll notice I recommend many books and authors I think may help you think through your organization's brand strategy and positioning. I've been an avid reader all my life and devour almost every book about branding I can find. Like everything new, the approach to brand positioning and brand strategy you'll find in these pages is built on the great ideas of others.

My hope is that I'll expose you to some of the classic brand positioning concepts you may not already be familiar with while teaching you how to apply them in a new way. I encourage you to read as many of these classic books as possible. Their authors are the people who inspired me—the heroes of ad-free branding—and they might inspire you as well.

Although the general concepts behind brand positioning had roots in the classic advertising campaigns of the twentieth century, Jack Trout first widely popularized the actual term *positioning* in a series of magazine articles appearing in *Advertising Age* in 1972. The concept truly hit the mainstream after the release of his (with co-author Al Ries) bestselling 1981 book *Positioning: The Battle for Your Mind*—the same book Red Hat's CEO gave me 20 years later.

Their book is a simple, elegant read, and I still refer to it regularly for inspiration. In the introduction, Trout and Ries define what positioning is and is not:

> "Positioning starts with a product. A piece of merchandise, a service, a company, an institution, or even a person. Perhaps yourself.
>
> But positioning is not what you do to a product. Positioning is what you do to the mind of the prospect. That is, you position the product in the mind of the prospect."

For Trout and Ries, this is the essence of good positioning—that it is not what you do *to a product*; it is what you do *to the mind of the prospect*.

So, to put it in simple terms, Trout and Ries think of brand positioning as the art of creating meaning for a brand in people's minds.

Why Does Brand Positioning Matter?

I believe almost all great brands are built on a foundation of great positioning. Sometimes great positioning is led by a branding genius such as Scott Bedbury (the "brands are like sponges" guy); sometimes a great leader and communicator with a very clear vision (like Steve Jobs at Apple) drives it into the organization; sometimes people stumble on great positioning by pure luck; and more and more often, organizations are developing positioning the way I describe in this book.

> "Positioning is not what you do to a product. Positioning is what you do to the mind of the prospect." — Jack Trout and Al Ries

Why does great positioning matter? In my view, there are four key reasons those who create ad-free brands should care about positioning.

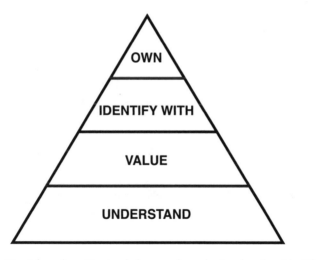

Figure 1.2 *Great brand positioning helps people understand, value, identify with, and ultimately even take some ownership of the brand.*

Great positioning helps people understand the brand—The best brand positioning is always simple and clear. The greatest product or organization in the world won't be successful if people can't or don't bother to comprehend why they should care about it. Your story must be able to break through the clutter.

Great positioning helps people value the brand—Getting people to understand the brand is the first step, but no less important is ensuring they *value* the brand. The best brands stand for things people care about or desire.

Great positioning helps people identify with the brand—Once people understand and value the brand, they must also understand how they fit in and how they can engage with the brand. They need to see some of themselves in it.

Great brand positioning helps people take ownership over the brand—It may sound like a brand's worst nightmare to lose control and have the brand community take over. But the most self-actualized brands of the twenty-first century allow the communities of people surrounding them to take some ownership of and responsibility for the brand. Essentially, the brand owners become in command and out of control of the brand.

Why on earth would brand owners be willing to give up control of their brands? The answer lies at the heart of the ad-free brand strategy.

IN COMMAND AND OUT OF CONTROL

The phrase "in command and out of control" perfectly describes the positioning approach you will see throughout this book. I originally read this phrase in the book *Blink*, where Malcolm Gladwell tells the story of the leadership approach of U.S. General Paul Van Riper, who explained his military strategy to his troops this way:

"The first thing I told my staff is that we would be in command and out of control."

By this he meant that the overall strategy and direction were so clear and well understood that he was able to leave many of the decisions about how to implement the strategy to others.

Positioning in a Post-Advertising World

When Jack Trout and Al Ries wrote *Positioning: The Battle for Your Mind* in 1981, traditional advertising was still a dominant force. In fact, as you glance through their book, you'll notice that most of the examples they use to illustrate positioning concepts are classic advertisements or advertising campaigns like the Avis "We're #2, so we try harder" or the 7-Up "Uncola" campaign.

AD-FREE BRAND HEROES PART 1: JACK TROUT AND AL RIES

Jack Trout and Al Ries, the duo who invented the term *positioning*, worked together for over 25 years and wrote numerous books both together and individually. While the book that defined the concept was their 1981 collaboration *Positioning: The Battle for Your Mind* (which was also updated with a 20th anniversary edition in 2001), I also recommend the following books for people who'd like to explore their ideas about positioning even more deeply:

- *Marketing Warfare* by Jack Trout and Al Ries (1986, 20th anniversary edition published in 2006)

- *The 22 Immutable Laws of Marketing* by Jack Trout and Al Ries (1994)

- *Differentiate or Die* by Jack Trout and Steve Rivkin (2001, 2nd edition in 2008)

- *The 22 Immutable Laws of Branding* by Al Ries and Laura Ries (2002)

- *Repositioning: Marketing in an Era of Change, Competition, and Crisis* by Jack Trout and Steve Rivkin (2009)

For a long time, people have expressed criticism for or even hatred of advertising because they view it as manipulative. And even the Trout and Ries definition of positioning as "what you do to the mind of a prospect" could be viewed as manipulation.

This is where the concept of *esse quam videri* (*"to be rather than to seem to be"*) comes in again. Twentieth-century positioning was about *telling* people who you were, mostly through advertising and PR, whereas positioning for ad-free brands is more about *being* who you are, with the help of those who care about your brand.

So, the Trout and Ries model of positioning is all about what you do to the mind of the prospect, while the best positioning efforts in the ad-free branding world will be less manipulative, more authentic, and more collaborative. In essence, the ad-free brand is less interested in creating meaning for a brand *in* people's minds, and more interested in creating meaning for a brand *with the help of* people's minds.

> The ad-free brand is less interested in what it does *to* people's minds and more interested in what it does *with the help of* people's minds.

Ad-free brands are managed as openly as possible, with the help and support of employees, partners, customers, and other members of the communities that surround our brands.

Sound kind of scary? Let me explain why it's not.

An Open, Collaborative Approach to Brand Positioning

At Red Hat, we built a successful business selling open source software. Since this is a branding book and not a computer book, I won't bore you with a lot of mundane details about how open source software is made. But I will share a few key ideas.

In the open source model, every piece of code you create is shared with a worldwide community of developers who can use your code to create their own products and services. In return, you can use the code written by others in the community to make your products and services.

The software development effort extends beyond the walls of the organization. Work is done transparently out in the open, everyone collaborates, and the rising tide lifts all ships.

It might sound crazy, but it works. The open source development model is responsible not just for Linux (the operating system that Red Hat built its business around), but also much of the rest of the software that keeps the Internet up and running, including wildly successful products like the Firefox web browser, the Apache web server, the WordPress blogging platform, and the Drupal content management system, among many others.

THE OPEN SOURCE WAY

What do we mean by the *open source way*? The open source way is a loose set of principles common to most open source projects that can also apply well beyond software development. The opensource.com website has defined five key principles and, while I wouldn't limit myself to just these five, I think they provide a great foundation for understanding the main tenets of the open source way:

1. **We believe in an open exchange.**
    We can learn more from each other when information is open. A free exchange of ideas is critical to creating an environment where people are allowed to learn and use existing information toward creating new ideas.

2. **We believe in the power of participation.**
    When we are free to collaborate, we create. We can solve problems that no one person may be able to solve on her own.

3. **We believe in rapid prototyping.**
    Rapid prototypes can lead to rapid failures, but that leads to better solutions found faster. When you're free to experiment, you can look at problems in new ways and look for answers in new places. You can learn by doing.

4. **We believe in meritocracy.**
    In a meritocracy, the best ideas win. In a meritocracy, everyone has access to the same information. Successful work determines which projects rise and gather effort from the community.

5. **We believe in community.**
    Communities are formed around a common purpose. They bring together diverse ideas and share work. Together, a global community can create beyond the capabilities of any one individual. It multiplies effort and shares the work. Together, we can do more.[6]

During the '90s, as people began to notice how well this approach worked for software development, the open source way began to expand to other areas as well in business, government, education, and beyond.

Wikipedia is probably the most famous example of an open, collaborative effort in part inspired by the success of open source software. But there are plenty of other great examples, including the Creative Commons (an open copyright model for creative works) and the MIT OpenCourseWare project (offering more than 2,000 college-level courses for free online).

> When you're free to experiment, you can look at problems in new ways and look for answers in new places.

If you are interested in learning more about how the open source way is inspiring projects beyond software development, visit http://www.opensource.com, a great site highlighting examples of the impact of the open source way in business, government, education, the law, and generally in our lives (disclosure: I'm a regular contributor to the business channel there).

---

6. This text can be found on the opensource.com website at http://www.opensource.com/open-sourceopen source-wa

At the same time many others around the world were beginning to experiment with applying the open source way in new and unique environments, at Red Hat we began thinking about how we could infuse the open source way into every part of the business—not just the software development model—so that it became part of the underlying DNA of the organization.

The rationale? If the open source model could help build better software faster, maybe it could help build anything better and faster. We began to experiment.

We used an open, collaborative approach to uncover the Red Hat corporate values, with great success. We began to define the key elements of the brand and culture by working collaboratively with employees from across the organization. We even openly designed the logo and brand identity for one of our biggest open source community projects, the Fedora Project, in an effort that included people both inside and outside the company.

What we were surprised to learn is that every time we engaged a community of people beyond our core group in one of these efforts, we not only achieved better results, but also created an incredibly important side effect—one perhaps even more important than the work product itself.

When we involved people in the process, we helped create an engaged community of people who would continue to ensure the project's success for years to come.

By openly and transparently involving people in the development of a project, we gave them a reason to care more about it. They saw their ideas in the final work. They felt like they had a say in its design. And, over time, they actually began to take ownership.

🔍 Tip

By openly and transparently involving people in the development of a project, you will often give them a reason to care more about it.

Over the years, we started running almost every project we could this way—the open source way—and the results of these projects formed the foundation of much of the brand, culture, and even the overall organizational "operating system" and management model of Red Hat.

LINUS'S LAW

In his classic essay about open source, *The Cathedral and the Bazaar*, Eric Raymond attributes the following statement to Linus Torvalds, the original creator of the Linux operating system:

"Given enough eyeballs, all bugs are shallow."

Meaning, with enough people looking at a project, the odds that someone can identify and see a way to fix its problems increase dramatically. This has certainly been proven true in the open source software movement, but we've found that Linus' Law applies even more broadly. We've found that when you open up a project to allow for contributions from people who care deeply about the end result, the best ideas can come from anywhere—and usually do!

Brands Out of Control

As I stated earlier, we didn't set out to build an ad-free brand at Red Hat. We did it because we didn't have the money to advertise. But in the process, we discovered a way to develop deeper, more meaningful relationships with the employees, partners, customers, and other communities surrounding the company.

We developed a way of building the brand that didn't simply tell people what the Red Hat brand was about and convince them to buy our stuff. Instead, we encouraged people inside and outside the organization to become participants in the brand, to contribute to its growth and evolution.

> **We were in command, but out of control**—By bringing the internal and external communities surrounding the brand into the process of defining it, we acknowledged the cold, hard truth of the second Internet revolution—that organizations no longer have complete control over their brands.

> **Instead of fighting, we embraced**—After all, shouldn't we be thankful for anyone who takes interest in our brands? Thankful that there are people willing to contribute to our brands' success? Thankful that there are people who care?

I admit the Red Hat situation was unique, and our success was the combination of many factors that included not just the open source model, but also incredible timing and a great deal of luck. But I also believe many of the open source principles we used to build the Red Hat brand will work for any organization of any size in any industry.

2

Ad-Free Brand Positioning Basics

Great ad-free brands will develop brand positioning that resonates with the communities surrounding the brand. But what exactly does that mean, and how do you construct effective positioning for your brand?

Thankfully, the basic concepts behind brand positioning are much simpler than you might think. By the time you finish Chapter 3, you should have all the tools and information you need to develop your own effective positioning, and by the end of Chapter 4, you'll have developed prototype positioning for your brand.

In this chapter, I cover the basic building blocks of brand positioning and then outline some principles that will help you set up your own brand positioning project for success.

My Introduction to Brand Positioning

One day during my time at Red Hat, when we were struggling through a particularly complex brand challenge, I came back to my desk to find a copy of the *Harvard Business Review* opened to an article about brand strategy with a handwritten note attached from CEO Matthew Szulik: "Perhaps you should consider finding someone like this to help you," the note said.

For the next day or two, I searched online, looking for brand strategy firms I might be able to enlist to help us work through our branding issue. I ran across all the normal agencies. I made a list. But none of them felt quite right, and I wasn't sure I could afford to hire one even if they were right.

Then it hit me—what if, instead of finding someone *like* the author of the *Harvard Business Review* article, I actually just contacted the author himself?

I did a bit of research and found that the primary author of the article, a Dartmouth professor named Kevin Keller, had also written a brand management textbook. So I found his email address and sent him a note to see if he'd be interested in talking about Red Hat.

AD-FREE BRAND HEROES PART 2: KEVIN KELLER

Kevin Keller, E. B. Osborn Professor of Marketing at the Tuck School of Business at Dartmouth College, is one of the top brand strategy experts in the world. He has advised many of the world's top brands, including Accenture, Allstate, American Express, BlueCross BlueShield, Campbell's, Disney, Eli Lilly, ExxonMobil, Ford, General Mills, Goodyear, Intel, Intuit, Johnson and Johnson, Kodak, Levi Strauss, Mayo Clinic, Nordstrom, Procter and Gamble, Red Hat, SAB Miller, Shell Oil, Starbucks, Unilever, and Young and Rubicam.

His textbook *Strategic Brand Management* has been called the "bible of branding" and is used at top business schools and leading firms around the world. Dr. Keller is also the co-author with Philip Kotler of the popular introductory marketing textbook, *Marketing Management.*""

I'd recommend anyone who is serious about their brand initiatives invest in a copy of *Strategic Brand Management* and consider purchasing reprints of some of his classic articles about brand management from *Harvard Business Review* and elsewhere. You can find a current list of Dr. Keller's published work here:

http://mba.tuck.dartmouth.edu/pages/faculty/kevin.keller/publications.html

To my surprise, Dr. Keller responded, and we were off and running. Bringing in Kevin Keller was one of the best business decisions I made during my time at Red Hat. Over the next few years, Dr. Keller became a key advisor on Red Hat's brand strategy, and he helped us work through many complex issues, including a few in uncharted territory.

I tell this story here because I use many of Dr. Keller's brand positioning terms throughout this book. In addition, this book contains advice, stories, and examples I learned from Dr. Keller during my time working with him at Red Hat. In the following section, I use Dr. Keller's terminology as I introduce the four key building blocks of brand positioning.

The Four Building Blocks of Brand Positioning

Those who spend all of their time thinking about brands and brand positioning can make the subject seem incredibly complex. Before you know it, these experts will fill you up with so much marketing jargon and so many impressive-sounding positioning principles and rules that your head may end up exploding from the pressure.

Yet the best-executed positioning won't always come from these sorts of experts. Great positioning is often developed by the people who know the brand best, the people who are most passionate about the brand, when they are allowed to play a key role in the positioning process.

So, where many experts might attempt to convince you that positioning is a complex process best left to people like them, my goal in this book is to show you basic brand positioning is *simple* and can be done by anyone—with or without marketing and advertising experience.

> ...basic brand positioning is *simple* and can be done by anyone—with or without marketing and advertising experience.

While any person in any organization can help create great brand positioning, whether he has a high tolerance for marketing-speak or not, to do so he must first understand some basic concepts.

I've attempted to simplify the jargon down to four key principles I believe form the foundation of solidly constructed brand positioning. I call these principles "the four building blocks" of brand positioning, and I refer to them often throughout the book.

The four main building blocks of good brand positioning:

1. The competitive frame of reference

2. Points of difference

3. Points of parity

4. The brand mantra

DON'T GET HUNG UP ON THE WORDS

When it comes to positioning terminology, I sometimes get questions like "what is the difference between a brand mantra and a brand essence?" or "is a point of difference the same thing as a key differentiator?"

My answer? Don't get hung up on the words; it's the concepts that matter.

For the sake of clarity, in this book I've standardized on a set of terms that work for me and have become comfortable for me to use in my positioning projects.

But often, I'll be working with a client who approaches positioning from a slightly different point of view, and when this happens I always gravitate toward the words most comfortable to the client (They *are* the client!).

The exact terms aren't important. What really matters is whether we agree on how to articulate brand meaning and understand what makes the brand stand apart.

Using the terminology from this book to describe your brand positioning won't automatically make it good brand positioning, and some of the best-positioned brands I have ever seen were probably developed by people who had never heard of a point of parity.

My advice? Use whatever words you like, but seek to deeply understand the concepts behind them.

The Competitive Frame of Reference

Where does your brand compete?

This can seem like a very simple question with equally simple answers, and it can be.

If you run a furniture store, you probably compete with other furniture stores. If you run a tattoo parlor, you are up against other tattoo parlors vying to attract the same customers as you.

Great brands can't be positioned in a vacuum; they must be positioned in *context*. The competitive frame of reference provides the context for positioning, and it is a fancy way of describing the market or context in which you choose to position your brand.

The furniture store and tattoo parlor are pretty cut-and-dried cases. But have you ever stopped and wondered to yourself, "exactly which market am I in?" and realized that you are really competing in a market or context that is not initially obvious?

> ✉ *Note*
>
> The competitive frame of reference is a fancy way of describing the market or context in which you choose to position your brand.

Let's look at one example of a less-than-obvious competitive frame of reference.

What Market Do You Think Starbucks Is In?

Most people would say Starbucks is in the coffee market because the primary product Starbucks sells is coffee. In the coffee market, Starbucks competes with grocery stores, convenience stores, fast food restaurants, and other coffee shops. The coffee market is tough, and in many of those places the profit margins are pretty slim.

In the coffee market, Starbucks isn't usually competitive on price. In fact, the company managed to convince the world that coffee that used to cost 50 cents a cup was actually worth $2 or more. Starbucks may no longer be the most expensive coffee in the world, but there are definitely plenty of places you can find coffee cheaper.

When it comes to taste, I'm not sure Starbucks has a huge advantage either, despite what their marketing folks might tell you. Only hardcore Starbucks addicts would tell you it is the best coffee out there. Everyone's tastes are different, but if you are like me, you probably wouldn't have too much trouble finding a cup that tastes better.

Convenience is pretty important in the coffee market simply because many people are in a rush to grab a quick cup on the way to work. And Starbucks stores are nothing if not ubiquitous. But in my experience, the only thing as ubiquitous as Starbucks is a line at Starbucks. So, even though you can find Starbucks stores everywhere, after standing in line, it'll still probably take you 10 minutes or more before you have your coffee in hand.

Thus, in a market where price, taste, and convenience are all very important, Starbucks doesn't look like a strong competitor. Yet Starbucks has more than 16,000 stores in 50+ countries around the world and does over $10 billion per year in revenues.[1] Almost makes it hard to believe that Starbucks could have grown this big by simply competing in the coffee market.

Well, in addition to competing in the coffee market, Chairman and CEO Howard Schultz has been known to say that Starbucks is competing to be your "third place." According to him, the third place is the other place you want to hang out besides your first place (your home) and your second place (your work).

In the competitive frame of reference of third places, Starbucks has a whole different set of competitors, only some of which are coffee shops. Starbucks competes with bookstores, bars, restaurants, parks, libraries—all the places you might want to hang out and spend your time away from home and work.

For years, Starbucks has been differentiating itself not just on its coffee, but also on the experience and environment it creates. That's why Starbucks focuses so much time with the music, ambiance, and complex drink names that make you feel like you are reciting chants when you order them. It is all part of creating an air of comfort, relaxation, familiarity, exclusivity, and all of the other things that you look for in your preferred hang-out spot.

Now, I personally have some pretty awesome first and second places to hang out in. I love my house and I love my office. When you add to this the fact that I am a bit of an introvert who values privacy and quiet time, I'm not really in the market for a third place. So Starbucks' differentiation as a third place probably matters less to me than a nice, tasty cup of iced coffee.

But every time I go into a Starbucks, I see tons of people who have their laptops open, or are reading newspapers, or meeting with friends or business associates. That and $10 billion in revenues per year tells me there must be a lot of other people who *are* in the market for a third place. Small business owners, salespeople who work on the road, people who need to get out of the house—clearly the Starbucks positioning in the third place frame of reference must be working or there wouldn't be a Starbucks on every corner.

In fact, as I write this, Starbucks has just announced a new logo and brand identity that actually removes the word "coffee" from the logo completely. I wonder whether this is actually a sign. Perhaps their effort to position themselves in the "third place" competitive frame of reference has been so successful that they're considering moving into even more markets that utilize their third place brand position, but aren't directly related to coffee at all?

Multiple Competitive Frames of Reference

In all likelihood, you'll decide that you have one primary competitive frame of reference where your organization will spend the majority of its positioning energy.

---

1. Data from Starbucks FY10 annual report, page 2.

But hopefully the Starbucks example opens your eyes to the possibility that you may want to position your brand in more than one frame of reference. By looking beyond the obvious competitive markets, you might even uncover new business opportunities or ways to broaden your horizons to include people who may never have considered your brand before.

Be open to the idea that you might want to develop different positioning for each frame of reference, or that you might choose to highlight different elements of the brand as you present yourself in different frames of reference.

If this seems complex, don't worry. In Chapter 4, I take you through a simple exercise that will help you determine the optimal competitive frame of reference (or references) for your brand.

Points of Difference

If you've ever been around anyone who talks about positioning, you've probably heard them talk about points of difference, differentiation, or the concept of key differentiators.

POINTS OF DIFFERENCE: THE ROOKS OF POSITIONING

If brand positioning was a chess game, points of difference would be the rooks. They are strong, powerful tools, and it is easy to understand how they work and see the impact of what they do.

A point of difference is a something about the brand that makes it different from other competing brands. But a good point of difference won't just revel in its different-ness; it must also be something your customers would value.

✉ *Note*

A point of difference is something about a brand that makes it different *and* would be valued by potential customers.

Let's look at an example that highlights good and bad points of difference.

Who Wants Mexican?

I love Mexican food and think it is awesome that I can go anywhere in the country and find a Mexican restaurant. But even though there are probably lots of people like me out there who love Mexican food, my guess is the Mexican restaurant business is pretty tough.

There is a lot of competition, and many of the restaurants tend to look (and often taste) alike. So, if you wanted to open a new Mexican restaurant, how could you ensure it'd stand out?

If you were thinking in terms of creating solid points of difference, you'd probably start by thinking about what customers would value in a Mexican restaurant. Since I'm a bit of a Mexican connoisseur, let me start with what *I* value in a Mexican restaurant. In order of priority:

1. Cleanliness

2. Freshness of ingredients

3. Tasty salsa

4. Good carne asada

5. Price

Say you happened to be opening this restaurant in a place where there were many other people who shared my idea of what is important in a Mexican restaurant. Let's also say that there were a lot of Mexican restaurants already open in the area competing for the attention of people who valued price, quantity of food, and good margaritas.

To stand out, you might consider cleanliness, freshness of ingredients, and tasty salsa as three things you want to focus on as points of difference for your restaurant brand. By focusing on these three things, you could make your restaurant very different in a way that potential customers would actually value. Victory!

By starting with what your potential customers value and then thinking about what makes you different, you have a better chance for success than if you start with just the things that make you different.

Here's another example to highlight this point. What if your claim to fame is that you know how to make an incredibly good, incredibly authentic Mexican posole (a stew) featuring pigs' feet? In fact, it is widely known that no one in the entire world can make a better pigs' feet posole than you.

You should be very proud. But you shouldn't for a second believe that your great posole is a good point of difference for your restaurant. Why? Most Americans aren't that crazy about pigs' feet, and no matter how good your stew is, they proba-bly won't buy it from you. Your posole is certainly different and probably very tasty (at least to those into that sort of thing), but it is not something your customers would value, so it is not a good point of difference. Get the idea? Or am I just mak-ing you hungry?

In the next few chapters, I show you some ways to ensure you are uncovering points of difference for your brand that will not only help you stand out but will also be valued by your customers.

Points of Parity

Now you are probably beginning to think about, and maybe even feel good about, all the points of difference that make your brand stand out. But while you've been busy thinking about how to make your brand stand out from your competition, your competitors are also busy developing points of difference that make them stand out from *you*. This is where the idea of a point of parity comes in.

Most simply, a point of parity is a point of difference a competitor has over *you* that you need to counteract. Sometimes points of parity are "table stakes"—characteris-tics you need simply to enter or compete in the market. Other times points of par-ity are advantages that competitors have been able to gain that are highly valued by customers.

✉ *Note*

> A point of parity is a point of difference a competitor has over *you* that you need to counteract.

It takes a strong person to admit to their weaknesses, and strong brands must admit their weaknesses, too. This is why great brands use not only points of difference to show where they stand out, but also points of parity to show where they are trying to be as good as their competition.

But highlighting a point of parity doesn't necessarily mean that you need to turn it into a key strength for your brand or that you need to beat your competitors at it. You shouldn't feel like you need to turn all your brand weaknesses into strengths.

In fact, one of the key things to understand about points of parity is that they don't represent places where your brand needs to be the best. Instead they highlight places where your brand must simply be good enough, so that, given the amazing points of difference you have in other areas, someone will still choose your brand over the competition.

✉ *Note*

Points of parity highlight places where your brand must simply be good enough, so that, given the amazing points of difference you have in other areas, someone will still choose your brand over the competition.

POINTS OF PARITY: THE KNIGHTS OF POSITIONING

If brand positioning was a chess game, points of parity would be the knights. They are sneaky, often attacking when you least expect it, and are at their most powerful when used in conjunction with points of difference.

Well-played points of parity are one of my favorite brand positioning tools. Points of parity are the jujitsu maneuvers of brand positioning, with the amazing power to nullify the strengths of opposing brands, while focusing energy back on the differences that make you stand out.

> Points of parity are the jujitsu maneuvers of brand positioning...

Make sense? Let's look at an example.

Wal-mart Versus Target

Wal-mart is one of the most intimidating competitors in retail. Over the years, they've developed a key point of difference around everyday low prices that is almost impossible for competitors to match. Their enormous size and efficient operations give them incredible pricing power with the ability to beat the prices of almost any competitor. Wal-mart has used this strength to become, based on annual revenues, the largest corporation in the world.

Faced with a massive competitor like Wal-mart, many companies would curl up in a ball and prepare to die. Yet Target, the second largest discount retailer in the United States, has actually prospered in this tough environment, ranking #30 in the Fortune 500 in 2010.

How has Target done it? I believe a large factor in their success is the combination of a very strong point of difference around design and fashion, coupled with great execution on a point of parity around price.

Is Target always the cheapest? No. As I've said previously, it's pretty difficult to beat Wal-mart on price. But are Target's prices "good enough" that, given how much better designed many of their products are and how fashion-forward much of their clothing is, many people in certain demographics choose to buy from them instead of Wal-mart? Absolutely.

Target is not trying to *beat* Wal-mart on price. They are simply trying to create enough parity around price that their point of difference around fashion and design becomes the deciding factor for many consumers.

It is a great example of using a point of parity and point of difference well together, and it's a 1-2 punch that has worked very well for Target.

The point of parity is one of the most overlooked tools in the brand positioning tool chest, but it can be one of the most powerful, especially when used in combination with a great point of difference. In Chapter 4, I walk you through an exercise that will help you uncover the best points of parity for your brand.

Current Versus Aspirational Points of Parity and Points of Difference

When we begin to develop points of parity and points of difference in Chapter 4, one thing to keep in mind is that you may develop points that the brand currently owns today *and* points that you hope to be able to achieve in the future. Brands shouldn't feel like they can only define themselves by what they are today.

By choosing points of parity and points of difference that describe who you are today and who you want to be down the road, you'll ensure the brand is not only well positioned today, but also has room for future growth.

The Brand Mantra

The final brand positioning building block is the brand mantra, which some refer to as the *brand essence* and others call a *brand promise*.

A brand mantra is short (usually 2–5 words maximum) and encapsulates the competitive frame of reference, the points of difference, the points of parity, and everything else about your brand into one thought. A brand mantra is to brand positioning what triple distillation is to liquor—they both remove the impurities, refining and simplifying to an essential form.

> ✉ *Note*
>
> A brand mantra is a short, 2–5 word encapsulation of everything about a brand.

A brand mantra is *not* an advertising slogan or tagline, and, in many cases, it won't be something you use publicly at all. Great brand mantras can change everything. They become rallying cries that define everything a brand is and will ever be. But, because they are part purification process and part poetry, they are also incredibly hard to make well.

A ROSE BY ANY OTHER NAME WOULD SMELL AS SWEET

In this book, I use the terms *competitive frame of reference*, *points of difference*, *points of parity*, and *brand mantra* to describe the building blocks of positioning. But feel free to use whatever terms you like. Here are some common alternatives:

Competitive Frame of Reference:	Market
	Competitive landscape
	Competition
Point of Difference:	Differentiator
	Key differentiator
Point of Parity:	Brand parity
	Table stakes
Brand Mantra:	Brand essence
	Brand promise
	Positioning statement
	Brand statement

According to Scott Bedbury (the "brands are sponges" guy from Chapter 1), the term *brand mantra* was coined during his time at Nike. The Nike brand mantra, *Authentic Athletic Performance*, is probably the most famous example, and Bedbury discusses it at length in his book A *New Brand World*. From the book:

> "Nike's brand mantra put a particular emphasis on maintaining authenticity, by which we also meant integrity and purity, front and center…. All products and activities associated with Nike likewise had to be athletic, not leisurely…. Finally, every Nike product had to exude world-class performance and meet the demands of the world's finest athletes, even though such athletes represented a microscopic piece of Nike's total business…. "Authentic Athletic

Performance" was a simple idea, but like so many simple ideas, its execution and implementation could be complex, not to mention challenging, daunting—and even painful, when it came down to forgoing revenue-generating activities because they violated these accepted core values."[2]

When used in its proper context, a good brand mantra is not simple sloganeering. If you asked most people to name Nike's brand mantra, they'd probably say "Just do it."

But "Just do it" is a tagline, not a brand mantra. It is an externally facing manifestation of *Authentic Athletic Performance* (and a pretty darned good one, I might add). It's a wonderful example of how great communications can be built on the back of a solidly constructed brand mantra.

> A brand mantra is at its most powerful when it becomes a deeply resonant piece of the DNA of the organization.

Still, if the brand mantra is simply used as a building block for campaigns, it is not living up to its true potential. A brand mantra is at its most powerful when it becomes a deeply resonant piece of the DNA of the organization. It can be used to rally an internal or external brand community to action or as a touchstone the organization returns to when making difficult decisions.

What businesses should you be in? What businesses should you not be in? How should you handle this crisis you've gotten yourself into? How do you make this painful choice? The brand mantra can be your guide.

Kevin Keller tells a great story of how Disney (Brand mantra: *Fun Family Entertainment*) at one point made the choice to get out of an investment business they had entered because, although it was vaguely family-related, it was neither fun nor entertaining.

This is my favorite example of a brand mantra that has been used to steer the brand and keep it on track.

THE BRAND MANTRA: THE QUEEN OF POSITIONING

If brand positioning was a chess game, the brand mantra would be the queen. It is the most powerful piece you have and, when properly placed, can win the game by itself. It is, however, one of the most difficult pieces to get into the action, especially early in the game.

2. From *A New Brand World* by Scott Bedbury, page 51.

In my experience, the best brand mantras are the rock stars of the positioning world. For people who don't have the patience for understanding competitive frames of references, points of parity, and points of difference, a poetic, authentic brand mantra makes everything else fade into the woodwork. It encapsulates every important point of difference, maybe an important point of parity, and even the competitive frame of reference, into a few short words.

Brand mantras are poetry. They are art. And they are powerful tools, not just for building brands, but for building organizations. Yet, as I've noted, great brand mantras are very difficult to achieve, and some positioning exercises never uncover one.

In upcoming chapters, I reveal some exercises and tips that can help your brand break the code and find a powerful brand mantra that works for you.

AD-FREE BRAND HEROES PART 3: SCOTT BEDBURY

Scott Bedbury, CEO of the brand consultancy Brandstream, is a branding legend who played key roles in the development of the Nike and Starbucks brands during the late '80s and early '90s.

Tom Peters has called Bedbury "perhaps the greatest brand maven of our time."[3] His book *A New Brand World*, published by Viking Press in 2002, is a great read for anyone who wants to be inspired by the possibilities brand positioning can create from someone who was a central figure in the development of two of the most iconic brands of our time.

Key Principles Behind a Successful Ad-Free Brand Positioning Project

Now that you have a taste of some of the most important brand positioning concepts, you are probably eager to get started working on positioning for your brand.

To design the best possible brand positioning project for your organization with the best chance for success, you'll need to recognize that, while the fundamental building blocks may stay the same, every positioning project will be a little different.

I've helped people with a wide variety of brand positioning projects in all sorts of organizations including large corporations, small businesses, non-profits, start-ups, websites, events, musical groups, and government agencies. I've even helped people position themselves.

---

3. This quote appeared in the "Praise for..." section at the beginning of Scott Bedbury's book *A New Brand World*.

In some organizations, I've run very formal positioning projects involving input from dozens of people and expensive research that took many months to complete. I've also done mini-positioning projects that were completed at no cost over a weekend.

When making a decision about how to set up your positioning project, I'd suggest you take the following principles into account:

Cast Your Net as Wide as Possible

Two-time Nobel Prize winner Linus Pauling once said, "The best way to get a good idea is to generate a lot of ideas." And I've already mentioned, Linus's Law, named for Linux founder Linus Torvalds, which states, "Given enough eyeballs, all bugs are shallow."

Can two Linuses be wrong? Contrary to what you'll hear from many branding experts—who like to run positioning projects behind closed doors and involve only agency types, marketing executives, or management committees—great positioning projects can be run out in the open.

My experience in the open source world has taught me that the more people you can involve in the positioning project, the more great ideas you'll uncover and the more flaws you'll reveal. Where traditional positioning projects are often very secretive projects run by a select few, I believe great modern positioning projects can be run as powerful meritocracies where the best ideas can come from anywhere, and often do.

> 🔍 *Tip*
>
> The more people you can involve in the positioning project, the more great ideas you'll uncover, and the more flaws you'll reveal.

Also recognize that, especially if you are a small organization or an organization of one, you can get even more ideas if you cast your net beyond the walls of your organization. Consider whether getting your customers, partners, friends, or even neighbors involved in your positioning project might give you ideas you could never get on your own. I cover this subject in more detail in Chapter 4.

Powerful brand positioning doesn't have to be the work of a lone genius and usually isn't. My goal is to break the (misleading) stereotype of the ad agency creative director who stumbles upon the perfect positioning while scribbling on a napkin and sipping a martini at an outdoor brasserie in Manhattan.

Powerful brand positioning doesn't have to be the work of a lone genius and usually isn't.

Great brand positioning is the result of collaboration between people who are *passionate* about a brand and is led by people who cast their net widely for the best ideas on how to position that brand.

The Best Ideas Should Win

When I talk about soliciting ideas from a large group of people for a positioning project, many people immediately assume I mean turning the project into a democracy where every person gets a vote and majority rules. Nothing could be further from the truth. Positioning by popular vote can be ugly, painful, and ineffective and is a great way to achieve a lowest common denominator of bland and mediocre ideas.

While I like to involve as many people as possible in the positioning project to ensure their ideas are captured, I also make sure the rules of the game are very clear. In a positioning project run the ad-free brand way, we create a meritocracy where the *best* ideas will win, not necessarily the *most popular* ideas (although in many cases both can happen at once, which I love to see).

Tip

In a brand positioning project run the ad-free brand way, the *best* ideas should win—not necessarily the most popular ones.

So we consult as many people as possible throughout the course of the project, communicate regularly, and keep them involved through the process, but never promise them they will get a vote. Does the fact that they don't get to vote make people less apt to contribute?

Believe it or not, I've never seen this happen. In my experience, people aren't used to being asked what they think. Usually they are thrilled to be asked, excited to even have the opportunity to contribute.

The People Who Care the Most Make the Decision

So, who chooses which ideas are the best ideas? I recommend you put together a small leadership group of people to make the final brand positioning decisions and recommendations (between 5 and 15, depending on your project size). These people are not always the most senior people in your organization, although some of them might be. They are the people with the deepest understanding of and most experience with the brand. Eventually, many of these people may become part of the long-term "command center" of your in command, out of control brand.

🔍 *Tip*

> Choose a diverse brand leadership group made up of people with the deep-
> est understanding of and most experience with the brand and culture,
> regardless of where they sit in the organization.

What should you look for? Good candidates could include employees who have
been with the organization for many years. They may be people whose daily job is
to manage the brand or brand-related assets. They might be people who are most
passionate about the brand and culture of the organization. These will also be the
people who will be your strongest advocates internally for socializing the brand.

Depending on how your organization is set up, this group may make the final
brand positioning decisions (my preference) or decide on the final recommendation to take to the executive team for blessing (more dangerous).

But I believe the worst way to make decisions
on a brand positioning project is to put a team
of just executives or just marketing people in
charge. For me, no job title should be a guar-
antee of a vote during a brand positioning
project (although executive *support* is a must).
If you want to achieve brand positioning that
truly reflects your brand in an authentic way,
put the people who care the most in charge.
They will almost never let you down.

> Put the people who care the most in charge. They will almost never let you down.

Value Diversity

The best positioning projects involve people looking at the brand from as many
angles as possible. For example, groups that talk to customers or community members every day, like sales, support, and customer service, often have more expertise
on the actual brand experience than marketing folks. There are all sorts of people
both inside and outside the organization who can bring points of view to the project
that might never have been evident to those whose day job is to manage the brand.

What is the best way to ensure you get the best ideas? Don't just get a lot of people
involved, but get lots of different types of people involved. Don't stop at collecting
ideas from this diverse group; consider including some of the best and brightest
people as part of the decision-making team.

Begin Your Positioning Rollout on Day 1

When you bring a diverse group of people into your project, in my experience you
will not only get a more diverse set of ideas, but will also pave the way for the
future success of the brand positioning.

John Lilly, former CEO of the Mozilla Corporation, has a saying: "Surprise is the opposite of engagement." I've used this statement as a guide over and over during positioning projects.

Involving people in the creation of positioning early in the process will give you a head start on rolling it out because you'll be building a strong set of advocates inside and outside the organization starting on day one. These are the people who, because they're involved, will help ensure your project's success. But by not involving people in the project who care passionately about the brand, you are taking dangerous chances that can actually lead to failure.

> "Surprise is the opposite of engagement."
> —John Lilly, Venture Partner at Greylock and former CEO of Mozilla Corporation

Building brand positioning in secret and then unveiling it as a dramatic surprise (the traditional favorite approach of advertising agencies, "Look, a spiffy new slogan!") is a horrible strategy in a world where the Internet and social media have given every individual powerful tools to publicly destroy your team's hard work.

I look to involve people early and often who I believe will play key roles during the brand positioning rollout. When properly engaged, these passionate brand advocates will work tirelessly for the brand. But when spurned, they can do more damage than your worst enemies.

THE GAP LOGO: A CASE STUDY IN SURPRISE VERSUS ENGAGEMENT

In October 2010, Gap provided one of the best examples I've ever encountered of "surprise is the opposite of engagement" in action.

In a startling announcement, the company unveiled a dramatically different logo for the Gap brand. The reaction from the communities of people surrounding the Gap brand was swift and disastrous.

Why did people have such a visceral negative reaction to the logo change? Was the logo really that bad? The firm in charge of the redesign had a deep understanding of and experience with the Gap brand and has an overall great reputation for doing quality work. So how did a project run by experienced brand professionals working with one of the largest consumer brands in the world go so wrong so quickly?

The answer? Gap *surprised* the people who cared about the brand the most.

While this concept seems so simple, I wonder if many in the advertising world still struggle with it. After all, if you've been doing big *Mad Men*-style brand "reveals" for the last 30 or 40 years (What's behind the curtain? Why it's a new logo!), the idea of working transparently *with* customers to define a brand represents a monumental transition in process.

Please don't misunderstand me. I'm certainly not suggesting that large companies start taking votes or resorting to crowd-sourcing their brand identities. The horror.

I'm suggesting twenty-first-century brands must take their community of loyal customers on the transitioning brand journey with them. They must let their communities come along for the ride, showing the people who love them the scenery they see; granting them the opportunity to share ideas, suggestions, comments; and even letting them get things off their chests along the way.

I don't think the brand community expects you'll give it the wheel to steer the brand. But the simple fact is this: if the community isn't invited on the journey, it will reject the destination. And now that social media has given brand communities loud voices and powerful organizing capabilities, real problems can be created for brands that surprise their communities.

Gap learned this lesson the hard way. Hopefully, as long as you keep the idea that surprise is the opposite of engagement in the back of your mind as you consider your brand strategy, you won't need to make the same mistake.

🔍 Tip

If the community isn't invited on the journey, it will reject the destination.

The Size of the Project Should Be Proportional to the Value of the Brand

If you are running a website that does $100,000 a year in revenues, should you go out and invest $40,000 doing research for your positioning project? Absolutely not. If you are positioning a brand responsible for millions of dollars of revenue, should you change your brand strategy based on a mini-positioning project you ran in your basement with the help of your dog over a long weekend? I wouldn't.

If the risks are small, keep the investment small. If the risks are larger, consider making a larger investment and potentially consider bringing in a professional branding firm to help facilitate the project.

Positioning projects usually involve an investment in both time and money. For many small organizations, time is easier to part with than money. For many large organizations, money is easier to part with than time. So if your money is short and your time is plenty, use this book and do most of the work yourself.

> ...if your money is short and your time is plenty, use this book and do most of the work yourself.

But if you have a budget, yet are pressed for the time or people required to do things right and the stakes are high, consider bringing in a professional partner to help you through the process. Sometimes an outside facilitator can also be an objective voice of reason and experience when things get emotional or next steps are unclear.

In some ways, you should consider your time/budget investment in much the same way you'd consider budgeting for a home improvement project. Could you put up your own drywall in the new guest room? Yes. Should you? Well, that depends on your experience, time, and patience.

The same concept applies here. While this book is designed around the idea that you can "do it yourself" in most cases, there are certain projects where you can achieve better results if you enlist professional assistance. I'll point these places out as we cover them.

The Four Phases of an Ad-Free Brand Positioning Project

An ad-free brand positioning project is made up of four phases:

1. Research
2. Positioning
3. Initial rollout
4. Continuing engagement

Smaller organizations may move through these phases relatively quickly, while larger, more complex organizations might take months before they make it to the continuing engagement phase. All ad-free brand positioning projects will go through these four phases at least once. But I encourage brands to think of brand positioning as an ongoing process, living by the open source adage "release early, release often."[4]

---

4. Like Linus's Law, the adage "release early, release often" was first popularized by Eric Raymond in his 1997 es "The Cathedral and the Bazaar."

> ✉ *Note*
>
> Think of brand positioning as an ongoing process, living by the open source
> adage "release early, release often."

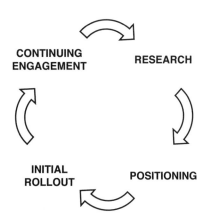

Figure 2.1   *The four phases of a brand positioning project are the research, position-ing, initial rollout, and continuing engagement phases. Ideally brand positioning is an iterative process where these phases repeat over time.*

The sooner you can begin to test new concepts and ideas with the communities of customers, partners, and contributors surrounding your organization, the better your ability to quickly make refinements that will ensure the effectiveness and rele-vance of the positioning.

In addition, I recommend ongoing diligence once the brand positioning has been effectively rolled out. You'll want to regularly update your research; re-examine your positioning concepts to make sure they remain relevant in the face of changes to your organization ; and continue to communicate, making changes to your approach as necessary. In this way, brand positioning becomes an ongoing cycle versus a one-time event.

Basic Training Is Now Complete!

You should now understand the basic concepts and principles behind the ad-free brand positioning process. In the next chapter, we take a closer look at the research phase, covering all the required homework that will help you better position your brand.

3

Brand Positioning Research

Do you already have strong ideas about the future direction of your brand positioning? Awesome! But I'd encourage you to put aside your current ideas about the brand for now. By doing some research homework, you often can learn new and interesting data about your brand that will help you establish more authentic, compelling, and enduring brand positioning.

The Four Key Questions

What kind of research homework do you need to complete before you begin to position your brand? Your homework will help you move beyond your own thinking and deeply understand what people inside and outside the organization think about the brand today—and what they might like it to become tomorrow. It will help you better understand the views of the community of people—customers, partners, contributors, shareholders, and more—surrounding your brand.

AUDIENCE VERSUS COMMUNITY

Because ad-free brands are interested in engaging with those around them, not simply broadcasting messages at them, I use the word *community* instead of the more typical word *audience* found in most marketing and branding books.

By thinking of those who surround your brand as members of communities rather than simply ears receiving messages, you'll already be starting the journey toward a better, deeper relationship with the people who engage with your brand.

A well-organized research phase answers the following four questions:

1. What does your brand community currently believe about or value in the brand?

2. What might your brand community believe or value about the brand in the future?

3. What does your organization currently claim about the brand?

4. What would your organization like the brand to become down the road?

In this chapter, I come back to the diagram in Figure 3.1[1] many times. When you feel like you've done the best job possible answering the four questions in this diagram, you'll have completed your homework and can move onto the positioning phase.

Why are the answers to these four questions so important? Great brand positioning has one foot in the present and one foot in the future. The research we're doing to answer these questions helps us understand exactly where each foot should be planted.

---

1. The diagram on this page is based on a concept covered in Chapter 3 of Kevin Keller's book *Strategic Brand Management*.

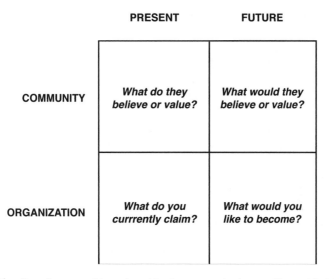

	PRESENT	FUTURE
COMMUNITY	*What do they believe or value?*	*What would they believe or value?*
ORGANIZATION	*What do you currrently claim?*	*What would you like to become?*

Figure 3.1 *A well-executed brand positioning research phase will provide information that answers these four questions.*

The Foot in the Present

By studying what your brand community members currently believe the brand stands for and what they value about it today, you'll begin to understand their current experience of the brand. Yet your community's experience of the brand can be very different than how you see or talk about the brand inside the organization. So the brand research will study the brand from both an internal and external perspective.

Often organizations will notice gaps or inconsistencies between the brand they claim to be and the brand their community sees or experiences—the brand promise –brand experience gap.

Once you deeply understand what your community currently believes or values about the brand and compare this to what you currently claim about the brand, you'll have a complete picture of where your "foot in the present" is planted. You'll see clearly how big the gap is between our brand promise and brand experience. Only then can you begin the work of building brand positioning that closely aligns the brand promise claimed with the brand experience delivered.

 Note

Brands often find gaps between the brand promise they are claiming and the brand experience they are providing. Ad-free brands aim to minimize or eliminate these gaps.

The Foot in the Future

But a brand that is only concerned with the present state of affairs is a brand in stagnation. You'll want your brand to grow, prosper, and remain relevant down the road. So you should also try to understand what the brand community might believe or value about the brand in the future.

> ...a brand that is only concerned with the present state of affairs is a brand in stagnation.

What directions might people give you permission to take the brand? Where do they not want you to take it? What would they value in the brand that you don't provide today? What does the organization do today that people would rather not see you continue to do down the road?

Equally important is that you strongly consider where you want to take the brand. Remember the apocryphal Henry Ford quote, "If I had asked people what they wanted, they would have said faster horses."

Sure, to remain relevant you should deeply understand what the community members want the brand to become, but do not become a slave to their vision. You might have entirely different and amazing places you'd like to take the brand that your customers or other community members can't yet envision.

So, in order to understand where our foot in the future is planted, you should seek to understand both what your community would believe or value in the brand and what you want the brand to become down the road.

Where Great Positioning Lives

Great positioning lives where all four answers intersect. It is a bridge between your current brand experience and the brand you'd like to become in the future. It deeply reflects the brand you currently see while lighting the path to what it could become.

Great positioning lives in all four of these quadrants at once. It can be like the North Star, guiding the organization toward the future, while paying homage to the past and making clear connections between things that resonate about the brand with both your organization and your brand community.

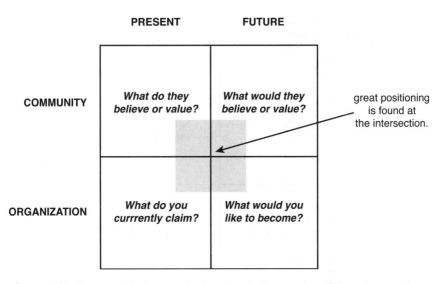

PRESENT   FUTURE

COMMUNITY

*What do they
believe or value?*

*What would they
believe or value?*

great positioning
is found at
the intersection.

ORGANIZATION

*What do you
currrently claim?*

*What would you
like to become?*

Figure 3.2   *Great positioning can be found at the intersection of these four quadrants. It connects the brand present with the brand future while providing a link between the community and organization's understanding of and beliefs about the brand.*

The Low-Cost, High-Value Approach

So how exactly do you discover the answers to the four key questions? Do you need to hire an expensive market research firm and spend hundreds of thousands of dollars on surveys and focus groups?

Here is the general ad-free brand philosophy on the question "how much should I spend?"

I always answer that question with an astoundingly simple approach that became the backbone of our entire brand strategy during my time at Red Hat. I call it the *low-cost, high-value* approach, and if you were to illustrate it, it'd look something like what you see in Figure 3.3.

The low-cost, high-value approach means that you always analyze potential strategies in terms of their cost and value. You then default to choosing strategies first that are inexpensive in terms of time and money yet bring you a lot of potential value, before selecting strategies that cost more, even if they bring you great value.

Pretty simple, huh?

For example, hiring a research company to set up a brand tracking study with 10,000 potential customers for your brand might provide you with a lot of useful information (high value). But the study can also cost you a lot of money and take up a lot of your team's valuable time (high cost).

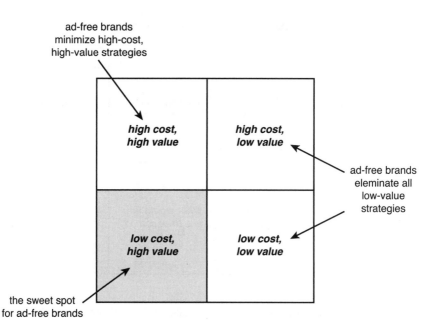

Figure 3.3 *Ad-free brands focus on low-cost, high-value strategies first before considering any other options.*

If you have the time and money, you might still decide to field the high-value brand tracking study, but only after you have exhausted all of the low-cost, high-value strategies that might help answer those questions more inexpensively.

So, the essence of the low-cost, high-value approach is to default to spending as little time and money as you can and consider high-cost strategies only when there are no other options that will get you the information you need.

You'd be surprised how many organizations are essentially blind to an entire category of low-cost, high-value research options because they prefer to stick to practices they used in the years before better options became available.

The reality is that the last 10 years have given us a variety of low-cost, high-value digital media resources that are perfect for doing brand positioning research and for rolling out positioning effectively.

I come back to this theme over and over again: we now have low-cost, high-value alternatives to effectively position brands that did not exist before the Internet. Positioning a brand is less expensive than it has ever been in history. Some people just haven't received the memo.

Ad-free brands, rejoice!

How Do You Decide How Much to Invest in Brand Research?

When you keep the low-cost, high-value approach in mind, the answer to this question should be clear: balance the amount of time and money you put into the research with the value of the brand you are positioning.

If you are trying to position a small web-based business just getting off the ground, you might attempt to answer these four questions with data you already have at your disposal. Perhaps you've already done some customer surveys; you've just completed a formal business plan; or you and your team even have strong, well-informed ideas about the direction you want to take the brand. You can use all of this preexisting information to answer the four critical questions I listed previously.

🔍 Tip

Balance the amount of time and money you put into the research with the value of the brand you are positioning.

But if you are attempting to position or reposition a brand where the stakes are high, especially if the brand is already generating significant amounts of revenue, the information you have at your disposal might not be enough.

If the stakes are high, but your time or money is short, don't despair. The ad-free brand positioning approach really shines in low-budget situations because you can always take advantage of the "release early, release often" principle that this open, transparent positioning process embraces.

> The ad-free brand positioning approach really shines in low-budget situations...

Don't have any money to invest in research? You can still create a starting brand position by answering the four questions with the best information you have at your disposal. Then immediately start testing the positioning with others in the organization and potentially even in communities outside the organization. Incorporate the feedback, revise the positioning, and try again.

Sure, you'll get good ideas from others that will help you make the positioning better, but you might also get the added side benefit of catching people's interest in the project. The earlier you get people involved, the more likely they are to be advocates during the later brand positioning rollout. We discuss this approach in more detail in Chapter 4.

Answering the Four Key Questions

Did you like doing your homework when you were in school? Me neither. But I was smart enough to recognize that if I didn't do my homework, I probably wouldn't pass the test. If I didn't pass the test, I might fail the class. If I failed the class, I might not get into a good college. If I didn't get into a good college, then I was probably going to end up living in a van down by the river or whatever other horrendous fate my parents were using to scare me into doing my homework that week.

So, I did my homework. And I did exactly as much as I needed to do to get a good grade. No more, no less.

I'm passionate about conserving resources during the brand positioning research phase, and I don't like seeing organizations spend any more money or time on research than they absolutely must.

In the next two sections, I've outlined what I believe are the best sources for the answers to the four questions. The first section highlights some of the key basic sources of data you might already have, while the second section highlights some of the more advanced methods for collecting new research data to inform your brand positioning.

If you are positioning a small brand or don't have a lot of time or money, you'll probably want to stick to the first section, using basic research you already have at your disposal. You should be able to make your way through your research homework relatively quickly.

If you are positioning a brand with more at stake, still start at the beginning—often you can take advantage of many of the low-cost, high-value research sources as well—but you will likely find you'll need to conduct some more advanced research to adequately answer the four questions.

Beside each source of information, I've provided a chart that shows which of the four questions this source can help inform. To help you plan your time and budget allocations, I've rated the estimated cost (in money and time) and potential value of each source using the following scales:

Financial cost:

$	low or no cost
$$	moderate cost
$$$	high cost
$$$$	extremely high cost

Time cost:

6	quick and easy
6 6	reasonably quick and easy
6 6 6	labor intensive
6 6 6 6	extremely labor intensive

Value:

★	low value
★ ★	medium value
★ ★ ★	high value
★ ★ ★ ★	extremely high value

Basic Research

Why spend a lot of money and time if you don't need to? As you go through the following list, you'll find plenty of sources of information that will help you answer the four questions quickly without costing you a dime. Here is a list of 13 basic research sources, followed by more details about each option.

1. Website content
2. Web analytics
3. Public relations materials
4. Marketing materials
5. Corporate online footprint
6. Brand elements
7. Existing brand community research
8. Existing employee research
9. Executive communications
10. Media coverage
11. Customer references
12. Brand footprint on Web and social media
13. Existing core ideology

Website Content

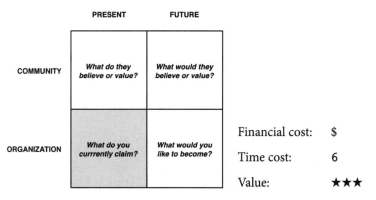

	PRESENT	FUTURE
COMMUNITY	*What do they believe or value?*	*What would they believe or value?*
ORGANIZATION	*What do you currrently claim?*	*What would you like to become?*

Financial cost: $

Time cost: 6

Value: ★★★

Want a quick snapshot of what you are currently claiming about the brand? If your brand is synonymous with your organization, look no further than the "About us" (or whatever you call it, "Company," "About," "Who we are," etc.) section of your own website. Sure you might wince and say, "Wow, I haven't updated that website copy in years." However, there is no better place to find the latest version of your brand's external story to the world.

In any brand positioning project I work on, the "About us" section is typically the first place I go. It usually represents what at some point was the most thought-through version of the organizational story found anywhere.

Often, this section is the first place your community might visit when they encounter your brand, so it is where many people get their first impression. I suggest printing all of the written copy on any pages in the "About Us" section of the website and going through it with a highlighter, noting key phrases and words that appear often or seem especially important.

If you are positioning a product brand or sub-brand, go to the main page for that brand and complete the same exercise. Consider spending time poking around the website and see what else you find that reflects the way your organization is currently positioning the brand. Note recurring themes.

If the brand you will be positioning is small—maybe you are a one-person company or are looking to position your personal brand—you might not have a traditional website. But you probably do have a LinkedIn profile, a Facebook page, a MySpace page, a blog, or a Twitter account. Let these take the place of the website in your analysis.

Web Analytics

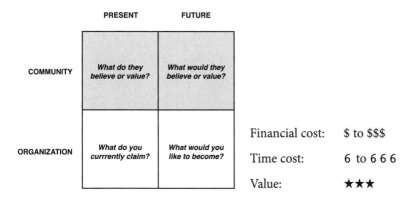

PRESENT   FUTURE

COMMUNITY	*What do they believe or value?*	*What would they believe or value?*
ORGANIZATION	*What do you currrently claim?*	*What would you like to become?*

Financial cost: $ to $$$

Time cost: 6 to 6 6 6

Value: ★★★

While examining the content of your website will help you understand what you are currently saying about the brand, studying the traffic to your website can help you reveal which elements of your brand story are resonating with your community. You might also reveal parts of your brand story you are currently under-telling.

For example, say you are the owner of a vintage furniture store. On your website, you currently tout your store as the best place in the state to find vintage furniture. When you look at your web data, you notice that the pages where you discuss your mid-century modern furniture collection are getting about 10 times the traffic of the other collections on the website. This data point might indicate an opportunity to position the brand with a mid-century modern point of difference.

You can easily get lost in web analytics. Some website hosting services offer complex visitor path tracking and analysis; they can tell you what sites visitors came from, where they live, how often they come back, and maybe even what they ate for breakfast. But even if your website is nothing more than a WordPress blog, you can still learn a lot from simple web metrics like page views and click-throughs.

Don't read too much into the analytics by themselves, though. In my experience often the best time to consult website metrics is when your non-web-analytics research uncovers an interesting trend, and you'd like to see if the web data offers any supporting evidence for that trend.

Public Relations Materials

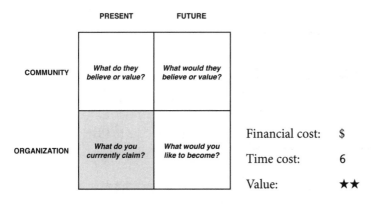

	PRESENT	FUTURE
COMMUNITY	*What do they believe or value?*	*What would they believe or value?*
ORGANIZATION	*What do you currrently claim?*	*What would you like to become?*

Financial cost: $

Time cost: 6

Value: ★★

Press releases and other press materials where you are tooting the brand horn often have brand positioning hints hidden in them. In particular, look at the press release boilerplate—the short section about the organization at the end of a press release that always stays the same. It might be one of the best simple, concise encapsulations of the brand you'll find.

As you read through press releases, look for short, elevator speech-like descriptions of the organization or product brands and why they matter. What do they emphasize first? Do you see similarities between what you read in your PR materials and what you saw when you reviewed the website? Are there phrases that appear over and over in the press releases?

HOMEWORK EXAMPLE #1: ENVICLEAN DRY CLEANERS

You are the proud owner of a regional chain of 30 dry cleaners called EnviClean. But as your company has grown, you wonder if the mission on which you founded the organization has made its way into every corner of your chain and think a brand positioning project might help. It's time to do some research and get started.

You decide you can complete all the basic research yourself. To begin to answer the question "What does my organization currently claim about the brand?" you conduct a deep review of your:

- Website content and analytics
- Store signage, brochures, and other marketing materials
- Presence on Twitter and Facebook
- Logo and brand identity

To answer the questions "What do my brand community members currently believe about or value in the brand?" and "What might they believe or value in the future?" you do a thorough search using Google and Twitter, finding all the positive and negative comments and reviews of your chain online.

When you founded EnviClean, you did so because you deeply believed that it was possible to create a dry cleaning chain that had a smaller environmental impact on the world. You founded the business with a key set of principles in place, including using environmentally friendly equipment and chemicals in your process and starting a recycling program for hangers and other dry cleaning byproducts. You use this core ideology behind the brand as a starting point for answering the question "What would my organization like the brand to become down the road?"

After doing your basic research, you've decided that you don't feel great about the answers to all four questions and need to collect a bit more information to complete your brand homework. So you select a few advanced projects as well.

First, you conduct a customer brand survey via email to better understand what your customers believe about your brand now and what they might value down the road. To say thanks for completing the survey, you offer each customer who completes the survey a coupon for 20% off an upcoming visit.

Next, you conduct an employee survey, separating out responses by job responsibility and level of tenure within the organization. This gives you more information about what the organization would like the brand to become down the road. What's more, the employee survey reveals even more stories from the front line that help you understand the current customer experience across the chain—bonus!

Finally, you go from store to store and conduct a series of interviews with some of the employees who filled out the survey to learn a bit more about the way they see the brand. This gives you even more detailed information about what the current experience is and what both customers and employees might value in the brand down the road.

While you realize that you could have done a lot more research, you feel like you now have the information you need to answer all four questions well. It's time to begin positioning EnviClean.

Marketing Materials

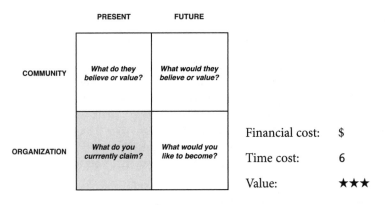

Your organization might produce marketing collateral—things like brochures, posters, advertisements, trade show signage, presentations, whitepapers, and other tools of the marketing trade—describing your brand.

Collect as many of these pieces as you can. Study them closely, and see if there are recurring themes used to describe the brand. What about the imagery used in these materials? Does it present a consistent view of the brand? If you see concepts used to describe the brand over and over, are they the same concepts used in the PR materials and on the website?

Corporate Online Footprint

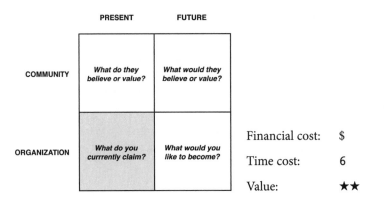

An organization's own website plays an increasingly smaller role every day in determining how an organization defines itself online. These days a brand's official footprint on the Web is spread more thinly across sites and services like Twitter, Facebook, LinkedIn, Google, Wikipedia, YouTube, job sites such as Monster.com, and a myriad of other corners of the Internet.

✉ *Note*

Your brand's web presence is no longer confined to your website.

Where does your brand have an official presence? How consistently do you present the brand in each place? Here are a few examples of things you might look for:

1. If your brand has a Twitter page, how does it describe the brand? If press boilerplate language is a good place to find brief descriptions of the brand, Twitter requires even shorter ones. The character limit for a Twitter bio is only 160 characters—brands must pack a lot of punch into a few short words.

2. If your brand has an official Facebook, LinkedIn, or YouTube page, how does it describe the brand? Is the description the same in each place? Note any differences and think about the possible reasons for the discrepancies.

3. When you type your brand name into Google, what does the first official entry say? Usually Google grabs 160 characters worth of content from the text or metadata (words hidden in the page source code that describe the content) of a webpage. Which text did Google choose? How does it represent the brand?

4. Usually official job postings on websites like Monster or CareerBuilder include a description of the organization. How do your job postings reflect your brand?

Brand Elements

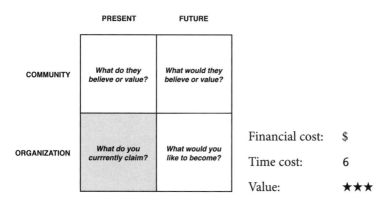

	PRESENT	FUTURE
COMMUNITY	*What do they believe or value?*	*What would they believe or value?*
ORGANIZATION	*What do you currrently claim?*	*What would you like to become?*

Financial cost: $

Time cost: 6

Value: ★★★

Take a close look at things that help represent the brand like brand names, logos, iconography, taglines, slogans, and branded features. Is there a structure connecting all these pieces together? Are they consistently used everywhere the brand is found? Are they consistent with each other?

Do they support the themes and ideas that you uncovered when researching the website, press materials, marketing pieces, and online presence? Could they do a better job of tying everything together?

Existing Brand Community Research

	PRESENT	FUTURE
COMMUNITY	*What do they believe or value?*	*What would they believe or value?*
ORGANIZATION	*What do you currrently claim?*	*What would you like to become?*

Financial cost: $

Time cost: 6

Value: ★★★

Probably one of the least expensive and least time-consuming datasets to study is the research you and your organization have already completed. I've noticed people have a tendency to want to design an expensive new survey to answer their questions when the organization just fielded a survey six months ago that covers 50% of what they need.

I find this wasteful. I always like to go back and look at any research that has been done in the last few years with customers, partners, and other community members before ever considering funding a new piece of research.

 Tip

Before you field an expensive new research study, check to see if there is some existing research that can inform your positioning.

The reality is that original research projects are often quite expensive—in time and money—and most organizations rarely make full use of the research in which they have already invested. So, before you make a decision to undertake a new study, ask around in your organization to see if you can get your hands on what you've asked people previously.

Sure, you might not like exactly how the questions were worded, you might not agree with the way the sample was selected, or you might feel like the data is no longer current or relevant. Simply accept these drawbacks, and keep them in the back of your mind as you study the data.

At worst, you'll get ideas for how to better word questions should you design an original research project of your own. At best, you'll find out you have enough information that you don't need to conduct new research at all.

Existing Employee Research

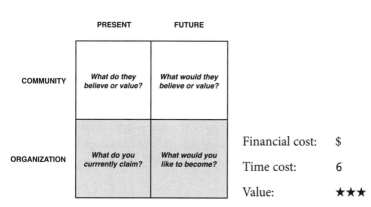

Just as existing research on customers and others in your brand community is a great source for hints as to what your community values about the brand, existing employee research is great for finding hints about what people inside your organization think about your brand today and what they'd like to see it become down the road.

Employee surveys and internal engagement surveys are particularly good sources of brand-related information, especially when they've provided opportunities beyond multiple-choice or yes/no questions for people to express their ideas freely.

Executive Communications

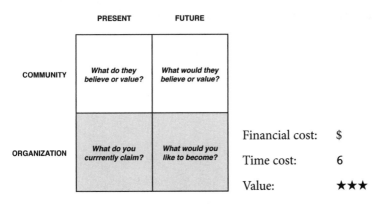

	PRESENT	FUTURE
COMMUNITY	*What do they believe or value?*	*What would they believe or value?*
ORGANIZATION	*What do you currrently claim?*	*What would you like to become?*

Financial cost: $

Time cost: 6

Value: ★★★

Executive communications are another great source for discovering what is currently being said about the brand and what the organization aspires to have it become in the future. Study the speeches your CEO gives at trade shows. Read the blog of your executive director. Examine state of the union–type emails from the president to employees. If any great quotes or important phrases appear regularly, make sure to note them.

Media Coverage

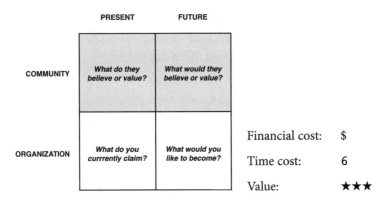

	PRESENT	FUTURE
COMMUNITY	*What do they believe or value?*	*What would they believe or value?*
ORGANIZATION	*What do you currrently claim?*	*What would you like to become?*

Financial cost: $

Time cost: 6

Value: ★★★

Have there been stories in the press about your brand recently? If so, see if they offer hints about how your brand is viewed from the outside. I always look for the "comma phrase"—the phrase immediately following the brand name at the beginning of a story.

For example a sentence might start like this: "Red Hat, *the open source leader*, was…" or "Red Hat, *the leading Linux provider*, was…". Do you think these comma phrases describe your organization accurately? Why or why not? Do stories in different media outlets refer to the organization the same way?

Media coverage is also a great place to collect quotes from customers, partners, or competitors that can be used to inform the positioning later.

Customer References

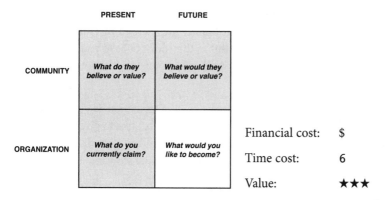

Financial cost: $

Time cost: 6

Value: ★★★

Customer references are a good source for data that helps us answer our questions. Typically, they include customer quotes that might highlight what customers view as the key benefit or benefits of the brand. They can also tell you a lot about what your brand is currently saying to the outside world because the folks who wrote them probably selectively picked a quote that highlighted the exact part of the brand they wanted to showcase.

Make sure to look at both written and video references if they are available. References on video are especially valuable because, when the customer is speaking, you can often gather as much from his body language and tone as you can from his words.

Brand Footprint on Web and Social Media

	PRESENT	FUTURE
COMMUNITY	What do they believe or value?	What would they believe or value?
ORGANIZATION	What do you currrently claim?	What would you like to become?

Financial cost: $ to $$

Time cost: 6 to 6 6

Value: ★★★

No basic research about the brand would be complete without a deep look at what people are saying about the brand online. There are infinite sources you can explore.

Google is your friend when it comes to finding the best stuff. Start by typing something into Google as simple as the name of your brand plus "reviews" and see what comes up. If your brand is a product, service, or store, you might find hundreds of reviews of your brand, both good and bad, on sites like Epinions (www.epinions.com), TripAdvisor (www.tripadvisor.com), and Amazon (www.amazon.com).

What do people like and dislike about your brand? Are there things that they especially value about what you do? Are there things they don't believe you do well? Are they calling you out on anything in your brand experience they do not believe to be authentic to the brand?

But don't stop there. Use Google to search for as much information as you can find about what people are saying about your brand on the Web. I like to give myself one hour to search Google for as many opinions about the brand as I can find using every relevant search phrase I can think of. At the end of the hour, I stop and analyze.

Did the same comments from the same people appear over and over in multiple searches? Were comments about my brand rare, or were they everywhere? Were people largely in agreement, or were comments all over the map? If you see especially revealing data points, take screenshots of them—you might want to use them when you present your research.

You'll want to track the conversation about your brand on an ongoing basis, and it doesn't hurt to start the process now. I'd recommend you set up what some have begun to call a brand *listening post*. A listening post is a set of tools that allow you to track the ongoing conversation, not just on the Web, but also in real-time conversations about your brand in social media.

You can construct your own listening post using a host of freely available tools. Start with Google Alerts (www.google.com/alerts), an amazing free service. Use Google Alerts to select one or more keywords (like your brand name) on which you'd like to receive alerts, and then Google will send you an email whenever something new is posted online including that keyword. If your brand is a popular one, set up some email filters so that you don't overload your inbox, or send the alerts to a secondary email address—perhaps one you set up exclusively for this purpose.

 Tip

You can construct your own listening post for free using a host of simple tools available on the Web.

To stay on top of the current pulse of your brand, you should follow what is being said about the brand on Twitter. There are plenty of good tools that allow you to set up custom searches of Twitter based on any keyword you choose. I find TweetDeck (www.tweetdeck.com) to have the cleanest interface, but Seesmic (www.seesmic.com) and HootSuite (www.hootsuite.com) are also popular. New tools are being developed daily, so by the time you read this, you might be able to uncover one that works even better for you.

A growing number of sites allow you to quickly search for your brand within and across multiple web and social media channels. Consider testing IceRocket (www.icerocket.com) to find what people have written about your brand in the blogosphere. Addictomatic (www.addictomatic.com) allows you to search for any keyword and then creates a custom page showing where that keyword has appeared across blogs, Twitter, YouTube, FriendFeed, and a number of other popular sources. SocialMention (www.socialmention.com) does pretty much the same thing but also attempts to track positive and negative sentiment, which is interesting and useful for our purposes.

Most brands should be able to find out everything they need to know about the brand footprint from the free services mentioned. But if you'd like to have much more sophisticated reporting, one stop for all your information, and budget is not an issue, consider subscribing to a professional-grade subscription service. These services are becoming quite popular in larger organizations, and the most-widely used is probably Radian6 (www.radian6.com).

One of my favorite brand-related sites is Brand Tags (www.brandtags.net). When you first come to the Brand Tags site, a random brand logo appears. You are asked to type in the first word that comes to mind about the brand you see.

After you do this for five brands, you'll see a link allowing you to look at the tag cloud for any brand, built upon the "first word that comes to mind" responses from all of the visitors who've ever come to the site. These clouds are some of the most interesting, revealing, unvarnished depictions of brands I've ever seen. Unfortunately, only widely recognized brands are included, so you might not see yours (although you can submit your brand for consideration).

If you manage a well-known brand, you will enjoy coming to this site to see your brand tag cloud. You also might want to look at the clouds for other brands similar to yours for ideas that can inform your research. Brand Tags is the most interesting experiment I've seen in exploring the answers to the question of what people believe about or value in famous brands.

Existing Core Ideology

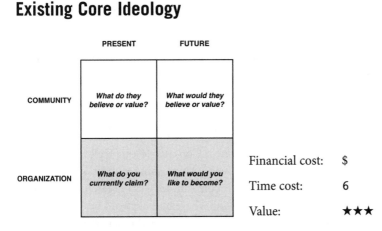

Has your organization articulated a core purpose or mission? Do you have a strong set of organizational values? If so, there is no better place to find clues about what your brand could become in the future.

Jim Collins and Jerry Porras introduced the concept of the core ideology in their book *Built to Last*, an extremely useful resource for those developing ad-free brands. They describe core ideology as the "core values and sense of purpose beyond just making money that guides and inspires people throughout the organization and remains relatively fixed for long periods of time."[2]

 Tip

> Your organization's mission and values can provide great clues to where your brand should go in the future.

You might have seen some evidence of the core ideology behind your organization or brand during your analysis of the "About us" section of the website, but many organizations don't publicize their mission and values externally.

Some other common places to look for the core ideology include the organization's intranet, new-hire orientation presentations, the organization's "who we are" presentation, annual reports, and feature-length press interviews with the CEO or other top executives.

But don't look too hard. If you have to search to find the mission and values of the organization, chances are they aren't deeply held and might not be particularly useful to you in your positioning efforts.

---

2. This definition is found in Chapter 3 of the book *Built to Last* by Jim Collins and Jerry Porras.

Advanced Research

Sometimes the basic research mentioned previously just isn't enough. In the event you were not able to collect enough data to answer the four questions using the basic research sources, you'll need to consider doing some original research to supplement the basic research. The following projects all cost more in terms of time and money but can provide much more detailed, valuable information as well.

Even if you can't afford to do all these projects, perhaps you can select one or two or do them on a smaller scale. Look at your existing body of research, and pick the projects that will provide data that helps answer any of the questions where answers remain cloudy.

Here is a list of 11 basic research sources, followed by more details about each option.

1. Brand inventory

2. Email survey

3. Web survey

4. Employee survey

5. External interviews

6. Internal interviews

7. Executive conversation

8. Employee conversation

9. External conversation

10. Brand tracking study

11. New core ideology

Brand Inventory

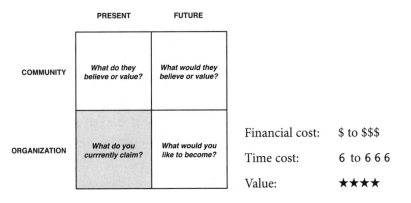

If your brand is bigger, is more complex, or is present in multiple countries, I suggest studying some of the projects included in the basic research already mentioned as part of a more formal brand inventory.

The brand inventory is a long, hard look in the mirror, examining from every angle possible how your brand presents itself to the world. It reveals how you make your brand look and sound by what you say, show, and do. It can help you answer questions like:

1. Are you consistent in how you present the brand?

2. Are you actually saying and doing what you thought you were saying and doing?

3. How does the brand look when we see it as a whole?

4. Does looking at everything together change the way you think about the story you are putting out there?

There is no better way to reveal how your organization is actually positioning itself today on the broadest possible scale than conducting a brand inventory. Figure 3.4 shows an example of materials collected during a brand inventory at Red Hat.

Typically a brand inventory results in a formal report or presentation highlighting examples of how the brand looks and sounds in every place it is found around the world. Even if you are just doing the report for yourself, consider keeping a copy of it on file so you can look back later to see how far you've come.

✉ Note

A brand inventory reveals how your organization is actually positioning itself to the outside world today.

While informal, basic research about how you are currently presenting your brand can be done quickly, a full brand inventory usually takes some time.

If you have a lot of time but not a lot of money, consider conducting the brand inventory internally. If you can't collect all the required materials yourself, enlist help from other departments and other offices around the world to send you every manifestation of the brand they can find.

Figure 3.4   *This photo shows the wall where we hung the materials we collected during our Red Hat brand inventory. We found that organizing the materials by brand and region of the world where they were created made it easy to get a clear picture of how consistently we were positioning the Red Hat brand around the world.*

If you are short on time but have money to spend, consider hiring an outside branding firm to do a brand inventory on your behalf. Although an external firm might not be able to connect with as broad a range of internal people to collect materials, it sometimes has the advantage of distance from the brand. Often when external agencies do your review for you, they notice things you might never have seen on your own.

As organizations get bigger, brand inventories can often reveal complications, inconsistencies, and other interesting and sometimes frightful things. You might find gaps or differences in the brand story from function to function inside the organization. Inconsistencies in visual brand and positioning in different parts of the organization or the world are both common.

...brand inventories can often reveal complications, inconsistencies, and other interesting and sometimes frightful things.

In a big organization, the most fun part of a brand inventory is getting the opportunity to see materials from all over the world created by people you've never met. You'll see some amazing stuff that you probably didn't know was being made. For you extroverts, the brand inventory gives you a good excuse to reach out to other folks who are living the brand every day and see what they are working on.

As you are doing a brand inventory, I encourage you to handle it in the spirit of brand enlightenment and not be the brand police. The goal is to see whether your organization is presenting a consistent brand position to the world, not to punish people for what they are doing wrong. Use it as an opportunity to educate.

If your brand inventory is all stick and no carrot, the reality is you will only expose a small subset of the work actually being created. So, if you want the true picture, be open-minded, be curious, and especially stay open to the possibility that the best brand implementations and the best ideas for the future of the brand can come from far-flung parts of the organization. You might be pleasantly surprised with what you find.

When we did our brand inventory at Red Hat, we put everything we collected up on a big wall in our workspace. Figure 3.4 shows what our wall looked like when it was done. The funniest thing we found during our Red Hat brand inventory was that someone had designed a pair of Red Hat tighty-whiteys with our Shadowman logo on the front. Probably not exactly on brand—I think Shadowman would actually wear boxers, not briefs—but we loved it.

HOMEWORK EXAMPLE #2: BUBBAPOP SODA COMPANY

You are the chief brand officer for BubbaPop Soda Company, a growing producer of soft drinks, now doing over $500 million a year in annual revenues. Until recently, BubbaPop was a regional company selling about 90% of its products in the southern United States.

But after a push by Mothers Against Drunk Driving, a group of NASCAR drivers began celebrating their wins by drinking bottles of BubbaPop instead of champagne or beer. The NASCAR drivers love your soda, and BubbaPop loves the free exposure.

This publicity led to more and more orders for BubbaPop across the country, which has made you think that perhaps BubbaPop should revisit its brand positioning to ensure it resonates with a larger, national audience.

Fortunately, you have been given a sizeable budget to complete this positioning project and you and your team can afford to research the brand extensively.

You encourage your team to spend a few weeks doing a pass through all the basic research options, and based on this work, you have a strong sense for what members of the current brand community value about BubbaPop and might value in the future. You also understand what people inside the organization think, but you would like to hear more.

Fortunately, you have a solid external agency that helps you with your branding initiatives because your internal team has a lot of balls in the air given the rapid growth of the brand. You decide to bring in your external agency to do a full brand inventory. They bring back a complete report that shows you an amazing amount of detail about how some new bottlers outside of the South have begun positioning BubbaPop—you had no idea this stuff even existed.

Your agency also has extensive research experience, so you ask them to help design and field a brand tracking study. This study will separate the country into five regions: the South, the Northeast, the Midwest, the Southwest, and the Northwest. It will also not only target current customers, but will study people you think might make ideal customers for your business down the road, as well.

Based on the results of the study, you realize there are rich opportunities for your brand well beyond your current vision. Exciting stuff!

You decide you need to learn more and ask your agency to conduct and record a series of in-person interviews across the country, covering both current and potential future customers.

At the same time, you ask the internal team to work with the human resources department to do a deeper study of the people who work for BubbaPop today. You conduct both an email survey and also help them analyze the results of a recent customer engagement survey. Then you go further, hosting a series of town hall conversations with employees in many departments and a series of one-on-one interviews with key employees from across the organization.

After almost eight months of analysis, you now feel like you have enough information to begin repositioning BubbaPop for the future.

Email Survey

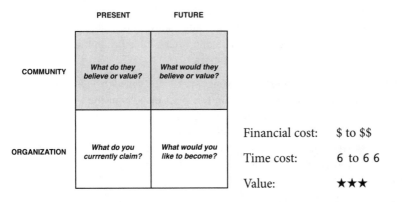

	PRESENT	FUTURE
COMMUNITY	What do they believe or value?	What would they believe or value?
ORGANIZATION	What do you currrently claim?	What would you like to become?

Financial cost: $ to $$

Time cost: 6 to 6 6

Value: ★★★

Do you have access to a list of email addresses for customers, partners, or others in the community of people surrounding your organization (and permission to use it)? If so, a short and informal survey is often a good way to collect some key information about your brand community members' current perceptions and opinions about your brand.

Be very, very careful about planning and executing this survey. It should be coordinated with others in the organization so that multiple emails or surveys are not going out at the same time. It should also be carefully worded and constructed—this is an opportunity for you to positively engage with those who surround your brand and every word you chose could have a positive or negative effect.

Think of this as one of the first steps in your brand positioning rollout. By asking people what they think of your brand, you are beginning to bring them into the brand positioning process. While some people will be annoyed to receive an email survey, others (especially if it is well executed) will be glad that someone is finally asking them what they think. This can be the beginning of a beautiful friendship.

To get the most possible respondents and most valuable results from your survey, be sure to choose your words carefully and limit the number of questions to the minimum needed.

If you are a for-profit company, also try to segment your survey (if your data allows it), separating actual customers from other parts of the community. There are often major distinctions between what people in general think about your brand versus what people who've actually spent money with you think. I'd put extra weight on the opinions of the latter group.

I've included a sample survey in the appendix that you might decide to use as a starting point.

🔍 *Tip*

Check out the sample email survey in the appendix for ideas.

I recommend linking from the email to a web-based survey. If your organization already has a web-based survey system in-house, by all means use it. If you don't have access to a survey tool, there are some great online services you can use.

My favorite is SurveyMonkey (www.surveymokey.com). It's free to get started and allows you to upgrade to a (still inexpensive) paid service that offers more flexibility to customize and give your survey a professional appearance.

Web Survey

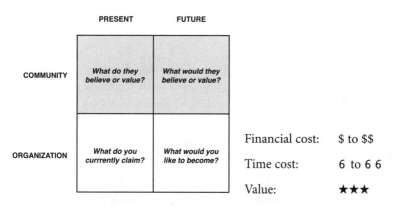

Conducting a survey on your website is another good way to get some data about your brand even if you don't have access to an email list. You can post a link to the survey on the homepage or on key pages throughout the site, or even stick the survey at the end of the order process.

As with email surveys, it is often hard to tell the paying customers from others in the community, so be sure to ask a question that will help you segment customers from other community members. And if you want to specifically target paying customers, you may want to consider placing the survey at the end of the order process.

If you don't have survey functionality built in to your website, set up an online survey using SurveyMonkey or another similar tool; then link over to it from your website. If you have a Twitter account or Facebook page, consider cross-promoting the survey via Twitter and Facebook as well.

Employee Survey

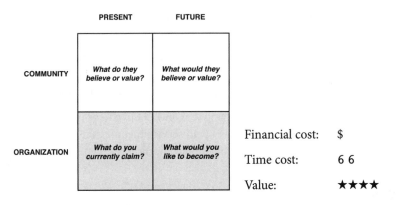

Ad-free brands rely heavily on the people closest to the brand—the employees of the organization—to tell the brand story. So, it is never too early to involve them in the brand positioning process.

I recommend, if all possible, you kick off the brand positioning project internally within your organization with an open call for people to let you know what they think about the current state of the brand and future possibilities they see for it. Transparently acknowledging that there are people within the organization thinking about the future of the brand who are interested in hearing the opinions of every employee can do wonders for your culture and morale.

An employee survey can prove to be one of the most valuable investments you make in the future success of your positioning project. By asking the people who care the most about the brand what they think upfront, you begin building a stable of future brand ambassadors who might be willing to help later during the brand positioning rollout phase.

I've included a sample version of what an employee survey might look like in the appendix.

 Tip

Check out the sample employee survey in the appendix for ideas.

Be sure to ask both multiple-choice questions (so you have some quantitative data to analyze) and free-response questions (so you can get a better sense for people's feelings, emotions, and ideas). Finally, be sure to use this as an opportunity to recruit volunteers who'd like to help further. This is a great opportunity to begin recruiting for your positioning rollout teams.

External Interviews

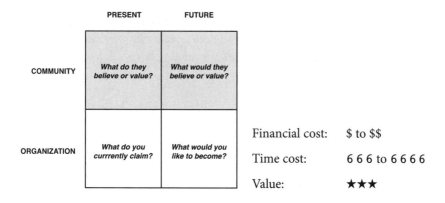

	PRESENT	FUTURE
COMMUNITY	What do they believe or value?	What would they believe or value?
ORGANIZATION	What do you currrently claim?	What would you like to become?

Financial cost: $ to $$

Time cost: 6 6 6 to 6 6 6 6

Value: ★★★

After you have completed an external survey via email or on the Web, you might find that you have uncovered some interesting data you'd like to explore further. Perhaps you are beginning to see the shape of your future brand positioning take place, but you'd like to learn a little more and ask some specific questions.

Interviews can be a great way to fill in the gaps in your knowledge, often providing good stories, quotes, and other examples that can be used in your positioning work. The downside is that they are extremely time-consuming. You must take into account not just the time to conduct the interview, but also writing the interview questions, finding interview candidates, scheduling, travelling, writing up notes or editing video, and analyzing the results.

My recommendation would be to conduct no more than 20 interviews at the absolute maximum, but preferably 5–10. If each interview is scheduled for 30 minutes, figure about 2–3 hours of total work per interview when trying to decide how much time you can afford to invest.

If you are planning to conduct an email or web survey, consider using the survey to ask for volunteers who would be willing to talk further with you about the brand. This ready-made list will save a ton of work searching for interview candidates. Even better, you might have a wider pool of potential candidates, so you'll be able to be more selective.

⊘ Tip

To save yourself time looking for interview candidates, ask people in your web or email survey if they'd be willing to provide additional feedback.

Carefully choose the candidates for your interview so that your interview pool covers many segments of the brand community. You'll likely want to have a strong focus on customers, but also consider interviewing partners, members of the news media who cover your brand, vendors, investors, board members, and other important constituents.

View these interviews as an opportunity for future brand engagement, and select people who you think can not only offer you deep insight into your brand, but also might be potential external brand advocates or sounding boards down the road.

ARE YOU COMFORTABLE NOT HAVING ALL THE ANSWERS? ARE YOU OKAY WITH ASKING FOR HELP?

I've noticed over the years that many people in business have trouble admitting they don't know everything. Our traditional business culture seems to value people acting like they have all the answers, while viewing those who ask for help or say "I don't know" as weak.

My good friend and business partner David Burney is fond of saying, "I'm comfortable not having all of the answers."

My view? Those who have all the answers will have a difficult time building engaged communities around their brands. But those brands willing to reach out for help, admitting they don't know everything and remaining curious to learn more from the people who care about the brand, will have a huge advantage.

In my experience, there is no better way to engage members of your brand community than humbly reaching out and asking them for help. By admitting you don't know everything, and showing others that you think they could provide useful feedback and advice, you begin to engage on the basis of trust and respect.

Many marketing people try to hide behind a veneer of trust and respect, making statements like "we value your input" or "we appreciate your feedback." But eventually the facade breaks down and they reveal their true passion—your money. A relationship based on a financial transaction is much less valuable than one based on trust. Good salespeople know this intuitively.

Ad-free brands are comfortable not having all the answers because they know every answer they get from people in their community moves them a step closer to engagement.

When at all possible, select interview candidates you can speak with in person. Conducting the interview in person not only allows you to make a stronger personal connection with the interviewee, but also gives you the opportunity to film the interview (if the interviewee agrees). Filming interviews is the best, albeit most expensive, option. When you capture the interviewee's comments on video, you can show highlights later during the brand positioning group session. Watching someone talk passionately about the brand can be powerful and far more effective than simply reading a quote.

If you can't afford to film the interviews, the next best option is to record the audio. Most smartphones, including the iPhone and Android-based phones, now have applications that allow you to do this easily. If you can't record the video or audio, at very least take good notes—you'll want to ensure you collect as many full quotes as possible in the event you'd like to use them later.

If your brand is a national or international brand, it might be cost- or time-prohibitive for you to attempt to conduct every interview in person. In this case, the next best option is to conduct the interview via phone or Skype (or a similar web-based conferencing tool). Although these options won't create quite the same personal connection, you can still capture great information and select from a wider pool of interview candidates.

I still recommend recording telephone or Skype interviews. Always ask the interviewee for permission before recording the session, of course. Many conference call services have an option to record the call, which is the easiest way, but in a pinch, a speakerphone in conjunction with a recording device like a smartphone will work well, too. Several downloadable applications allow you to record Skype sessions. The best one I've encountered that works on both PCs and Macs is called IMCapture (http://www.imcapture.com).

You might be tempted to conduct interviews via chat/IRC session or even email. While chat sessions are acceptable (given you can copy and save the text of the session), I'd stay away from interviewing via email. If you are going to just send questions via email, you eliminate the personal engagement benefits of the interview process and might be better off simply conducting a standard web- or email-based survey.

External interviews are great for enhancing the information from an email or web survey because they give you an opportunity to explore things further. For example, if the survey results show you there is a particular brand attribute people clearly value, you might want to use the interviews to go deeper into why they value it. You might also want to delve deeper into areas that help you answer what people might value in the brand in the future.

While in-person and telephone/videoconference interviews take a lot of time, they can be extremely valuable, both in providing great data and stories and as a first step toward engaging with people in your brand community. Every time you ask for help or show you are interested in those who are interested in you, a door to a future relationship opens.

Every time you ask for help or show you are interested in those who are interested in you, a door to a future relationship opens.

Internal Interviews

	PRESENT	FUTURE
COMMUNITY	*What do they believe or value?*	*What would they believe or value?*
ORGANIZATION	*What do you currrently claim?*	*What would you like to become?*

Financial cost: $ to $$

Time cost: 6 6 6 to 6 6 6 6

Value: ★★★

Just as external interviews can provide good color to the results of an external survey, internal interviews can help you flesh out many of the things you learned in your internal employee survey.

Many of the rules for external interviews also apply to running internal interviews with employees. Try to hold them in person, try to record if possible, and choose a broad cross-section of key internal folks.

When choosing people for internal interviews, keep in mind that one of an ad-free brand's goals is to engage employees in the positioning process as early as possible. Interviews provide a great vehicle for starting these relationships with employees who might become brand ambassadors down the road.

You should interview people from a variety of job functions within the organization and at all levels (not just executives). Try to focus on the people who know the brand best, are passionate about the brand, or have an enormous amount of historical perspective about the organization. Remember that people in traditional brand-related roles like marketing or PR are not necessarily the people who know the brand best. I've found tenure to be one of the most reliable indicators of brand knowledge, but it also doesn't hurt to interview some smart folks who are relatively new to the organization to get some fresh perspectives.

If at all possible, try to interview the top executive of the organization, or maybe even the whole senior executive team, especially focusing on those who have a long tenure with the organization. Consider including a board member or two if your organization has them.

One thing to look out for: the selection process for internal interviews can be politically sensitive, so you might end up having to interview more people than you originally budgeted for to stay on everyone's good side.

You might find you need to conduct personal interviews with each and every executive to ensure everyone feels like they had their say. There's no sense in making enemies now—go ahead and invest the time, do the extra interviews, and you'll find it ends up saving you time down the road because you'll have more advocates for the project (and fewer roadblocks) at the executive level.

In your internal interviews, you'll often come across "ah-ha!" moments where someone articulates a point, an example, or a concept that you didn't have the words to describe before. When this happens, be sure to note both the example and the person who provided it. Every time you use this example down the road you'll need to very publicly give this person credit for providing the idea.

 Tip

Each time you use a piece of knowledge you collected from an internal interview, very publicly give credit for the idea to the person who provided it.

Showing where ideas came from and giving credit to members of the community is an essential element of the engagement process that I discuss further later.

HOMEWORK EXAMPLE #3: YOUR BEST FRIEND, CHAUNCEY

Your best friend, Chauncey, was just laid off after 20 years as a middle manager in a telecommunications firm. Chauncey is depressed and worries his job prospects are dim. He wonders who would want to hire a 46-year-old former telecommunications manager.

As a good friend, part of your job is to help Chauncey feel better. So you take him out on Friday night for a few beers and let him know that you might be able to help him using what you've learned about positioning. He looks at you for a second like he is going to break a bottle over your head, but then sighs and says, "What do I have to lose?"

So you ask the bartender to bring over a pile of napkins and you access the Internet on your phone. First, you take a quick look at Chauncey's LinkedIn page to see how he currently positions himself. You write down some of the key words he uses on a napkin labeled "What Chauncey currently says about himself."

He's also brought along a copy of his resume to the bar (desperate times call for desperate measures), so you take a look at that, circle some key words, and write a few more things on the "What Chauncey currently says" napkin.

You've known Chauncey for a long time, and you actually play golf with his former boss at the telecommunications firm once a month or so, so you know a lot of the things his former company valued about him. In fact, when the former boss and you played golf last week, he told you how hard it had been to let Chauncey go and how much he loved his work, and he mentioned a few things that he really missed. You write these things down on a napkin labeled "What people like about Chauncey" and add a few thoughts of your own.

Next, you get back on your phone and search Monster.com job listings for telecommunications managers across the country. Some key phrases appear over and over in these job listings. You write them down on a napkin labeled "What people are looking for in a telecomm executive" and circle the areas where you and Chauncey believe he has the strongest skills and qualities.

By now, you are several beers into the evening, and Chauncey has begun to talk passionately about his dreams for the future. A couple of the things he says really resonate with you, and you think employers will find them compelling, too. You write down some of these ideas on a napkin labeled "What Chauncey wants to become."

Finally, you spread out the four napkins on the bar in a square and talk to Chauncey about how you need to create positioning for him that connects all four of the napkins together. But that's enough for tonight—you agree that you can continue the conversation on Sunday afternoon during the football game.

Research complete, check please!

Executive Conversation

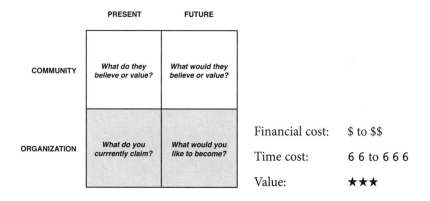

	PRESENT	FUTURE
COMMUNITY	What do they believe or value?	What would they believe or value?
ORGANIZATION	What do you currrently claim?	What would you like to become?

Financial cost: $ to $$

Time cost: 6 6 to 6 6 6

Value: ★★★

To be successful, a brand positioning project needs support or sponsorship from the highest levels of the organization. If your organization is just you, you have this covered. But in large organizations dealing with hundreds of complex issues on a daily basis, senior leaders often are dealing with urgent crises right in front of them and spending time on a long-term-benefit project like brand positioning can seem like a luxury.

It is important to build broad executive support for the positioning project as early as possible. While I recommend that most people wait to bring executives together to talk about positioning until the research phase is completed, in certain cases where you need strong executive support to get the project started or keep the project moving, it makes sense to gather executives together for a conversation about the brand sooner rather than later.

📩 *Note*

Successful brand positioning projects should have support at the highest levels of the organization.

I'd recommend you wait to host this session until you have some data to present—perhaps you've completed the basic research and can show the results of it, or maybe you've even completed an internal or external survey. Use this data as the jumping off point for the conversation. Give the executives some information they can react to; show them some early ideas. Explain what brand positioning is and why it matters, and show them the benefits the organization might see from better brand positioning.

The executive conversation might generate some great ideas that help you steer the next pieces of research you complete. But even more importantly, you'll be building executive support for the project, which will come in handy down the road.

Employee Conversation

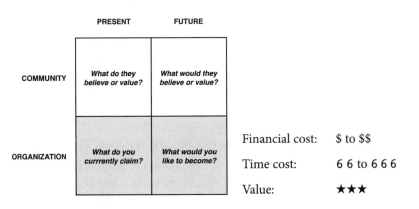

If you don't have the time or budget to do in-person interviews with individual employees, consider bringing them together in a group or series of groups to have conversations about the brand together. These groups should be small, no more than 20 people or so, where everyone can face each other (this is not a presentation; it's a discussion).

You can bring people together by department (consider asking to be invited to host department team meetings in different parts of the organization), by office location, or by tenure. Or you can randomly select people to attend with no criteria at all. You might even want to host the conversation over lunch or snacks. The promise of free pizza or catered food often brings folks out of the woodwork who wouldn't otherwise attend.

Come prepared with a set of conversation-starting questions designed to elicit more information about interesting areas that you've identified in previous research. Make sure you actively facilitate the conversation. If it starts veering into a place that doesn't help you, ask another question to redirect the conversation. But give the discussion a lot of room—you don't want to accidentally cut off a discussion that can lead to an interesting place. I've provided some ideas in the appendix for the types of questions that can often get an internal brand conversation started.

Tip

For internal conversation-starting ideas, check out the list of sample discussion questions in the appendix.

As with interviews, consider recording the conversation or at least take good notes. If you are the facilitator, you'll probably have your hands full, so ask a colleague to take notes for you.

External Conversation

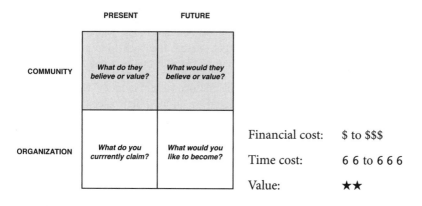

	PRESENT	FUTURE
COMMUNITY	*What do they believe or value?*	*What would they believe or value?*
ORGANIZATION	*What do you currrently claim?*	*What would you like to become?*

Financial cost: $ to $$$

Time cost: 6 6 to 6 6 6

Value: ★★

If an opportunity arises to bring together members of the community for a conversation about the brand, you might want to consider taking advantage of it. External conversations might be exclusively for customers or partners, or they might be for anyone in the brand community.

What are some common examples of where external conversations might make sense? Perhaps your organization is hosting or attending a trade show, and many of the people you'd like to talk to will be there. Maybe you are having a large group of customers visit your headquarters for an event; a conversation could be added to the agenda.

🔍 Tip

Check out the list of sample discussion questions for external conversations in the appendix.

Hosting conversations with members of the brand community can be a good way to get a lot of information from a large number of people very quickly.

One important point: these conversations are *not* focus groups, where you show something to people and they react to it. Instead, organize these conversations more like design-thinking sessions. These conversations are for building things, not for tearing them apart. I discuss this design thinking approach to facilitation more in Chapter 4.

AD-FREE BRANDS DON'T LIKE FOCUS GROUPS

A lot has been written about the dangers of focus groups, especially whether they provide reliable results. While I can see where focus groups might provide value in certain situations, ad-free brands should usually stay away from them. Why?

First, focus groups are expensive. I believe there are much cheaper ways, especially in the age of the Internet, to get reliable feedback from people in your brand community—I've outlined many of them in this chapter.

But even more importantly, the culture of the focus group is totally wrong for an ad-free brand. The stereotypical focus group, in which executives sit behind one-way glass as someone asks a group of paid "target customers" to react to a logo or slogan, is about as far from engagement as you can get.

Ad-free brands love feedback. But they prefer to get it out in the open, where every question asked is an opportunity to engage a real person, not "observe" a "target consumer" in an unnatural habitat. Focus groups only collect information, ignoring one of the biggest benefits of feedback—it can form the foundation of a relationship.

Brand Tracking Study

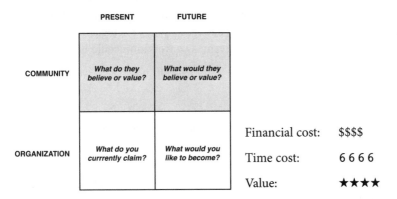

	PRESENT	FUTURE
COMMUNITY	What do they believe or value?	What would they believe or value?
ORGANIZATION	What do you currrently claim?	What would you like to become?

Financial cost: $$$$

Time cost: 6 6 6 6

Value: ★★★★

The Rolls Royce of brand research is the formal brand tracking study. A brand tracking study is typically a rigorous survey, often conducted via phone or email and sometimes including paid participants. A brand tracking study is much longer and more complex than the surveys we covered earlier. It will provide you with statistically valid data and much more detailed information about the current state of your brand than almost any other research tool.

There is no substitute for a well-executed brand tracking study to help you learn about your brand, but they do not come cheap. A brand tracking study should be designed by professional research experts experienced in carefully crafting and ordering questions. Sometimes very small details that most of us would overlook can skew the results in important ways. By working with a professional, you can ensure the cleanest possible results.

One of the great benefits of a brand tracking study is that it allows you to define a starting point showing the state of your brand as it exists today. It is called a *brand tracking study* because it allows you to track your progress from that starting point on an ongoing basis. Typically, brand tracking studies are conducted about once a year, but if you need more data points, you can do them twice a year. If budget is an issue, you can also do them less often.

There are very few things more valuable than being able to see the progress of your brand over time by looking at the answers to questions that have stayed the same over a period measured in years. For brands that can afford to conduct a formal brand tracking study, there is no better tool for measuring your ongoing progress.

Can you design a brand tracking study on your own? Yes. But this is one place where, if you have the money, you might find the investment in professional assistance well worth it. Most research firms are not only good at designing effective brand tracking surveys, but are also very good at analyzing the results. They'll be able to do things with the data you would never have considered and can reveal knowledge that would have been invisible without their help.

New Core Ideology

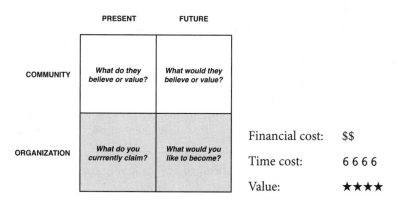

In the previous basic research section, I mentioned that one of the best places to look for clues about the current and potential future state of your brand is in your core ideology—your organizational purpose and values.

If you read that section and wondered whether your organization even *has* a deeply held core mission and values, it might be a good time to take a few steps back.

The best ad-free brands have a soul. In my experience, it is difficult to clearly articulate the soul of your brand if no one has articulated the soul of the organization as a whole through a well-developed core ideology. Most ad-free brands drink deeply from the well of meaning, and they die of thirst without it.

Getting the core ideology right is perhaps even more important for small organizations, as a clear core ideology provides a solid foundation for future growth and expansion.

If you are in a large organization, you might not be in a position of power or influence where you can lead a project to determine or refine the core ideology of the organization. But in a smaller organization, this can be a much easier project to tackle.

The first rule of any project to design the core ideology of an organization is that it must have support and sponsorship from the highest levels. Do not attempt a project to define the core ideology without this support. You will be wasting your time.

I highly recommend you read the book *Built to Last*, by Jim Collins and Jerry Porras, before you attempt to define or refine your organization's core ideology. It provides a compelling model for ad-free brands to use in developing not just the core ideology, but much of the other cultural infrastructure of the organization as well. I'll come back to the concept of core ideology in Chapter 8.

HEROES OF AD-FREE BRANDS, PART 4: JIM COLLINS AND JERRY PORRAS

Great ad-free brands have souls. Perhaps no two people on Earth have done a better job studying and writing about organizations with souls—those with a deeply held core ideology—than Jim Collins and Jerry Porras.

Their book together, *Built to Last*, might be one of the greatest business books ever written. Not only does it provide a blueprint for how to create a powerful, enduring core ideology for your organization, but it also offers some great tips on building an enduring cultural and management model.

Jim Collins wrote another favorite business book of mine, *Good to Great*, which explains how to turn your organization into one of the very best organizations in the world.

Jim Collins's most recent book is a much darker one titled *How the Mighty Fall: And Why Some Companies Never Give In*. He has also written a short book that might be of interest to those in non-profit, government, and education; it's titled *Good to Great and the Social Sectors*.

Now Take a Breath...

Whew. It is easy to get overwhelmed by all the possible sources of information about your brand. It will likely be difficult for any organization to complete all the research projects listed here, and I do not suggest you attempt it.

Instead, I've provided a reasonably comprehensive list of possible sources for research data. Choose the ones most suitable given your budget, timeframe, and the resources at your disposal. In the appendix, you'll find a handy checklist you can use to select the research options that are right for your organization.

🔍 Tip

See the appendix for a checklist you can use to organize your research project.

You'll also notice I used the phrase *reasonably comprehensive*. No list could possibly contain all the possible places where you might find valuable research data to support your positioning project. I've tried to pick some of the best general research ideas, but I'm confident you'll uncover some additional sources of research to explore.

For example, perhaps you have a chain of stores; touring several could yield useful information. Maybe you decide to spend a day listening in on customer service calls. Or closely examine your organization's elevator and on-hold music for clues. Be creative, and use the projects mentioned here for inspiration, not as a definitive list.

After you've completed your research projects, you'll have a vast amount of information that can seem overwhelming. How do you organize it? How do you ensure that the most meaningful data rises to the top?

It's time to synthesize your research data into the most useful format possible.

THREE VERY DIFFERENT HOMEWORK EXAMPLES

In this chapter, I've shared three examples of very distinct positioning research projects. EnviClean is what I would refer to as an average-sized research project. While the EnviClean research involved a decent amount of time spent by one person over a period of a month or two, it cost little money (other than the discount for people who completed the survey). Yet it was still able to produce an enormous quantity of valuable research. I view this as a fairly typical positioning project for an average ad-free brand.

The BubbaPop Soda Company example is a much higher-end project by a company in an industry that usually does a lot of traditional advertising. BubbaPop has the budget to spend and a team of people whose time can be allocated to the research project. BubbaPop is such a big business that it can't afford to make the wrong positioning decisions, so the time and financial investments are well worth it.

I created the Chauncey example to show you that positioning doesn't have to be a rigid and formal exercise. In fact, once you understand the basics of positioning, you'll find all sorts of ways to apply it in everyday life, to the great annoyance (and occasional gratitude) of your friends and family.

We'll check in on EnviClean, BubbaPop, and Chauncey again later.

Synthesizing the Research

By the time you are ready to begin synthesizing your research, you might have collected hundreds or thousands of pages of research, a hard drive's worth of spreadsheets and presentations, a roomful of organizational swag and marketing materials.

My advice? Get a room.

Literally, try to find a dedicated space inside your office where you can begin to hang materials on the wall, sort them into piles, and write up your ideas.

Figure 3.5 *Start organizing your research by which pieces inform the answers to each of the four questions covered here.*

The physical act of organizing materials often helps you draw connections between them.

You might want to create a wall like the one we created for the Red Hat brand inventory (shown previously in Figure 3.4). Consider hanging things by where they were created, or how old they are, or whatever other variables are important to you. You might want to reorganize them multiple times in different configurations to see if that gives you new ideas.

If you can't afford the space or don't want to create a big messy room, you can create the equivalent on your computer. Organize your research into folders, one folder for each of the four questions. Make duplicate copies of or shortcuts to research that informs the answer to more than one question, and put one in each folder that applies.

Once you have all the research that informs the answer to each question in one place, it's time to start doing some analysis.

If you are like me, you aren't starting from scratch, but have been beginning to analyze the data and information as you've collected it. But looking at all of the data at once will help you see it differently, making new connections and revealing things you might not have noticed before.

At this point, your goal is to synthesize all your sources of information into the clearest, simplest possible answers to the questions.

> ...looking at all of the data at once will help you see it differently, making new connections and revealing things you might not have noticed before.

Are the data points revealing common themes, ideas, or opportunities?

 Note

> The goal is to synthesize all your sources of information into the clearest, simplest possible answers to the four questions.

For example, say you own a bubblegum distributor. In your surveys and interviews with employees, it was clear that people strongly valued the playful culture of the company that makes work seem less like work. Employees indicated that this is a major reason they have stayed with the organization.

In your surveys and interviews with customers and other external communities, it is clear that this playfulness shines through to the outside world. One of the things people seem to like most about your bubblegum brand is how fun and playful it seems to them. A few people even indicated in their interviews that the company must be a creative and fun place to work and that spirit shines through.

In this case, you've found data supporting the idea that both your external communities and your employees both respond well to the playfulness of the brand. Perhaps this is currently a part of your brand that you don't highlight today. If so, it might be something that you'd want to consider highlighting more down the road. Even if you already know this is a brand strength, you now have the data to prove it. Playfulness can end up being a key point of difference for your brand.

By the time you've finished analyzing each of the four piles of data you've collected, you'll be starting to draw some conclusions about how to answer the four key questions.

This is a great time to give yourself a three-part test.

1. Attempt to summarize the answer to each of the four questions in a paragraph of three sentences or less.

2. Once you've completed all four paragraphs, next attempt to summarize the answers to each question using only *one* sentence.

3. Finally, write down the *five most important words* that summarize the answer to each question.

I've included a sample test you can use in the appendix. If multiple people are analyzing the research together, have each person take the test separately and then compare and discuss your results.

 Tip

Check out the appendix for a sample test that will help you answer the four questions succinctly.

This is also a great time to get others involved in the project. If there are people who, through interviews, surveys, or elsewhere, have expressed interest or offered to volunteer, bring them in to look at the research with you. If you consider some pieces of research to be sensitive, confidential, or simply too dense for the average person to make it through, consider giving them "research-lite"—a smaller subset of relevant data—to explore.

 Note

If there are people who, through interviews, surveys, or elsewhere, have expressed interest or offered to volunteer, bring them in to look at the research with you.

If you are feeling daring, consider bringing people from outside the organization in at this stage to look at the research with you. Assuming you've edited any materials that are confidential to the organization, sometimes getting a broader perspective really helps, and you can also begin the process of engagement with your external brand community.

After you've completed the test, and perhaps encouraged others to do so as well, you'll probably be closing in on a simple set of concepts that will form the basis for the next phase, in which you will actually develop the brand positioning.

One final step: take a blank copy (you'll find one in the appendix) of the four key questions chart and fill in your one-sentence answer to each question and the five words you chose.

 Note

In the appendix you'll find a blank copy of the four key questions chart.

Next, for each box you'll need to collect some evidence you can use to support your answer. Are there key data points like the results of some of the survey questions? Perhaps you heard certain statements over and over. Or perhaps you have a particularly expressive customer or employee quote that summarizes a larger point. You should collect the best evidence possible that supports the conclusions you've drawn because you'll need good examples to use when you present your research results during the positioning workshop in the next phase.

Congratulations on Completing Your Research Homework

Doing the right homework for a brand positioning project can be a grueling, yet ultimately rewarding, experience. Not only will you better understand your brand from a wide range of perspectives, but you'll also be in a great spot to begin the next phase of an ad-free brand positioning project: the design of the positioning itself.

4

Designing Brand Positioning

Now that you've survived the research phase, some of the most grueling work of the positioning process is behind you. The research part of positioning is very much like panning for gold. You usually have to shake a lot of pans full of rocks to uncover a few nuggets that make it all worthwhile.

But once you have the raw materials, you can start designing beautiful things with them. If the research phase is like panning for gold, the positioning phase is where the jewelry is made, where we use the gold we've found to design effective brand positioning.

Three Approaches to Designing Brand Positioning

In the last chapter, I provided examples of how three very different brands might approach their research homework. Similarly, there are multiple paths brands can take to designing great brand positioning. In this chapter, I cover three approaches I believe will work for the majority of brands:

- The lone designer approach

- The internal community approach

- The open community approach

Each of these approaches has strengths and weaknesses. You can also combine multiple approaches in one positioning project, as you'll see later in the chapter.

The Lone Designer Approach

Are you a small organization or an organization of one? Perhaps you are attempting to position a website or simply get a small company off the ground on a foundation of solid positioning. If you found during the research phase that you were doing most of the work yourself and don't want or can't afford to bring others into the positioning process, you may be a good candidate for the lone designer approach.

The lone designer approach is exactly what it sounds like: a positioning process run by one person alone or by a very small group. The advantage of this approach is that you have complete control over the process. You won't have to spend much time arguing with others over the exact words in your brand mantra; you won't need to conduct time-consuming collaboration sessions; and you will only go down rat holes of your own choosing. The lone designer approach can be very efficient and is the least resource-intensive of the three approaches.

> ✉ *Note*
>
> The lone designer approach is a positioning process run by one person alone or a very small group.

The downside of the lone designer approach is that it gives you no head start on rolling out your positioning to your brand community. By making your positioning process a black box and revealing only the finished product, you are taking some risks. First, the positioning you design might not resonate or, worse, might be ignored because you didn't include input from others beyond the initial research. Second, you may have trouble getting others to help you roll it out or take ownership over its success because they had no role in creating it.

Usually I recommend the lone designer approach only to small or new organizations with no access to a preexisting community of employee or community contributors who care about the brand. If you already have a community of supporters around your brand—even if it is small—strongly consider one of the other two approaches (internal community or open community).

In a pinch, the lone designer approach can also be used to design "quick and dirty" brand positioning with the idea that a community of people inside and outside the organization will help refine it later. This is the "release early, release often" approach I described in Chapter 2. If urgency requires you to build a positioning prototype on your own, be sure to bring others into the process as soon as you can.

For me, the lone designer approach is a lot more akin to the traditional advertising agency approach to brand positioning ("Surprise! Here's our fancy new brand positioning!"), and it will not help create an atmosphere for engaged community participation.

Frankly, that's just not how ad-free brands roll.

The Internal Community Approach

You understand the powerful impact that engaging members of your brand community in the positioning process might have on your brand. You believe your organization is progressive enough to allow employees to help with the brand positioning process. But you just don't think your organization is ready to open up the brand positioning process to the outside world. If this sounds like your situation, the internal community approach might be the best option for your brand.

The internal community approach opens up the positioning process to some level of participation from people inside the organization. It may broadly solicit contributions from every employee, or it can simply open up the process to a hand-selected group of people representing the employee base.

 Note

> The internal community approach opens up the positioning process to participation from people inside the organization.

The internal community approach to brand positioning is a smart, safe approach for many organizations. It makes brand positioning a cultural activity within the organization, allowing you to collect a broad range of interesting ideas and begin to sow the seeds for future participation in the brand rollout down the road. In addition, it can become a compelling leadership opportunity, helping develop future leaders of your brand as well.

While this internal approach is still community-based, it is usually perceived as less risky than an approach involving external contributors. You might find it easier to sell the internal approach to executives who fear opening up the organization to the outside world or think doing so will give the external community the perception the organization is confused or doesn't know what it is doing because it is asking for help (remember: ad-free brands are comfortable not having all the answers).

The internal community approach recognizes that the most important community to engage first is always the internal community. Don't worry, you'll still be able to build an effective ad-free brand even if you don't run your positioning project with the help of people outside your organization.

 Tip

The most important community to engage first is always the internal community.

The Open Community Approach

Even though I'll be the first to admit that it is not right for every brand, the open community approach is by far my favorite approach (as you can probably tell by now) and is a very effective one for ad-free brands.

The open community approach opens the positioning process to contributions from members of both the internal and external brand communities. Running an open community brand positioning project is similar to running an internal community one. Both approaches have the advantage of bringing in a variety of viewpoints. Both can create valuable brand advocates who will be helpful down the road. The open community approach just takes things as step further and allows people outside the organization to contribute as well.

The benefit of this approach is that it can usually form the beginning of a constructive dialogue with *all* the people who care about your brand—not just those who work for your organization. It can help you build relationships based on trust, sharing, and respect with people in the outside world. And it can save you money and time by revealing flaws in your positioning much earlier in the process. (Remember Linus's Law? "Given enough eyes, all bugs are shallow.")

TO OPEN EXTERNALLY OR NOT TO OPEN EXTERNALLY? THAT IS THE QUESTION.

When a positioning project is in capable, responsible hands, my belief is that fears about opening up the process to the outside world are often unfounded. As you'll see later in this chapter, it all comes down to how you engage the external community. Properly engaged, an open community brand positioning project can become an extremely valuable connection point between the outside world and the brand.

But I'm also a pragmatist and realize many executives will not be ready to take that risk. Many won't be as comfortable not having all the answers as you are, and many will also fear the risks of increased transparency.

To be clear, there are also many organizations that simply *shouldn't* take the risk of opening up the brand positioning process to the outside world. Perhaps they have secrets, strategies, or other things an open brand positioning process might reveal that could do them harm or give a competitor a huge advantage. Perhaps your brand community is just not very happy with you and is likely to be a negative participant in the process.

Think about the decision between an open community and internal community approach as a series of tradeoffs. An open community process often leads to a more engaged external community and more effective positioning but can also be risky. An internal community process is safer but gives you fewer advantages when it comes to external community engagement. Neither is good nor bad—you'll simply need to choose the one that feels right for your brand.

The downsides of an open approach? If the project is poorly organized or badly communicated, it really will realize the fears of some executives and show the outside world you *don't* know what you're doing.

An open positioning approach requires a deft, highly skilled, effective communicator and facilitator. It requires coordination between different parts of the organization that are in touch with the outside world to ensure communication is clear and consistent.

But although the risks of opening up your positioning process to the outside world are higher, the rewards can be much bigger as

> A brand is not what *you* say it is—it's what *they* say it is.
>
> —Marty Neumeier, *The Brand Gap*

well. By transparently opening a relationship between your brand and the outside world, you are embracing the future of brand management, accepting the role of your brand community in the definition of your brand, and proactively getting your community involved in a positive way. You are beginning a conversation.

AD-FREE BRAND HEROES PART 5: MARTY NEUMEIER

As you are planning your brand positioning workshop, consider buying some copies of Marty Neumeier's book *The Brand Gap* to hand out to your participants ahead of time. In addition to providing one of the most succinct definitions of what a brand is that I have found ("A brand is not what you say it is…it's what they say it is."), this book provides a simple, quick read on what branding is and why it is important.

He calls the book a "whiteboard overview," and it is perfect for the busy executive; it is beautifully designed and can be read cover-to-cover in 30 minutes or less. And if everyone in your team reads it, you'll ensure the team shares a common perspective and is using similar terminology in discussions about your brand positioning.

If you enjoy *The Brand Gap*, also be sure to look for Neumeier's other two books, *Zag* and *The Designful Company*. Both provide great, inexpensive inspiration for ad-free brands.

Mix and Match

In this chapter, I've presented three ways to design brand positioning as discrete approaches. But don't feel like you need to choose just one. I encourage you to mix and match pieces of each approach as it makes sense for your brand.

For example, you might start by creating a proof of concept of how positioning might work for your leadership team using the lone designer approach. Based on this work, you receive the okay to open the next round of the process to a group of leading thinkers within your organization. And when that produces interesting results, you receive permission to open the aperture even wider. In this scenario, by the time you have completed your project, you've used all three approaches.

You might decide you only want to open up one or two small parts of the process to the outside world but make most of the project only visible to people inside your organization. That works, too. For example, perhaps you share your points of difference with your brand community, but you keep the discussion about points of parity as an internal one.

Every organization is different, and every positioning project is different. As you read through the next section, think about how you might mix and match elements of each approach to create a hybrid that works even better for you.

The Brand Positioning Workshop

In this section, I walk you through a typical approach to designing brand positioning through a brand positioning workshop. Because many of the basic concepts for running a workshop are common to each approach, I simply illustrate how one workshop would work, using the internal community process. Then I show you what you'll want to change if you are using the lone designer or open community approach instead. I also show examples of each of the three approaches in action throughout this chapter.

Planning a Brand Positioning Workshop

I like to begin the positioning phase with a half- or full-day kickoff workshop. But what should you try to achieve during this workshop? Who should you invite? What should the schedule look like?

The Invite List

The brand positioning workshop might be the first in-person meeting of the extended team that will be responsible for your brand positioning. You'll need to choose your participants carefully because many of these people will likely continue to work with you during the positioning rollout and might stay involved with the brand for years.

I prefer to limit the workshop to 25 participants or less, with the ideal size being 10–15 participants. When considering potential invitees, look especially for people who:

- Have extensive experience with and knowledge of the brand
- Have worked with the organization a long time
- Are in leadership roles or who have great cultural influence within the organization
- Have great passion for the brand, and have actively expressed interest in working on or improving it

- Represent a different point of view than you, either from a different part of the world or a different part of the organization

Although it is important to have management or leadership in the room, it is not necessary, or even advisable, that all members of the team be senior managers.

The best working groups are diverse, involving people from many different departments, bringing many different perspectives, from different management levels. If you've read Tom Kelley's book *The Ten Faces of Innovation*, you might want to consider looking to his 10 innovator personas for models of people to invite (and his description of the devil's advocate for whom to avoid).

AD-FREE BRAND HEROES PART 6: TOM KELLEY AND TIM BROWN OF IDEO

It is much easier to run a positioning process as a lone designer than one involving many other people. But my preferred approaches to designing brand positioning are community-based. To be successful, community-based projects rely heavily on the skills of a strong facilitator who can lead others through the process without shutting down creative thought on one hand or allowing the project to run wild on the other.

My community-based positioning approaches have been deeply inspired by the work of the masters of collaborative design at IDEO. In his book *The Art of Innovation*, IDEO general manager Tom Kelley breaks down the process IDEO has used to generate some of the most compelling innovations of our time, things like the computer mouse, for example.

Tom Kelley's second book, *The Ten Faces of Innovation*, is a great read for anyone who will be facilitating a brand positioning workshop. It teaches you how to negate the power of devil's advocates—the people who often shut down creativity and innovation during a brainstorming or ideation session. It also helps you understand how to effectively utilize the skills of all types of people in your project.

The newest book from IDEO's executive team is *Change by Design: How Design Thinking Transforms Organizations and Inspires Innovation* by president and CEO Tim Brown. This book is a great read for those unfamiliar with the design thinking approach to innovation. In reading this book, you'll quickly realize that my approach to brand positioning draws heavily from design thinking principles. If you've never tried design thinking before, this book will provide a great introduction.

When considering to what extent you should involve your senior leadership team in the workshop, carefully consider the culture of your organization. You'll probably want to have some management representation because executive presence will add credibility to the process and ensure management understands what is going on with the project. But executives can also unwittingly hinder an otherwise productive session.

Especially in hierarchical organizations, some executives have difficulty leaving their titles at the door and can shut down a constructive dialogue with a few badly timed words. If at all possible, select executives who are open-minded, creative, and nonhierarchical. But if an executive expresses interest in joining, by all means invite him or her—excluding someone who is interested in participating in the process will only cause you problems later.

Instead of leaving the executive out, try to sit down with him or her ahead of time and provide some guidelines for ensuring the workshop is successful. I've found most people want what's best for the brand and will leave their titles at the door and refrain from being a devil's advocate if you bring them in on the plan and ask them for their help ahead of time.

A few things you might mention in your conversation:

- People naturally look to leaders in a room, so the quieter the known leaders are during the workshop, the more others will step in to fill the space with their ideas. This is a good thing.

- Leaders should be extra careful about criticizing or challenging ideas during a workshop. Even if one idea isn't good, the public criticism from a known leader might stop others from contributing their great ideas, stifling the overall creative output of the team.

- Leaders should view themselves as part of the team. They should contribute according to the exact same rules that everyone else is using during the session.

To put some general parameters around the typical workshop makeup, use the following as a rough guide. Include:

- 40% people who work on the brand every day, including people in marketing, communications, and PR roles. Ensure all senior brand leaders are part of the group, but also include some doers and some people with the potential to be future brand leaders.

- 30% current cultural leaders from across the organization who might or might not have experience working on brand-related projects. Especially look for people who have been with the organization a long time, represent a different viewpoint that can often be overlooked, are passionate about the brand, and are widely respected and listened to across the organization. Try to choose a mix of people representing different generations if possible.

- 30% members of the senior leadership team. If at all possible, ensure this includes your entire chain of command, up to and including the head of the organization (your boss, boss's boss, etc.). Also look for executives who are curious, interested in the process, and open to great ideas coming from anywhere.

After you have your team selected, identify which people the session can't do without and plan around their schedules first. If there are a few people who were on your list who can't make the session, have some backups waiting in the wings.

A Crash Course on Design Thinking

Because the ideal brand positioning workshop is built on top of a design thinking innovation model, let's start by exploring some of the basic concepts behind design thinking. While a complete study of design thinking is beyond what we can cover here, if you are interested in learning more about the subject, consider reading one of the following great books:

- *The Design of Business: Why Design Thinking Is the Next Competitive Advantage* by Roger Martin
- *Change by Design: How Design Thinking Transforms Organizations and Inspires Innovation* by Tim Brown
- *Design Thinking: Integrating Innovation, Customer Experience, and Brand Value* by Thomas Lockwood

What is design thinking? Design thinking is a process by which groups can collaboratively solve problems or explore opportunities by *building ideas up* instead of tearing them down.

Because of its "building up" approach, design thinking is quite distinct from the analytical problem-solving process used regularly in the business world. Typically, analytical thinking attempts to break something down into its component parts in order to study it.

> Design thinking is a process groups can use to collaboratively solve problems or explore opportunities by building up ideas.

Why is design thinking a valuable tool for ad-free brands to use in brand position-ing? Simple: it is optimized for collaboration and inclusiveness. Because it celebrates all ideas and contributions and allows for the best solutions to come from every-where and anywhere, it is a great way to generate fresh ideas from diverse groups of people and to turn them into valuable members in the process. Design thinking is a wonderful way to engage people in a positive way, and it helps build relationships that can endure beyond any one project.

Compared to the standard method of generat-ing ideas and solving problems within organi-zations, a well-run design thinking project is often greeted as a breath of fresh air.

Although different people have slightly differ-ent views of how the design thinking process works, most typical design thinking projects will roughly follow these seven steps:

> ...a well-run design thinking project is often greeted as a breath of fresh air.

1. **Define:** Define the problem or opportunity.

2. **Research:** Complete or review the necessary research.

3. **Ideate:** Generate as many ideas as possible.

4. **Prototype:** Build models that test the concepts.

5. **Choose:** Choose the models that are most effective.

6. **Implement:** Try out the models in the real world.

7. **Learn:** Study the results, and use them to begin the process anew.

During the ideation step, you should follow many of the design thinking rules you'll find in the sidebar on this page. But once your group has generated a lot of ideas and is beginning to prototype and choose positioning for the brand, you can begin to apply more traditional decision-making principles to select the best ideas.

David Burney's Design Thinking Rules

One of my business partners at New Kind, David Burney, is a master facilitator of design thinking projects. David introduced me to design thinking and the work of IDEO and taught me everything I know about facilitating design thinking sessions.

At the beginning of any design thinking project, David writes a set of rules on the board that helps get everyone in the room on the same page. The rules apply to every-one (including executives) and help create an optimal environment for creativity. You might want to consider sharing these rules at the beginning of your workshop as well.

1. **Avoid the devil's advocate:** The devil's advocate is someone who (purposely or accidentally) shoots down the ideas of others without taking any personal

responsibility for his actions. The devil's advocate often begins his objection with the phrase "Let me be the devil's advocate for a second…". The devil's advocate often intends to be helpful by pointing out flaws in an idea, but ultimately this focuses people's attention on what won't work rather than exploring unexpected ways that it might work.

2. **Make agendas transparent:** Everyone in the room should make their personal agendas as clear as possible.

3. **Leave titles at the door:** No one person's ideas are worth more than anyone else's.

4. **Generate as many ideas as possible:** During ideation, you are not trying to generate the best ideas; you are trying to generate the *most* ideas.

5. **Build on the ideas of others rather than judging them:** If someone else has an idea you like, build on it. If you don't like an idea, share another one rather than critiquing.

6. **Stay on time:** Don't let your ideation session spiral out of control. Each ideation session should be timed and should have a clear ending point.

7. **State the obvious:** Sometimes things that can seem obvious reveal great insight from their simplicity.

8. **Don't sell or debate ideas:** Selling and debating ideas takes time away from generating new ideas.

9. **Stupid and wild ideas are good:** Sometimes the craziest ideas lead to the best ideas.

10. **DTA stands for death to acronyms:** Avoid acronyms—they are exclusionary because people who don't know what they stand for will quickly be lost. If you must use an acronym, write what it stands for somewhere everyone can see it. Keep a running list of all acronyms used during the session.

11. **Always understand in which stage of the process you are:** When you are ideating, you are not critiquing ideas. But when ideation is over and you begin the process of selecting the best ideas, you'll need to discuss the merits of each idea in a more traditional, analytical way.

12. **Play is good, have fun:** The more fun you are having as a group, the more creative ideas you'll generate.

The Workshop Agenda

Typically, a brand positioning workshop lasts either a full day or a half-day, depending on how much time you can convince people to invest. The more time you have, the more you'll be able to accomplish while you have everyone together.

In a half-day, you'll probably be able to get through an ideation session that provides good ideas you can use to develop your brand positioning. You might even be able to build a brand positioning prototype by the end of the session if you move quickly.

In a full day, you should actually be able to complete a brand positioning prototype, including developing the competitive frame of reference, points of difference, points of parity, and possibly a brand mantra, for the brand.

A typical agenda might look something like this (the description after each item shows how the activities relate to the design thinking process):

1. **Background**—Define the problem.

   - Introductions.

   - Why are we here?

   - What is brand positioning?

   - Why will good brand positioning benefit us?

   - Definition of key terms.

   - Rules for the day.

   Allow 15–45 minutes to complete the background.

2. **Research**—Share the research you've completed ahead of time.

   - Present the results of the research phase.

   - Discussion.

   Allow 1–2 hours, depending on the quantity of research, making sure to leave time for the team to discuss its own interpretations of the research if you can.

3. **Positioning working session**—Ideate and build positioning prototypes.

   - Competitive frame of reference

   - Points of difference

   - Points of parity

   - Brand mantra

   Allow 2–5 hours to ideate and build prototypes, depending on how much you'd like to accomplish collaboratively in the session.

4. **Next steps**—Outline the process by which the team will choose and implement the positioning.

   Allow 30–60 minutes to cover next steps.

Conducting the Background and Research Pieces of the Workshop

You've planned and scheduled your brand positioning workshop, your invitees have all arrived, and you have the perfect set of people in the room to begin developing your brand positioning. The clock strikes 9 a.m. It's time to begin.

Background

I always start the workshop with an introduction that ensures everyone in the room knows each other and has a common understanding of both brand positioning and the goals for the project.

Positioning is something that means different things to different people, so—especially because you'll be bringing together folks from many disciplines—getting everyone on the same page up front is extremely important.

Research

Once everyone shares a common understanding of the goals for the project, the next step is to share the results of your research. I recommend you put together a presentation highlighting the most important findings from your research homework.

In the test you took at the end of Chapter 3, you used your research to answer the four key questions that inform great brand positioning. I suggest you organize your presentation into four parts, one devoted to the data that informs each question/answer. Start with the questions:

- What does your brand community currently believe about or value in the brand?

- What might your brand community believe or value about the brand in the future?

- What does your organization currently claim about the brand?

- What would your organization like the brand to become down the road?

Follow each question with data points from the research that informs the answers to the questions.

Don't just create a boring PowerPoint presentation filled with dense slides full of data. If you present your research in an uninspired way, you'll make everyone silently wish they

> If you present your research in an uninspired way, you'll make everyone silently wish they hadn't shown up.

hadn't shown up. Ensure your research presentation tells an interesting story, and by all means, make it fun. An inspiring presentation will also inspire better ideas when the time comes for ideation.

Include quotes you found during your research, and accompany them with either pictures of the people you are quoting or video or audio clips if you have them. Show photos you took during the process, or even take the group on a tour to see your brand inventory wall if you created one.

When you are preparing the data, consider working with a designer on the presentation so complex information is as clear as possible. If other people worked with you on the research, consider giving them roles in the presentation as well.

Keep in mind that if your presentation of the research is not fun and interesting, people won't listen, and if they don't listen, they won't have the information they need to make informed positioning choices.

After you've finished your presentation, you then have a choice. You can either reveal your "answers" to the four questions (the summary sentences you wrote in the test at the end of Chapter 3 and the thinking behind them) or hold off and let the group form its own conclusions.

You'll have the best read on which approach is appropriate for your organization. I've found that some groups just want the answers and would rather have you synthesize the research for them. The advantage of this approach is that it saves time, so I especially recommend it for half-day workshops.

The downside of revealing your synthesis of the research is that it stops people from thinking through the data and drawing conclusions on their own. Just as doing your math homework helps you think through the underlying math principles and aids in comprehension, forcing people to process the data on their own might help them more deeply understand and retain the information.

The advantage of allowing the team to draw its own conclusions is that every person will interpret the data differently. Sometimes others will come to conclusions you never even considered, and you might benefit from a totally new view you wouldn't have otherwise noticed (there's Linus's Law again).

If you have the time, one nice option is to stop at the end of each of the four research question sections and host a 5- to 10-minute discussion during which you ask other people to take the test from Chapter 3 on the spot. Write all the words people come up with on a whiteboard or somewhere else where everyone can see them. Ask each person to answer all four questions in one sentence; then have everyone put their answers up on the whiteboard as well.

After everyone has given you their ideas, you'll need to be sure to share your ideas, too. Be careful not to position your answers as the "correct" ones, but simply one more viewpoint (although one from someone who spent plenty of time doing the homework). You might even want to mention only ideas that didn't already come up from the group.

I've found most of the time the answers the group comes up with will have a lot in common with my answers. But I've also found that in many cases, the group will develop answers that are improvements over mine or even change my thinking entirely. If you can afford the time, you might find these discussions well worth the investment. Plus, the discussions also break up what can otherwise be a long research presentation (now matter how fun you've made it), and they help people become more engaged in adding their own ideas and perspectives into the positioning process.

And remember: your group will be even more engaged if you give sincere credit to those people who come up with great ideas along the way. Remember who contributed by name. It shows that you are listening and reminds people that their individual contributions are valued.

I can't stress it enough: research can be boring, but it certainly doesn't have to be. Please, please make exploring the research fun. You'll need the energy level in the room to be high for the creative session that comes next.

The Positioning Ideation Session

Hopefully, you've managed your time well on the background and research because the bulk of your day should be spent on the most fun, interactive part of the project: the positioning ideation session.

At this point, you should quickly review the design thinking rules again with the team. During this session, everyone should be encouraged to actively contribute—all ideas are important. The initial goal is to generate the most ideas possible, not necessarily the best ideas, so do everything in your power to stop people from critiquing the ideas of others.

If devil's advocates in your group (including senior executives) begin to analyze or critique, you should gently encourage them to suggest better ideas of their own rather than critiquing so you can keep the ideas flowing. In the best groups you'll notice that the group itself even begins to police this, so you won't have to every time.

You should split the ideation session into four sections, one covering each of the four building blocks of positioning from Chapter 2:

- The competitive frame of reference
- Points of difference

- Points of parity

- The brand mantra

The Competitive Frame of Reference

To review from Chapter 2, *competitive frame of reference* is a fancy term to describe the market or context in which you plan to position your brand. You'll also remember that, while most brands will have one primary competitive frame of reference, you might also find yourself competing in multiple frames of reference. The competitive frame of reference is the thing you should ask the group to tackle first.

Begin by reviewing the definition of a competitive frame of reference; then start the ideation by asking your group to answer some questions based on the data they saw in the research. Record every idea. You can use a whiteboard, large Post-it notes, or even a computer with a projector to record ideas. But make sure you capture *everyone's* ideas, no matter how good or bad you think they are. To ensure people feel engaged in the process, it is important to show people that every contribution is valued equally. Also, sometimes a very bad idea is just the thing that sparks a very good idea in someone else.

Here are some sample questions to ask:

- If we asked our brand community, including customers, partners, and other important members, in which frame of reference would *they* say our brand competes?

- When we first walked into this room today, in which frame of reference did *you* think our brand competed?

- After reviewing the research, have you changed your mind? If so, what caused your view to change? In which competitive frame of reference do you now believe the brand competes?

- Do you see the brand competing in frames of reference in the future where it may not be competing today? What are they?

- According to the data, does the external brand community see the same future opportunities?

- If the external brand community did not see those opportunities, do you still believe they are important to the future of your brand anyway?

After you've discussed each of these questions fully, and as many ideas from the discussion are written down where everyone can see them, next have each person attempt to complete the following sentences, writing their answers down on a sheet of paper individually first.

- I believe our brand competes in the _____ competitive frame of reference.

- Our brand communities think of us in the _____ competitive frame of reference.

- I'd like to see our brand in the _____ competitive frame of reference in the future.

- Our brand communities would like to see us in the _____ competitive frame of reference in the future.

Encourage everyone to share their answers. Were the answers largely the same across all four of these questions? If so, you might have just figured out your competitive frame of reference. That wasn't so hard.

Were the first two answers basically the same, but the last two different? If so, you may be looking at an opportunity to transition the brand from your current frame of reference to a new one. Now might be the time to begin the process. You can choose to make your new frame of reference your primary one and your old one a secondary frame of reference.

Ideally, you'll find one or two competitive frames of reference with a foot in the present and a foot in the future, setting you up to remain competitive now and in the future.

Once all the possible frames of reference the group has identified are listed on a whiteboard or somewhere else everyone can see them, it's time to take a vote and see what the group thinks is the right competitive frame of reference for the brand. Do *not* position this vote as binding. The vote is informational, intended to help the group see where it stands and give a voice to people who might not be able to get a word in or might be afraid to speak up. It is not intended to be a democratic, decision-making vote on the final choice.

My favorite way to vote is with Post-its (although you can choose another way to vote as well). Handing someone a physical token like a Post-it to vote with is a symbolic gesture. It's empowering and it makes the act of voting active and visible for everyone. Plus it also gets people moving around and forces them to actively engage and think about their choices.

Give each person in the room three Post-its, and tell them they have one vote per Post-it. They can use all three of their votes on one competitive frame of reference option or split them across multiple frames of reference. After everyone has their votes up, it should be pretty clear what the consensus of the group is. You'll probably see one or two frames of reference that stand out.

Thank everyone for their input, but don't necessarily promise that the frame of reference with the most votes is the chosen one unless you've decided this team is that final decision-making body for your positioning.

You'll need to sit down after the meeting with your decision-making team (which might be you alone, or the executive team, or even a subset of this group) to make the final decision. Just because the process is collaborative doesn't mean the final decision has to be democratic, and if you make it democratic remember that you'll have to live with the results of the vote, so I don't recommend it for most projects. Just be sure the final decision-making process is clearly articulated to participants ahead of time, and I don't expect you'll have any problems—most people are just excited to have their voices heard.

🔍 Tip

Taking pictures of the results of your ideation session is a good way to ensure that all the ideas from the session are captured in context.

Before you move on from the competitive frame of reference, be sure to capture all the information shared in the ideation session, especially if you have to erase anything. Either ask someone to take notes and share them with the team or—even better—take pictures of everything so you can share the pictures later.

POSITIONING EXAMPLE #1: BUBBAPOP SODA COMPANY

As the chief brand officer for BubbaPop Soda Company, you were lucky enough to have a large budget to spend on your positioning homework. But when it comes to running a positioning workshop, you fear BubbaPop is not ready to open its positioning process to the outside world. The carbonated beverage market (which your group determines is the competitive frame of reference, by the way) is extremely competitive, and you don't want people who work for your competition to be aware of what you view as your strengths and weaknesses. Plus, your executive team would never go for it.

Still, you want to be sure to gather ideas from a large group of people inside the BubbaPop organization, so you elect to run your positioning workshop using the internal community approach. You have the budget to fly people in for the workshop, so you select a diverse group of people including not just marketing people and executives from headquarters, but also salespeople and people from your distribution network who are out in the field.

The session is fantastic. You get a wide range of ideas to choose from, including many you'd never considered before. Most of the group members leave very excited about continuing the process with you. You let everyone know that you'll set up a Basecamp project (www.basecamphq.com) so everyone can access the materials from the meeting, including research, notes, and photos of the ideation sessions, and promise to continue the discussion online.

By the time you and your executive decision-making team have chosen a positioning prototype, you've convinced the executives that it would be worthwhile to get some feedback from the outside world. So, you conduct a follow-up survey in which you ask a series of questions that help you test your brand positioning with customers.

The chosen positioning seems to really resonate with them. In fact, you received particularly good feedback on one of the points of difference the team had wavered on, and you decide to include it based on this feedback. The whole team feels confident that the chosen positioning now reflects both the internal vision for the brand and one that resonates with your brand community. It's time to move on to the positioning rollout.

Points of Difference

After you've determined the best competitive frame of reference for your brand, you'll next need to turn the team's efforts toward uncovering the things that make you different from your competition in the frame of reference you've identified.

Remember from Chapter 2 that a point of difference is not simply something that makes your brand different; it also must be something that your audience would value. Explain the concept to your workshop group.

Start by asking the group to list as many key competitors in the frame of reference as they can. Encourage people to get creative, naming obvious and not-so-obvious competitors. When you feel like you've exhausted the ideas and have them all written out where everyone can see them, get the group to complete a simple exercise.

Ask each person to write down, based on what she learned from the research, up to five words or short phrases answering the following questions:

- According to the research, what makes us different and better than our competitors today in the primary competitive frame of reference?

- What might make us better than and more valued by our brand community in the future in this frame of reference?

Always be sure to add the "in this frame of reference" part of those questions. It is very easy for people to get sidetracked with things they like or think people would value about the brand but lose sight of the specific context in which you are attempting to position it.

Write all the ideas that are generated where everyone can see them. Do you see any common themes emerging? Consider taking a Post-it vote and see which terms are resonating most as differentiators for the brand. Make sure people understand that these descriptions must not only make the brand different, but must also be things the audience would value. Also encourage people to think about things that differentiate the brand currently as well as things that describe ways the brand might stretch to become even more valuable down the road.

Look at the top 5–10 words or phrases receiving the most votes. Could any of these be combined to communicate one thought? With assistance from the team, attempt to reduce the number of points of difference down to two to four key ideas by combining similar ideas.

Finally, take the two to four points of difference you have identified, and ask the group to tell you, by a show of hands, whether the point of difference is true about the brand today or whether it is an aspirational point of difference you hope the brand will strive to reach. It is okay if you have one or, at most, two aspirational points of difference, but you should think very carefully about having too many points of difference that are aspirational because they will not resonate with your brand community as true. Mark an *A* beside any points of difference that are aspirational.

Again, thank everyone for their input, take pictures of or transcribe the notes, and—unless this is the decision-making body—get ready to work on the points of parity.

Points of Parity

You'll remember from Chapter 2 that points of parity are points of difference that competitors might have over you that you need to counteract. They are places where you only need to be as good as your competitors (not better) and they might also be table stakes that you need to show you've paid to play in the market. Define the term for your workshop group.

Start the ideation exercise for determining points of parity by asking the team the following questions. Ask them to individually write down their answers on a piece of paper:

- According to the research, what are our competitors' biggest advantages over us in our primary competitive frame of reference?

- What does our brand have to be good at just to stay competitive in this frame of reference?

Ask people to share the ideas they've developed, and write them where everyone can see them. Take a Post-it vote to see which ideas are most popular. Attempt the reduction exercise again—could any of the ideas be combined to communicate one thought? Work with the team to reduce the number of points of parity down to one to three key ideas.

Finally, take the one to three points of parity you have identified and ask the group to tell you, again by show of hands, whether the point of parity is true about the brand today or whether it is aspirational. It is okay to have an aspirational point of parity, but the majority of your points of parity and points of difference should be things the brand can already deliver today. Make sure to identify any points of parity that are aspirational by writing an *A* next to them.

You might even find that there aren't *any* points of parity you need to achieve within your competitive frame of reference, and that's okay, too. Some brands only have points of difference. Thank everyone again for their input and ideas, and take pictures of or transcribe the notes from this session.

Testing the Positioning: Desirable, Deliverable, and Differentiated

There is one final exercise you should complete before you leave points of difference and points of parity behind. I learned this way of testing your chosen brand positioning from Kevin Keller.

Write up the two to four key points of difference and the one to three key points of parity where everyone can see them together. Rather than looking at them separately this time, have the group look at them as one whole. When you put all the points of difference and points of parity together, can they pass this test?

- **Is this positioning *desirable* to your brand community?**
  Do the points of parity and points of difference reflect characteristics your brand community would want?

- **Is this positioning *deliverable* by the brand?**
  Does your brand experience already deliver on this positioning? If not, and if you've identified aspirational points of parity or points of difference, can you make changes to the organizational strategy that will ensure this positioning will reflect the actual brand experience at some point in the near future?

- **Is this positioning *differentiated* from your competitors?**
  Does this positioning distinguish your brand from everyone else in the competitive frame of reference?

Desirable, deliverable, and differentiated: great positioning will be all three at once. If your group agrees that your positioning passes the test, you are ready to move on. If not, you might want to go back and review your points of parity and points of difference again.

Desirable, deliverable, and differentiated: great positioning will be all three at once.

POSITIONING EXAMPLE #2: ENVICLEAN DRY CLEANERS

During the research phase, you learned that many in the EnviClean brand community view EnviClean as more than just another dry cleaner. Because of your focus on environmental responsibility, there is a core group of customers who are deeply loyal to your brand and would never consider another dry cleaner. Your brand survey also helped you identify these people, and many of them indicated they'd love to help you figure out how to make the company even better.

So, you decide to do something most other dry cleaning chains would never do. You ask some of these loyal customers to join your internal team in a workshop. Because you are asking these customers to spend a day of their time with you at EnviClean headquarters, you offer to give them six months of free dry cleaning in return. Ten customers take you up on the offer.

Your session ends up being a turning point for the brand. Many of these customers have a great deal of experience with environmental organizations and issues, and they bring ideas and environmental best practices that you can not only quickly incorporate into the positioning, but also use to improve the brand experience.

The interaction between the customers and members of your internal team is fantastic as well. You notice many people exchanging excited conversation and business cards during the breaks. At one point, the manager of one of your locations approaches and tells you that he and one of his customers just came up with the idea for a community council made up of loyal customers who can help keep EnviClean up-to-date with the latest environmental responsibility trends. You think this is a fabulous idea, and at the end of the day, one of the next steps you announce is the creation of an external community council for the brand. You ask if anyone would be interested in participating, and 7 of the 10 customers raise their hands.

By the end of the day, everyone is tired but pumped up, and the customers and employees alike all seem eager to continue the conversation. You've built a promising prototype of the EnviClean brand positioning, and you promise to keep everyone up-to-date on your progress, both through internal team meetings and quarterly meetings with the community council. It is time to begin the positioning rollout.

Wow—Nice Work

By the time you've reached this point in your workshop, you are probably exhausted. If you a running a half-day workshop, you are probably also running out of time. If the energy level is low or time is short, it might be best to save the brand mantra for another day.

It's hard to determine a competitive frame of reference, points of difference, points of parity, and a brand mantra all in one morning. But if you are running an all-day session or have been able to move through things quickly, keep on rolling.

The Brand Mantra

The final exercise of the day will be an attempt to create a brand mantra. Warn the team ahead of time that this exercise might or might not be successful on the first attempt. Some brands don't come up with a compelling brand mantra right away, and it is such an important part of your positioning (remember, if this were a chess game, the brand mantra would be the queen), it is not something to rush. But I have seen fantastic ideas for brand mantras come out of brand workshops, and it is worth taking the time to gather ideas. You never know what a group will uncover.

KEVIN KELLER'S FIVE CLASSIC BRAND MANTRAS

For this chapter, I asked branding expert Kevin Keller to share five favorite examples of real brand mantras. He not only provided the mantras, but also included a few sentences describing why each works so well. In his words:

- *Nike: "Authentic Athletic Performance"* One of the best brand mantras of all time, developed by Nike's marketing guru Scott Bedbury in the late 1980s (he would later become Starbucks' marketing guru). Bedbury actually coined the phrase *brand mantra*. It did everything you would want a brand mantra to do—it kept the Nike brand on track, it differentiated the brand from its main competitor at the time (Reebok), and it genuinely inspired Nike employees.

- ***Disney: "Fun Family Entertainment"*** Adding the word *magical* would have probably made it even better, but this brand mantra—also created in the late 1980s—was crucial in ensuring the powerful Disney marketing machine didn't overextend the brand. Establishing an office of brand management at that same time with a mission to "inform and enforce" the brand mantra gave it real teeth.

- ***Ritz-Carlton: "Ladies & Gentlemen Serving Ladies & Gentlemen"*** The Ritz-Carlton brand mantra has a clear internal and external message, an especially important consideration for services brands. It is simple but universally applicable in all that Ritz-Carlton does and highly aspirational.

- ***BMW: "Ultimate Driving Machine"*** BMW's brand mantra is noteworthy in two ways. One, it reveals the power of a *straddle* branding strategy by combining two seemingly incompatible sets of attributes or benefits. When launched in North America, there were cars that offered either luxury or performance, but not both. Two, it is also a good example of how a brand mantra can be used as a slogan if its descriptive nature is compelling enough as is.

- ***Betty Crocker: "Homemade Made Easy"*** Another example of a brand mantra that was effective as a descriptive ad tag line, Betty Crocker's brand mantra remarkably staked out three points of difference ("quality," "family," and a "rewarding baking experience") as well as a crucial point of parity ("convenience") at the same time.[1]

Start by having the group review the suggested points of difference and points of parity they voted on earlier. Set a timer for 30 minutes, and then give the team the instructions to brainstorm as many short, two- to five-word phrases as they can think of that could be good candidates for the brand mantra. The group should keep the following principles in mind:

- These phrases should encapsulate multiple points of difference and points of parity if possible, focusing on key points of difference first.

- The best brand mantras don't just capture the positioning, but also are *inspirational*. So try to come up with phrases that might also inspire both the internal organization and the brand community.

- Remember that you aren't writing advertising copy, and you definitely aren't writing taglines. Brand mantras are internal positioning statements that are used to capture the essence of the brand, not sloganeering (although, as Kevin Keller's earlier examples highlight, there are certain great brand mantras that can eventually translate externally).

---

1. Source: Kevin Lane Keller, personal correspondence

Now go. Have the team give you as many phrases as it can, working as a group, and write down every single one. Write down the dumb ideas, write down the funny ideas, and write down the great ideas. Even if suggested phrases are more than two to five words, write them down anyway—they could lead to something shorter and tighter. Remember not to allow people to judge, discuss, or debate ideas. The goal is to come up with as many ideas as possible.

Stop after 30 minutes. Take a Post-it vote to determine the group's favorites. Tell people to only vote for mantras they think pass the "desirable, deliverable, differentiated" test.

Finally, thank everyone once again for all the great ideas and contributions—and don't forget or take pictures or good notes of all of the ideas.

Next Steps

By now, if the day has gone well, there are probably many people who are pretty excited about the future of the brand. But this workshop is just the beginning of the process. Before everyone leaves for the day, you should ensure that this is the first step of each person's involvement, not the last.

First, you'll need to set expectations for what will happen with all the ideas collected during the meeting. In most groups, you won't necessarily have made any final decisions about the competitive frame of reference, the points of difference, the points of parity, or the brand mantra during the meeting (although you probably have some leading candidates). Be clear with the entire group on what the decision-making process is so they understand how they fit in.

If final decisions will be made by the executive team based on this group's recommendations, say so now. If you'll be reviewing the ideas the group has come up with and then a smaller group will get together to make the final decision, let everyone know. Whatever your decision-making process, be sure it is clear to everyone in the room before folks leave. Remember that surprise is the opposite of engagement, so it is important to be sure people understand and accept how their contributions and ideas will be used to create the final positioning.

 Tip

Make sure the decision-making process is clear to everyone in the room before they leave.

Unless your positioning workshop group is small and your project is simple, I don't recommend you make final decisions in the room during this initial meeting. Sometimes new ideas emerge after people have an opportunity to reflect and sleep on it.

I also don't recommend you tell the group you will be making the decisions by yourself. Collaborative input deserves an open, collaborative decision-making process, even if it doesn't include everyone.

You might want to consider naming a small group of people (or even let the larger team decide on a small group) to make the final recommendations. This group might be made up of people who added the most value during the workshop or were the most passionate contributors. Or, if your organization is hierarchical, you might want to allow the executive team to make the final decisions.

You'll also find the decision-making group is most effective when it includes at least one person (but ideally many people) with a gift for words. Sometimes a good writer or an organizational poet can use the raw ideas from the meeting to further craft the positioning using words describing what everyone was thinking but no one was able to express perfectly in the meeting.

Be clear with the team not just about the decision-making process, but also about the next steps. Now that you've built a prototype for the brand positioning, you'll need to refine it further. In most cases, it is best if this smaller, decision-making body works on refining the ideas of the larger group.

POSITIONING EXAMPLE #3: YOUR BEST FRIEND CHAUNCEY

Even though your research consists of four napkins you scribbled on at a bar, you still feel confident that you'll be able to help your friend Chauncey position himself well for the job market.

By the time you and Chauncey get together for the football game on Sunday, you've thought a bit more about how he might position himself. Because you really are that much of a branding nerd, you guide this conversation the same way you would a full-scale brand positioning workshop, but with just the two of you participating. First, you determine the competitive frame of reference by discussing the types of people Chauncey thinks he will be competing against in the job market, and you get him to show you 10 job descriptions online that he thinks would be a great fit for him.

Once the competitive frame of reference is clear, you go back to the napkins and use the ideas on them to inform a discussion about the characteristics and experiences that will really separate Chauncey from other job seekers going after the same positions. You ask him where he thinks other job seekers will have an advantage over him and ask him about the table stakes that hiring managers will be looking for in any candidate. Based on this, you clarify Chauncey's points of parity and points of difference.

Finally, while a brand mantra is probably not exactly the right thing for Chauncey, a single positioning statement will do the trick. By the fourth quarter of the game, you and Chauncey have drafted a five-word statement that he can use at the top of his LinkedIn page and on his resume summing up who he is and what he has to offer to potential employers.

Chauncey's confidence is coming back, and he is getting more and more positive about his employment prospects as you talk. By the time the game is over and you head home, it is clear that first thing Monday morning, Chauncey is going to be ready to begin applying for some open positions.

When Good Positioning Workshops Go Bad

I've described a pretty rosy version of a brand workshop so far. But I've also witnessed brand positioning workshops that didn't go so well. Perhaps some people were driving agendas they just couldn't leave behind. Perhaps organizational politics were brought into the room, causing rifts and heated disagreements. Perhaps the facilitator lost control of the group or an executive hijacked the process partway through.

As much as we want everyone to get along and come to a consensus, it doesn't always work out that way. If your first positioning workshop doesn't go as well as you hoped, don't despair. Collaboration isn't always pretty. Remember that your goal isn't to get everyone to agree or to choose the most popular ideas. Your goal is to ensure that the *best* ideas win.

> Your goal isn't to get everyone to agree or to choose the most popular ideas. Your goal is to ensure that the *best* ideas win.

If things didn't go so well, reflect on the experience. What went wrong? Did certain executives dominate the conversation, stifling good ideas? Were the ideas people chose during Post-it votes very different from the ones you believe are best for the brand?

Developing brand positioning can be like playing jazz. You may need to improvise and go where the music takes you. You might find you need to reduce the size of your group to move forward effectively. You might need to have conversations on the side to help guide the group toward a shared vision. You may even need to consider whether *you* are part of the issue and, if, by opening your mind to possibilities you haven't considered before, you might solve the problem.

Completing the Process

Using the decision-making process everyone agreed upon, you've now decided on the competitive frame of reference, points of difference, points of parity, and maybe even the brand mantra for your brand. You are sure this positioning is desirable, deliverable, and differentiated.

Don't keep this great positioning to yourself. Ensure that each person who was involved in the brand positioning workshop gets to hear the results of the process directly from you.

Once the decision-making group has made its recommendation, you might consider convening the whole workshop group again, ideally within a few weeks, to review the positioning. This meeting can be much shorter—sometimes as short as an hour. Use this meeting to solicit additional input and ideas from the team, and see if the chosen positioning resonates with them. If necessary, make modifications based on the input you receive.

Instead of bringing the whole group together, you might decide to reach out to people individually or in smaller groups to review. Be sure to recognize the efforts of the entire team, and highlight and give credit to the people who contributed significant ideas along the way.

This brand positioning process has been a team effort, and if you want to ensure that the people who participated in your positioning workshop stay with the process through the brand positioning rollout, it is important that they feel their ideas and contributions are recognized and valued.

Many of these people will become advocates for the brand positioning as it is introduced into the organization. Not all questions and objections will be addressed to you directly; some will come up in meetings and small conversations. Because these individuals had a role in the process, they'll likely be able to answer questions and address objections quickly and credibly, further extending the reach and effectiveness of the positioning.

Modifying This Process for the Lone Designer Approach

If you decided that the lone designer approach to brand positioning is the right one for you, how do you modify the process I've outlined to complete your positioning project?

Simple. Take the entire workshop process I've just described and complete it by yourself. Ask yourself all the same questions. Complete your ideation exercises in a notebook or on a computer instead of at a whiteboard.

The entire process still works if you do it by yourself. The downside is that you won't have the benefit of a diverse set of ideas, and your positioning can suffer because of it. If you chose the lone designer process because you are a small organization without enough people for the internal community approach to work well, read the following section before you get started. You might find you have opportunities to expand your rollout team and collect more ideas by involving people on the outside.

Real Positioning Case Study #1: Differentiated Positioning for The Redwoods Group

Throughout this book, I illustrate key brand concepts using fictional examples like EnviClean Dry Cleaners, BubbaPop Soda Company, and Chauncey to show the full breadth of positioning and rollout possibilities. But I'm also eager to share examples of real positioning exercises as well, even though they might not always fit perfectly into our model. In this chapter, I share two case studies of real-world positioning projects: The Redwoods Group and the Fedora Project.

Kevin Trapani grew up in the YMCA community, as a Y camp counselor, lifeguard, swim coach, and aquatics director. After spending the first part of his career working for a variety of insurance companies, Kevin founded The Redwoods Group in 1997 to service what many in the insurance industry would categorize as "unattractive" customers: YMCA camps and Jewish community centers (JCCs). Most insurance companies weren't interested in these customers because of the high degree of risk due to the threat of child sexual abuse, drowning deaths, and vehicular accidents, among other issues.

Even though these YMCA camps and JCCs represented an untapped business opportunity for insurers, Kevin didn't start Redwoods just to make money. One of his goals was to give back to organizations that had done many good things for him over the years. So, he began the business with a dream to serve others, giving away as much as 50% or more of the company's profits to social causes each year, paying employees to do at least a week of community service on company time every year, and improving safety and saving lives at YMCA camps and JCCs, among other charitable contributions. Eventually, Kevin turned Redwoods into a B-corporation, an innovative new breed of company using the power of business to drive social benefit.[2] *Businessweek* named Kevin one of the Most Promising Social Entrepreneurs of 2010.[3]

Clearly, Redwoods is not your average insurance company. So, when the company embarked on its first formal positioning project, it was a relatively simple task to uncover positioning that would be desirable to customers, deliverable by the brand, and differentiated from competitors.

---

2. You can learn more about B-corporations here: http://www.bcorporation.net/

3. http://images.businessweek.com/ss/10/06/0608_socialentrepreneurs/22.htm

After extensive research and a series of workshops, the positioning team settled on the following positioning framework: First, Redwoods would be positioned in the "specialty insurance" competitive frame of reference, although there would also be broader positioning for the organization in the "social entrepreneur" frame of reference.

Next, the team clearly identified two points of parity: price and coverage. While Redwoods would not always deliver the lowest price because it was providing other services competitors didn't offer, the price and coverage options had to be good enough that, given their strengths on the points of difference, customers would still choose them.

By this time, it was fairly clear what made Redwoods different from other special insurance providers—Redwoods is a mission-based company that truly cares about the health and well-being of YMCAs and JCCs and the people they serve and shows this through its actions, not just its words. Eventually the team settled on three words to describe the key points of difference: *love*, *serve*, and *transform*.

The thinking went this way: Love is mostly missing in the modern business world. Thus, by creating a business rooted in a deep, authentic love and sense of responsibility—for customers and their clients, for employees, and for all the communities it serves—Redwoods will serve these segments better than any other insurer could. This act of serving that is deeply rooted in love would in turn help transform these communities, and Redwoods itself in the process.

Love, serve, transform became not just the points of difference that separate Redwoods from its competitors, but now essentially have become the brand mantra of the organization that guides decisions and actions within the organization.

Modifying This Process for the Open Community Approach

I expect many organizations will begin to embrace an open approach to brand positioning over the coming years. As organizations begin to operate more transparently and the lines between organization and community become more and more blurred, an increasing number of organizations will want to take advantage of the benefits of involving the outside world in their positioning and brand-building process.

There are many ways to do this.

Opening a Window into Your Brand Positioning Project

Even if you are running an internal community positioning project like the one I previously outlined, you might want to take advantage of opportunities to get feedback and input from your external community.

During the research phase, you might have already involved your external community in the project through research or interviews, and that is certainly a good start. You may have also asked for volunteers who might like to give you further opinions and advice in the future. Once you've developed an initial prototype of your brand positioning in the brand positioning workshop, you might want to consider whether it makes sense to approach some of these volunteers again to test your positioning prototype.

One decision you'll need to make prior to opening the process to the outside world is whether to explain that you are asking for the brand community's advice because you are working on brand positioning. Don't feel like you have to explain what you are doing in terms of brand positioning if you are using this open-a-window approach.

One risk of using brand positioning language is that you also open yourself up to a whole set of questions like "What is brand positioning?" and "What is a brand mantra?" that will take you a lot of time to explain—and neither you nor members of your brand community will have the time to give satisfactory explanations like you can give in a positioning workshop.

Without much time to fully introduce context behind your questions, you might have difficulty convincing people accustomed to traditional marketing (and thus suspicious of an ulterior motive) to participate openly. Or using brand positioning language might prompt them to give more business-school-style answers when what you really want are their natural, authentic responses in their own language.

Should you hide the fact you are working on a brand positioning project? No, there's no big secret to protect. But if you are using the open-a-window approach, you'll find that avoiding the use of brandspeak in places where you don't have the time for full explanations can save you time.

For example, if I reached out to a community member, either via phone, email, or a follow-up survey, I might avoid talking about brand positioning altogether. Instead, I'd approach the subject like this:

> "We have been working on a project to better understand what people like about [Our Brand], and I know you answered a survey we sent out recently. I'd like to share some ideas we are considering based on information we learned from this survey and other research. Would you be willing to help us further by telling me if these ideas resonate with you,

or if you have additional thoughts that might help us improve how we talk about [Our Brand]?"

You'd follow this introduction with a series of questions testing how the community member feels about the competitive frame of reference, points of difference, and points of parity you've chosen, without necessarily using those words. Here's an example of how you might do this:

- **For the competitive frame of reference:** "In our research, we've found many people like you view [Our Brand's] primary competition as brands like [competitor 1], [competitor 2], and [competitor 3]. We view all of these together as [competitive frame of reference]. Does this sound right to you? Why or why not?"

- **For a point of difference:** "We've learned that one of the things other people like you believe separates [Our Brand] from our competitors in the [competitive frame of reference] is [point of difference]. Do you agree with this assessment? Why or why not?"

- **For a point of parity:** "If you were to consider other brands in the [competitive frame of reference], would [point of parity] be a primary reason?"

You might decide you want to test the brand mantra as well, but keep in mind that people may evaluate it as a tagline and color their opinions through that lens. In my view, you'll get the most useful feedback from testing the competitive frame of reference, points of difference, and points of parity.

In the appendix, I've provided a sample questionnaire that may help you design a survey or interview questions to test your brand positioning.

 Tip

Check the appendix for a sample questionnaire that can help you design a survey or interview questions to test your brand positioning.

A word of caution: remember that what your brand community thinks is only one set of data points. Don't make a knee-jerk change to your positioning simply because of feedback you receive if it conflicts with your organizational understanding of and goals for the brand as identified in your research.

> Don't make a knee-jerk change to your positioning simply because of feedback you receive...

The advantage of opening a window into the brand positioning process is that you get the benefit of continued feedback on your brand positioning from the community of people it is intended to resonate with. By evaluating your brand positioning prototype with your brand community before considering it finished, you might learn additional information that helps make it better.

The downside of this approach is that, although you might get useful information, you won't be able to begin to engage with your brand community as deeply as you could. You'll simply be collecting information, not building a relationship. If you'd like to understand ways you can build even deeper connections with members of your brand community, read on.

Opening a Door into Your Positioning Project

Brands interested in building highly engaged communities should do more than open a window to the outside world. They should open a *door* and invite people on the outside to come inside and participate in the process. Imagine running the same internal community positioning project from earlier in this chapter, yet inviting trusted customers, partners, and other community members into the process with you.

Perhaps your organization has user groups with members who have a deep knowledge of what you do. Perhaps certain key customers come into your store two or three times a week and tell you how much they love it. Perhaps some people regularly write articles or blogs about your organization. Consider letting them directly into the positioning process.

Run this open project exactly the same way you'd run the internal community project. When running an open-a-door positioning project, I do tend to use the language of brand positioning so that everyone has a common understanding (although I profusely apologize for the positioning jargon upfront).

Just as with the internal community workshop, start by providing background to get everyone on the same page and showing the research; then begin collaboratively working on the positioning itself.

You might feel some of your research results are too sensitive to share with an outside audience. If so, you may choose to handle this by simply leaving out certain bits of research that are inappropriate to share with the outside world. Or you might choose to go ahead and show the data but not hand out copies of the research or associated presentations for participants to take home. Or you may choose to go a step further and ask people to promise to keep the shared information private to this conversation.

Sharing promotes trust and an honest exchange on both sides. By showing people research they would not have otherwise had the chance to see, you are asking for their discretion and showing them trust and respect. This may ultimately help them feel more valued, engaged, and invested—and likely better brand advocates.

However, if you go so far as deciding that people need to sign nondisclosure agreements (NDAs) or other legal documents in order to participate, you've probably lost your chance for a relationship based on trust. If you are worried enough about the potential threats of disclosure to force people to sign NDAs, you might be better off just leaving out some of the sensitive data or not running a project involving outside participants at all. Legal documents are not good for promoting collaboration and engagement.

The risks of involving people from outside your organization are pretty clear. Some organizations are worried about secrets falling into the wrong hands. Some are worried that involving people from the outside world in the positioning project might make it appear that the organization doesn't have all the answers already, is unorganized, or lacks direction. Some worry that the community members might express opinions or ideas that conflict with the direction people inside would like to see for the organization. But, for organizations that manage the process well, involving outside contributors can be an incredibly smart strategy.

If you have the time and budget, you might even consider running both an internal community workshop and an open community workshop and comparing the results you get from each.

 Tip

> If you have the time and budget, consider running both an internal community workshop and an open community workshop and compare the results.

A funny thing happens psychologically when the walls between the organization and the community come down: the organization is forced to start thinking not in the language of writing messages or giving speeches, but instead in the language of *regular conversation*. By getting in the same room with members of your brand community and having a *human conversation* about the brand, you are forced to communicate person-to-person instead of organization-to-target market.

It is a humanizing activity that can do wonders for setting up a more open, collaborative relationship with your brand community. During this workshop, the organization willingly exposes that it does not have all the answers already, showing a vulnerable side to its trusted community. Because it is so rare for organizations to show this side, community members are often pleasantly surprised, setting the stage for more authentic dialogue.

For community members, when the organization asks for help and ideas and community members agree to give them, these folks undergo a psychological change as well. The act of providing input to the future of the brand gives people a stake in the future of the brand. By involving outside community members in the future of the brand, we often help them care more about it. It is no longer *your* brand that they use. It becomes *their* brand, too.

> The act of providing input to the future of the brand gives people a stake in the future of the brand.

This is where the ad-free brand building process is so powerful: When we engage people in the brand-building process, we help them move to the pinnacle of the brand pyramid (see Figure 4.1). We help people own the brand.

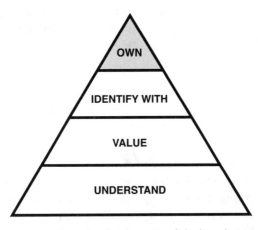

Figure 4.1 *Engaging people in the development of the brand gives them ownership of the brand. This engagement helps the brand relationship reach the top of the brand-benefit pyramid.*

Completely Opening Your Brand Positioning Project

The next frontier will be reached by brands that go beyond opening the brand positioning process to selected members of their brand community and transparently open the entire process to the outside world. The first completely open brand positioning projects are already underway; see the Fedora Project case study I've included here for one example.

In a completely open brand positioning project, everything about the process—research, dialogue, positioning prototypes, and more—is publicly available to the outside world. Anyone who wants to see inside the process can (including competitors). Usually the project is hosted on a website, blog, mailing list, or wiki, and the information about the project is publicly available for comment.

While this approach may seem very scary, certain brands can use it to great effect. Community brands, such as the Fedora Project, are one example of a place where a completely open process can be the catalyst for the rapid growth of the brand community. Nonprofits and other organizations relying heavily on input from volunteers can also see huge benefits from this approach.

> While this completely open approach may seem very scary, certain brands can use it to great effect.

A completely open approach magnifies the risks of an open process, but it also maximizes the potential benefits of creating a highly engaged community of contributors. The brand community has the power to take co-ownership of the direction of the brand with the organization and will become deeply invested in the success of the brand. The walls between the organization and its community might disappear entirely.

Real Positioning Case Study #2: Open Positioning for the Fedora Project

The Fedora Project is an open source development project sponsored by Red Hat and run by a group of contributors including Red Hat employees and outside community members. This project has created one of the most popular free Linux computer operating systems in the world. Because the relationship between Red Hat and the community of Fedora volunteers is a unique collaborative effort, everything is run in the open, where anyone who is interested can participate, no matter whether they work for Red Hat or not.

In September 2005, the Fedora team began a process to design a new brand identity and decided to run the design project out in the open—something largely unheard of in the brand identity and logo design world at the time. The team started a public conversation on mailing lists, asking contributors to begin by describing the core attributes of Fedora. More questions and extensive research within the Fedora community followed.

Eventually, the ideas were narrowed down to four core traits, which were named the Fedora Ideals: open, free, innovative, and forward-looking. Many community members contributed design ideas and one designer, Matt Muñoz (who is now one of my business partners at New Kind), was tasked with consolidating the diverse inputs—including concepts, ideas, and even logo designs—into one brand identity. Matt documented the whole process online,[4] so everyone could see how he arrived at the final logo. This brand identity has since been dramatically extended and expanded by the Fedora design team, which now has taken complete ownership over the ongoing brand identity project.

Figure 4.2   *The now ubiquitous Fedora logo, designed as part of an open, collaborative brand identity project.*

A few years later, in January 2008, Fedora project leader Max Spevack hosted a session at a Fedora conference (Fedora calls them FUDCons) with the goal of improving the clarity of the Fedora story and creating tools to help the story be more consistently told around the world. Based on the discussion that began at this FUDCon session, and using the original work as inspiration, the Fedora community members created a simplified version of the Fedora story based around Four Foundations: freedom, friends, features, and first. Soon after, the Fedora Design team began collaborating on a graphical representation of these Four Foundations. This imagery helped socialize the ideas through the community quickly. [5]

Throughout this process, everything was run out in the open, on mailing lists and wikis where anyone who was interested could contribute, and many people did. Community members quickly embraced both the brand identity and the Four Foundations because they had a role in creating them (standing in sharp contrast to examples like the Gap logo mentioned in Chapter 2 that was sprung upon an unsuspecting community). Today the Four Foundations of Fedora are as well recognized as the Fedora mission statement, maybe even more so. The Fedora logo and brand identity are recognized and embraced by millions of Fedora users around the world.[6]

Did the Fedora community use the language of brand positioning to run these projects? No. But the concepts behind the Four Foundations align very closely with brand positioning. In the competitive frame of reference of Linux operating systems, "freedom" is a very clear point of difference for Fedora, and something that community members treasure deeply. "Friends" represents the collaborative, community-based approach Fedora takes (as evidenced by the novel way it approaches

---

4. You can read more about the original Fedora identity design process here: http://fedoraproject.org/wiki/Logo/History

5. You can read more about the Four Foundations of Fedora here: http://fedoraproject.org/wiki/Foundations

6. You can find more statistics about Fedora usage here: http://fedoraproject.org/wiki/Statistics

brand identity and positioning). In my view, "features" is a point of parity, showing that Fedora does at least as much "stuff" as any other distribution. "First" represents a point of difference around innovation and leadership.

The Four Foundations together—"Freedom, Friends, Features, First"—represent a great brand mantra that is catchy because of the alliteration but also is inspirational for community members.

Figure 4.3 *This graphic depiction of the Four Foundations of Fedora became a powerful way to socialize core traits of the Fedora brand.*

Fedora project team members didn't know or get hung up on the vocabulary of brand positioning. But this project is a fantastic example of a brand positioning project being jointly led by a company (Red Hat) and a community (the Fedora community), with the community taking on more and more ownership as the project matured. I believe this open collaborative approach to brand positioning will become more and more common as other organizations discover its advantages[7].

Running Your Positioning Workshop Virtually

You might find it difficult to get all the people from the internal or external brand community you'd like to participate in the positioning workshop in the same room. It also may be too expensive or difficult logistically.

Getting people together in the same room is the best option by far because it creates a powerful shared experience that can galvanize your core group of brand advocates. But if it is impossible, here are some ideas for ways you can run your positioning workshop virtually.

- **Webcast:** Set up your session as a webcast using a tool like WebEx (www.webex.com) or GoToMeeting (www.gotomeeting.com). Many webcast tools now allow presenters and participants to communicate online and share documents, websites, and other information during the session. Some even allow you to work on a virtual whiteboard. If you've used webcast software before, however, you'll recognize that

7. Thanks to Paul Frields (a former Fedora Project Leader), Robyn Bergeron, and Matt Muñoz (a partner at New Kind and designer of the original Fedora logo) for their help on this story

communication often isn't as good as it would be with an in-person session or a phone call. If you are having technical trouble or not everyone has a built-in microphone on their computer, consider setting up a conference call people can join to participate via phone while they are watching the webcast online.

- **Videoconferencing:** If your group is small, videoconferencing might be an option. Consider Skype (www.skype.com), which offers an inexpensive group conferencing option. Webcast providers such as WebEx and GoToMeeting also offer videoconferencing options. If you have a big budget and want the Rolls Royce of virtual collaboration, take a look at Cisco Telepresence (www.cisco.com/telepresence).

- **Conference call:** This is the least desirable option. With just a phone call, you'll have trouble engaging the group well, people won't be paying close attention, and it will be difficult to share ideas and vote during the process.

- **Online collaboration tools:** While I do not recommend trying to run an initial brand positioning workshop as a discussion on a mailing list, forum, or wiki, you might find that these tools are perfect for follow-up meetings or conversations. My favorite online follow-up method is to create a group on BaseCamp (www.basecamphq.com); invite all the workshop members to join the group; and post all the research, brainstorming, and ongoing conversation on BaseCamp where everyone can review when it is convenient for them.

Phase Two Is Now Complete

By now you've completed your brand positioning workshop and have developed a solid prototype of your brand positioning that you are ready to begin to share and test with your internal team and external community. Congratulations, you are now ready to move on to the brand positioning rollout phase.

5

The Internal Brand Positioning Rollout

For most ad-free brands, the internal rollout of the positioning is as or more important than the external rollout. Why? Because every employee of an ad-free brand must live the brand every day for the positioning to be effective. This is a prerequisite for any brand that wants to operate the ad-free way. Ad-free brands must channel the spirit of esse quam videri: to be rather than to seem to be.

In the old days, positioning was largely the work of the marketing team, advertising agency, or PR firm. Employees simply enjoyed seeing the ads, reading the press releases, and checking out the new website along with everyone else.

No more.

> Every employee of an ad-free brand must live the brand every day....

In an ad-free brand, employees play the most important role in the success of the brand positioning. All employees must be aligned on the brand positioning for it to be effective. They must play the same music, together as one orchestra, conveying the positioning not just through their words, but through their actions as well. In this chapter, I share a set of strategies that will help your organization begin playing the brand positioning music together.

Building the Brand from the Inside Out

Earlier, I described ad-free brands as brands built from the inside out. What exactly does this mean?

Imagine for a second that a brand is a powerful star at the center of a solar system, maybe one like our Sun. If we've done a great job defining our brand positioning, we've described the gravitational pull at the very center of that star.

This gravitational pull is always drawing people closer to the heart of the brand. As people move closer, the brand releases energy, in much the same way a star sends out heat and light.

So, the goal of our internal brand positioning rollout is, as best we can, to mimic the thermonuclear fusion within a star.

> The goal of our internal brand positioning rollout is to mimic thermonuclear fusion within a star.

We want to pull people closer to the center of the brand using the brand positioning as a gravitational force. Then just like with atoms in a star, after the core group of people at the center of the brand is sufficiently dense, a reaction occurs, resulting in a continuous stream of brand energy released over time, as shown in Figure 5.1. The denser you can make the core near the center of the brand, the more energy is released.

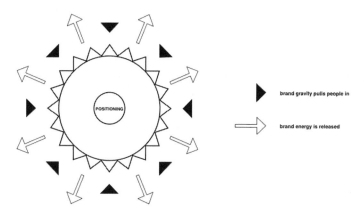

Figure 5.1   *Great positioning helps pull people toward the core of the brand. After the group of people near the center is sufficiently dense, a reaction begins, releasing a continuous stream of brand energy.*

If you aren't the least bit interested in astrophysics, or that explanation did not resonate with you, let me try another, simpler one:

At some point, if enough people begin to deeply understand and live the brand in their daily work, magic happens.

American showman and circus entrepreneur P.T. Barnum was no astrophysicist, but he understood the power of this magic moment. His explanation: "Nothing draws a crowd like a crowd."

Aligning a core, closely aligned group of people around the brand positioning is the only way to set off this particular reaction. And there is no better place to start rolling out your positioning than with those people who already work for your organization and have a vested interest in its success.

Building a brand from the inside out means building the brand by creating energy from the passion of the community of people closest to the brand—those who work for the organization—and using the gravitational force this group creates to pull even more people close to the center of the brand.

Thinking Like a Conductor

The goal of the internal brand positioning rollout is to embed the core positioning deeply within the minds and actions of each employee of the organization so that it comes out consciously and even unconsciously in their interactions with the external brand community.

This is very hard. You can't force people into "living the brand." No one likes to be told what to do. I certainly don't.

You can't force people into 'living the brand.'

Ad-free brands work from the core principle that those who are not invited on the journey will usually reject the destination. So, broad participation in the brand-building process is a prerequisite for the brand positioning to really take off. Unfortunately, the larger the organization, the harder it is to achieve consistency in the way the brand positioning is rolled out.

Let me switch metaphors from stars to orchestras. I like approaching the brand positioning rollout by channeling the mindset of the conductor of an orchestra. An orchestra conductor is able to create amazing, complex, and beautiful music just by using a tiny baton.

The conductor's role is to organize, motivate, and inspire a group of people to make music together. The conductor chooses the piece of music, interprets the piece, gives every person in the orchestra a part to play, and helps each musician rise to the level of his or her talent or experience.

An orchestra in which every musician plays the same notes would be boring, to say the least. In an orchestra, the diversity of instruments—woodwinds, percussion, strings, and brass—allows for the complex and beautiful expression of music. Yet many organizations attempt to roll out their brand positioning by expecting everyone to toe an explicit company line, sticking to a rehearsed speech.

This kind of approach does not play well for ad-free brands.

To me, the rehearsed expression of the brand positioning comes off as canned, corporate BS that most people will ignore. To be effective, ad-free brands take advantage of the talent and voice of each employee, allowing each person to utilize his or her own strengths, interests, and passions to explain or begin to live the brand positioning.

The goal is not getting everyone to play the same notes—it's getting everyone to play in the same key. Different people prefer the sounds of different instruments and types of music. One of the benefits of having many people playing in your orchestra is that you are likely to create tunes that appeal to all types of people, which will in turn attract even more people.

🔍 Tip

The goal is not getting everyone to play the same notes—it's getting everyone to play in the same key.

When you create a situation where many people are communicating and living the positioning in their own ways, you increase the chance that other people will begin to hear, understand, value, and live it themselves.

An orchestra will get better with practice. With a four-person rock band, like in a small organization, it is fairly easy to grab an instrument, pick a key, and start jamming together. But in a symphony orchestra with as many as 100 players, it takes some work to get everyone playing as one.

Getting 100 people playing well together in an orchestra takes practice and time, and in a large organization, it can take even more time and practice. Later in this chapter, I highlight some examples of ways to embed the brand positioning internally within your organization to ensure people are getting the practice they need to make brand positioning music together.

But let me leave you with this thought: As you build your brand positioning rollout team, encourage the team not to think of itself as the sole group responsible for articulating and living the brand positioning. Instead, encourage the rollout team to think of itself as the conductor of an orchestra, helping many different instruments create a complex, beautiful piece of music together.

🔍 Tip

Encourage your rollout team to imagine itself as the conductor of an orchestra, helping many different instruments create a complex, beautiful piece of music together.

Activating the Core

By this point in the process, you will likely not be starting from scratch in building a core group of people close to the brand positioning. Instead, by involving other employees in the research and positioning phases, you've begun to establish a strong core of people who already understand and are excited about the brand positioning.

You've begun to put together your rollout team, the conductor of your brand orchestra.

If you used an open community approach to positioning, this core group might even include people from outside the walls of your organization. But for the purposes of this chapter, we'll be focused only on activating people inside the organization (we'll get to the outside folks in Chapter 6).

The Brand Positioning Rollout Team

After your brand positioning prototype is finalized, you should look back at the group of people who participated in your positioning workshop. You will probably want to ask the majority of these people to continue on as part of the brand positioning rollout team.

Include any person from that workshop who expresses interest in continuing to work on the rollout team unless you have a compelling reason to exclude someone. For example, if one member was a destructive force during the workshop (a devil's advocate, for example), you *might* want to leave him or her off the rollout team. But don't assume just because someone was negative during the workshop that he or she is not a candidate for the rollout team.

When choosing people for the rollout team, I often try to choose one hater. By *hater*, I mean someone who expressed doubts about the brand positioning project specifically or perhaps tends to express doubts about *every* project he or she encounters.

Why knowingly bring in the enemy? Two reasons:

- The hater will be your canary in the coalmine, proactively exposing places where you might get a negative reaction from the larger internal brand community and allowing you to course-correct before you roll out more broadly.

- I've seen many cases where a hater who is properly engaged actually ends up being one of the biggest supporters of the project. This can be a powerful thing.

But one hater is plenty—you don't want to have too many negative influences because they will begin to demotivate members of the team who are excited about the project. Eventually, you'll find that your hater will either begin to enjoy the process (even if reluctant to admit it) or will leave the project.

You should also use the brand positioning rollout as an opportunity to bring new people into the process and begin to expand the number of people who understand the brand positioning within the organization. Look for many of the same things you looked for in workshop participants, including people who:

- Show clear excitement and energy for the process and have embraced the positioning resulting from the workshop

- Work in brand, communications, or human resources functions (especially internal communications)

- Have broad power or influence within the organization

- Have a reputation for coming up with great ideas

- Have a reputation for doing real work

- Have good diplomatic, facilitation, or organizing skills

- Are natural storytellers

If there are members of your senior leadership team who participated in the positioning workshop and would like to continue as part of the rollout team, that is great—it never hurts to have the ongoing executive support.

But the primary role of senior leaders during this phase is to provide support, visibility, and encouragement to the project, and, unless they are eager to stay involved, they probably don't need to attend every rollout team meeting (consider giving them a regular update instead).

Convening the Rollout Team

With team members chosen, next bring them together as a group, setting aside a few hours for the first session. Start with a recap of the brand positioning basics; then go over the final brand positioning prototype you've chosen, including the math for how you arrived at it.

Because some people in the session won't have seen the positioning before, you should align them with those who participated in the workshop. If you've made significant changes to what workshop attendees saw during the session and haven't updated them since, they'll want to hear how and why you've changed things. Be as transparent as possible about the reasons for any changes.

By the time you have finished this introduction, the whole team should be aligned around a common understanding of the brand positioning. I say *should be* because occasionally people will begin to debate or challenge the chosen positioning during this session. The best way to handle objections is to make it clear that you have all passed the point in the process where you are debating the positioning prototypes—that isn't the role of this group. If your team is familiar with design thinking, consider explaining which design thinking step you are working through (described in Chapter 4).

Explain that many from this group and others have already defined the problem, completed research to inform the positioning, ideated possible solutions, built prototypes for positioning, and chosen a prototype they'd like to implement. This rollout team's function is to implement the prototype built—not to design a new one.

Let them know that, after you've begun rolling out the prototype and have started to receive feedback, the group can decide to make some changes, and the sort of ideas they have for modifying the position will be valuable when they've reentered the ideation stage.

Collecting Rollout Ideas

After you have the entire team aligned, you'll be ready for the fun part: beginning to ideate ways to embed the positioning into your organizational DNA. This is where having people involved who deeply understand the organization's culture and history matters most.

A FEW THOUGHTS ON EMBEDDING POSITIONING AND LIVING THE BRAND

When it comes to rolling out brand positioning internally, I'm a big fan of subtlety versus beating people over the head. And I'm also a big fan of living the brand instead of talking about it (as you might have guessed by now).

That's why I like the words *embedding* and *living* to describe the internal rollout. An ad-free brand positioning internal rollout should not be an advertising or promotional campaign. Effectively embedding brand positioning is not as simple as putting posters on the walls or having an executive tell the organization about the new positioning at a staff meeting.

The rollout must be deeper than that, and it must be authentic to the culture of your organization. As you'll see from the examples later in this chapter, embedding brand positioning is not just a communications activity; it can be an exercise in organizational design as well and should not just impact what people *say*, but what they *do*.

On the front cover of the second edition of the *Red Hat Brand Book*, we wrote a simple sentence: "You are the Red Hat brand." By this, we meant that the content within those pages was simply a description of the brand, but the real brand was being lived by the people of Red Hat through their thoughts, feelings, and actions.

You want to get people to live the brand, not just talk about it.

Although your brand rollout ideation can extend beyond the initial kickoff meeting, I suggest you keep the ideas flowing using the rules for managing the ideation process that I shared in Chapter 4 (avoid the devil's advocate, all ideas are good, and so on).

> You want people to live the brand, not just talk about it.

As you continue ideating over the course of a few weeks, manage the ideation process online using a wiki or a tool like Basecamp (www.basecamphq.com) to collect people's thoughts and ideas. Meet with the team regularly, preferably once per week so that everyone can stay up-to-date with the team's progress.

Internal Rollout Project Ideas

I'd like to share some specific ideas for embedding brand positioning within your organization that I've used before with great success. While not all of these techniques and projects will be right for your organization's brand and culture, I provide them as examples and inspiration. Consider describing some of these ideas to your rollout team to help get the ideation process started.

As with the research ideas from Chapter 3, some of these ideas are easier to accomplish and less expensive than others. When it comes to internal rollout, I still look for low-cost, high-value rollout projects. Most of the projects you'll see here don't cost much money, but some of them will take the time of people within the organization.

If your organization has money but not time, consider bringing in an external firm to help brainstorm rollout ideas that might work within your culture. Although many of the best ideas will come from the internal team, an external agency might have more time to develop these ideas and will also be able to share projects that have been successful for other clients with similar brands and cultures.

I begin with the projects I believe are most important to consider.

Creating a Brand Story

There is no more important tool for rolling out brand positioning internally than a brand story. Remember that we are trying to create gravity around the brand; you'll find that effective brand stories are the best gravity-creators there are.

Think about your own organization for a minute. Are there legends or stories that have been told and retold over the years? How the brand got its name? How the founders of your organization first met? The original problem they were trying to solve by developing your product? Perhaps your particular worldview or internal values became very clear at one moment in the organization's history. Most organizations have internal legends, stories, and fables that are already being told.

Your existing stories and legends are powerful because they are illustrations of who you are and why you do what you do. Often, these stories serve as building blocks for a brand story.

A brand story is an attempt to articulate the brand positioning by answering the deepest truths about the brand, things such as:

- Who are we?

- Why are we here?

- What do we care about?

- What do we do?

- Why does it matter?

✉ *Note*

A brand story is an attempt to articulate the brand positioning by answering the deepest truths about the brand.

In all likelihood, your brand story is already partway being told in the form of the stories and legends that follow the brand around everywhere it goes. By the time your rollout team has begun to think about the brand story, your job will be simply to find and finesse that story and to mold it into something that helps support the brand positioning. If your chosen positioning remains true to the historical legacy of the brand, this will not be difficult.

To better articulate how a brand story can emerge over time, let me share my own story about the Red Hat brand story.

How the Red Hat Brand Story Emerged

When I started at Red Hat in 1999, co-founder Bob Young was still with the company. Bob is a wonderful storyteller who loves to share anecdotes and metaphors to illustrate his points. So, within my first week at Red Hat, my head was filled with all the basic Bob Young stories about Red Hat.

He told one story to explain the value of open source, which we referred to as the "Hood Welded Shut" story. In it, he compared buying normal software to buying a car with the hood welded shut. If you wanted to get inside the software code and try to fix or improve it, you couldn't. The underlying source code didn't come with it—the hood was welded shut.

But by buying open source software, which came with the source code, you could get under the hood yourself to see what might be wrong or, if you didn't have the skills or desire, pick anyone of your choosing to work on the code for you (not just the company that welded the hood shut in the first place).

People loved this story because it was at its heart a story about freedom from control, about having a choice. This resonated with anyone who has ever been forced to upgrade to a version of a software product they didn't need, dealt with a bug that did not get fixed for years, or had been otherwise bullied or ignored by a software company.

Stories like this one were great illustrations of the raw materials of what would later become core traits of the Red Hat brand, concepts like freedom, choice, liberation, and value.

Over the years, Red Hat began to collect more and more legends that illustrated who we were and what made us different. Former chairman and CEO Matthew Szulik loved to tell the story of the day he hosted an important meeting with one of the biggest technology companies in the world, and the head of our support organization walked in to the meeting wearing a t-shirt that read, "I'd rather be masturbating."

Matthew used this story as an illustration of the difference in culture between Red Hat and the other big technology companies of the day. But I also suspect Matthew liked that story partly because he was scarred by the experience, partly to show how far the company had come, and partly because it was a great (if demented) illustration of how much freedom people enjoyed at Red Hat.

In 2001, I was asked to be a part of a project to define the values of the company. At that time, Red Hat was still very small, probably about 500 employees. Our group decided to approach defining the values the open source way. Meaning, we opened the process to the entire company, allowing everyone to contribute ideas.

Interestingly enough, we found people continued to use many of the legends and stories we'd heard over the years (like those I illustrated) to explain why they thought certain concepts should be closely held as company values. Over 10 years later, the values that emerged from the ideas and stories of those early employees are still deeply ingrained in the Red Hat culture.

The following year, I participated in a project to define the Red Hat brand. We used the research, the results, and many of the same people who contributed to the values project to help build a first prototype of the Red Hat brand identity and voice. This project ultimately resulted in something called the *Red Hat Brand Book*, an attempt to answer those big "who are we and why we are here"-type questions and codify the visual and written language of the brand.

Over the years, we completed multiple versions of the *Red Hat Brand Book*, which began as a combination brand story and brand standards guide (see Figure 5.2). By the time we released the third version in 2009, we had separated out the Red Hat story into a separate book[1] from the brand standards guide (which became a manual describing the voice and look of the brand).

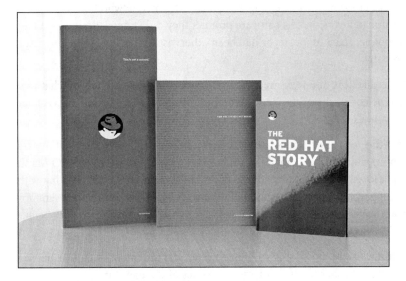

Figure 5.2   *Three versions of the Red Hat story created over almost a decade. The first two versions were both called the* Red Hat Brand Book *and combined the company story with the brand standards. By the time we completed the* Red Hat Story *book in 2009, we had made the decision to split the brand story, which could be broadly used by employees and others in the brand community, from the brand standards, which had a narrower audience. (Photo by Jonathan Opp)*

At the same time we were writing physical brand books, we were also working on projects where we shared parts of the Red Hat story in many media.

We created short films between two and four minutes long that articulated elements of the story. Some of these, like one called "Truth Happens,"[2] caught on; it was eventually translated into many languages and passed on by hand (before the days of YouTube) to many people all around the world. I guess you could call that "viral marketing," but we never thought of it that way. We weren't trying to use the film to sell anything; we were just telling a story (in fact, Red Hat wasn't even mentioned in "Truth Happens" until the Red Hat logo appeared at the very end).

---

1. If you'd like to see the *Red Hat Story* book, I highlighted it in a blog post a few years ago: http://darkmattermatters.com/2009/07/29/sharing-your-brand-story-and-heres-ours/

2. You can watch "Truth Happens" and some of our other short brand story films here: http://www.redhat.com/videos/truth_happens.html

We created unique events and experiences like the original Red Hat Road Tour 2002 (What happens when you put four passionate open source folks and a driver named Cookie in a rented RV and drive across the country meeting customers, developers, and partners? Answer: Assorted zaniness and positive corporate karma) and the follow-up Red Hat World Tour 2004 (What happens when you put four passionate open source folks and a filmmaker named Alphonse on a plane to talk to friends of Red Hat on four continents in a two-and-a-half-week trip circumnavigating the globe? Answer: More zaniness and a smaller planet). The stories from these events helped people live the brand story with us, and we captured them online with regular blog updates.

By the time we produced the *Red Hat Story* book in 2009, we'd realized that the best medium for telling the story was *every* medium. So, we produced both a book and a short film highlighting the basic brand story behind Red Hat and used these two vehicles as the foundation upon which many other extensions of the brand story could be built, inside and outside the organization.

Sharing Your Brand Story

I share this Red Hat story to show you that an authentic brand story won't just be made up on the spot by your brand rollout group. Great brand stories have a lineage and a heritage that are built over time and with the hard work and perseverance of many people.

In attempting to articulate a brand story, your group's job will be part historian, part archeologist, and part sculptor, taking the existing building blocks that have been provided to you by those who built the brand and merging them with the new brand positioning you've developed. You'll need to mold these two views together into an overarching brand story that is both authentic to the brand's past and relevant to the brand's future at the same time.

🔍 *Tip*

Your brand story should be authentic to the brand's past and relevant to the brand's future at the same time.

It is hard work creating a great story that will get passed on from person to person. You'll need to recruit the best storytellers you can find to the cause, including your organization's top writers, designers, and poets (or if you work with an outside firm, bring their best folks in, too).

CREATING GREAT STORIES

If you don't have much experience with storytelling or you'd like to get more deeply inspired on how to create great stories, consider reading one of the following books:

- *Made to Stick* by **Chip and Dan Heath:** An extremely inspirational and informative book for any storyteller, it explains why some ideas take on lives of their own and others never catch on, while providing great advice for how to tell stories that "stick."

- *Conversational Capital* by **Bertrand Cesvet, Tony Babinski, and Eric Alper:** Written by the brand strategists who helped build the Cirque du Soleil and MGM Mirage brands, this book will teach you how to use stories and experiences to manage word of mouth about your brand.

- *Resonate* by **Nancy Duarte:** This short, wonderful book will teach you how to use techniques normally found in movies and books to build great, engaging presentations and stories.

As you saw from my Red Hat experience, there are many media you can use to tell the brand story, but I usually recommend designing it first in one of the following formats.

- **Physical Story Book**—If you have an internal creative team of writers and designers, they'll probably view a brand story book as a fun assignment to work on and an opportunity to do some of their best creative work for the brand. Even if you don't have an internal design team, it has never been easier to design and produce a brand story book you can distribute inside and outside of your organization. After you write the brand story, consider designing it and printing it using an online book publishing service like Lulu (www.lulu.com) or Blurb (www.blurb.com). These services allow you to easily produce a bound, professional-looking brand story book. Even better, you can print on demand so you'll print and pay for only the copies you actually need. Perhaps because I am a writer and former editor myself, I have a great affinity for a printed brand book I can hold in my hands, keep on my desk, and refer to whenever I need a litmus test of what is "on brand." It becomes a reference guide, always at my fingertips.

- **Brand Story Film**—As it has become less expensive to create and distribute impactful digital media content, the brand film has become a great way to distribute the brand story. I use the word *film* rather than *video* on purpose because it better captures the spirit of what you should aspire to accomplish. For me, the word *film* evokes a spirit of capturing stories while the word *video* makes me think about people trying to sell me stuff. Brand films should be short—five or six minutes at the longest, but more likely between two and four minutes. If you can't boil down the brand story to that length, you probably have some work to do to simplify it first (or consider turning it into a series of brand story videos that you release over time). The main benefit of the brand film is that it can capture an emotional, personal angle of the brand that is hard to see in words and images alone. Films can engage the senses in ways that words on a page can't. With films, you can feature real people talking about the brand, and you can even use music and movement to enhance the experience. However, producing an effective brand story film takes time, talent, and money, and it won't be the right option for every organization. Personally, I love the combination of a brand book and a brand film that tell the same story but use the strengths of each medium to their fullest potential.

- **Brand Story Presentation**—Where books and films are two of the most common media for sharing stories in our lives, the slide presentation is perhaps the most ubiquitous way of sharing information in the corporate world. Although I prefer the book and film for the core articulation of brand stories, you might find that a more traditional slide presentation format is the most useful or inexpensive way to distribute your story.

However, when I say "slide presentation," I'm not talking about a PowerPoint deck with endless pages, bullets, and clipart. This presentation should be just as beautiful a story as a book or a film, relying on images and bursts of meaningful text. Even if the presentation is the only articulation of the brand story I'm producing, I still try to design it as if I am producing a book or a film. This is not an exercise in death by PowerPoint.

🔍 Tip

Even if your brand story is a slide presentation, you should still produce it using a storytelling mindset.

Although I don't typically love when a presentation is the only articulation of the brand story, I often begin developing the brand story first using presentation software such as Keynote (for Mac users, but you can also use PowerPoint or OpenOffice) as my writing platform. Using presentation software rather than just a word processor to write your story forces you to think as a writer and a designer at the same time and can help you develop ways to visually articulate stories and save some words.

 Tip

Using presentation software rather than just a word processor forces you to think as a writer and a designer at the same time.

A Few Final Thoughts about Brand Stories

I've spent a lot of time discussing brand stories here because investing time articulating a brand story that beautifully and poetically demonstrates the brand positioning is one of the most valuable investments your rollout team can make.

But before we leave the subject, I'd like to share a few final tips on how to ensure your brand story becomes a powerful tool for embedding your brand positioning deeply within the organization.

- **Make it short and simple**—To be effective, the brand story must be easily consumable and repeatable by internal and external audiences. If your brand story is the length of *War and Peace*, you might have created a brand story that few people will finish.

- **Make it relevant**—The best brand stories become part of a larger narrative and are set against a backdrop of events, issues, or experiences that will be shared by many in the brand community. The stories can be grounded in deeply human movements like freedom, hope, peace, opportunity, or faith. Or they can be closely tied to the issues important to your brand community.

- **Follow a typical storytelling arc**—Great brand stories are often adventures following a typical storytelling arc. For example, against a backdrop of events, a hero attempts an adventure, is threatened by a villain, encounters a crisis (or two), and ultimately triumphs. Imagine the narrative path of your own favorite movies or books. Who are the heroes and villains? What struggles do they face? How do they overcome them?

- **Be concrete**—Great stories marry deeply held philosophical concepts with real examples, illustrations, and people. Don't just use the story to preach the brand philosophy; show it in action through characters, events, crises, and resolutions.

If the brand positioning is the piece of music that your orchestra will be playing together, a brand story can help keep everyone playing in the same key. You should come back to the story over and over when you are developing new ways to roll out the positioning and use it as a litmus test for whether the articulation or experience of the positioning is true to the brand.

Mapping the Brand Experience

One of the most valuable projects your rollout group can work on together is mapping the experience of the brand from the point of view of many types of members of your internal and external brand communities.

An experience map is an attempt to document interactions with your brand from the point of view of members of your brand community. Experience mapping projects can quickly grow enormous and complex, but I recommend you begin with a small prototype project just involving your brand positioning rollout team.

✉ *Note*

An experience mapping project is an attempt to document interactions with your brand from the point of view of members of your brand community.

Start your project by asking the group to name as many of your brand's community member types as they can. Some of the most common community member types include

- Customers

- Potential customers

- Partners

- Users

- Contributors

- Investors

- Employees

- Press

Take a vote to choose the one member type you'd like to map first. Next, ask people to brainstorm every interaction they can think of that members of this community might have with the brand.

Common examples might include things like:

- The website

- Customer service

- The receptionist

- Service or support calls or emails

- Twitter or other social media

- Retail stores

- Sales calls or emails

- Newsletters or update emails

- Advertising (if you still do it!)

These examples are very general, but you'll want your group to get as specific as possible. For example, if you've chosen customers as the community type whose experience you'd like to map, you might decide to break down their experience of interacting with salespeople into in-person sales, phone sales, and partner sales.

Then, within each type of sales, you'll find several additional individual points where people interact with community members. For example, the first point of contact, the follow-up call, and the contract negotiation would all be interactions you can map. You may find that some of the best places for you to create brand experiences aligned with the positioning are places you would have never suspected.

One of my favorite examples from my time at Red Hat was when our extremely innovative legal department decided to redesign the entire contracting process so that it would be in tune with the brand and culture of organization. Amazing.

This team took the spirit of open source and applied it to legal documents, procurement processes, and negotiations. In doing so, they managed to simplify the language of the contracts, increasing the transparency of the process, encouraging collaboration rather than conflict, and much more.

After you have an exhaustive list of as many places where your community-member-type comes into contact with the brand, begin to map each interaction visually to see how they fit together.

This visualization can be as simple as drawing a line across a whiteboard and mapping the interaction points as a time continuum that looks something like Figure 5.3.

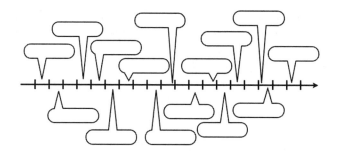

Figure 5.3   *Your experience map might look like a continuum of events over time.*

It can also be more of a web of connections, contact points, and experiences that looks something like Figure 5.4

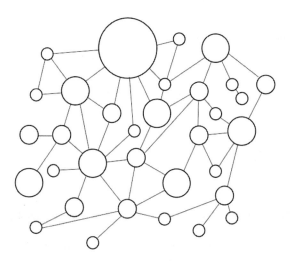

Figure 5.4   *Your experience map might look like a web of connections, contact points, and experiences.*

My business partner at New Kind, Matt Muñoz, works with clients to deeply understand the community's experience and then designs and builds wall-sized maps that illustrate the experience for our clients. People often put these maps on the walls in their offices and ask employees to make suggestions, additions, and modifications to the experience by writing directly on the maps. Consider putting up drafts of your maps as well so your rollout team can make comments and improvements.

Depending on the complexity of your brand, you might find that one of these formats works better for your mapping project than another—just pick the one that is most comfortable for you and run with it.

After you have the brand experience mapped out, your group will probably start to see many places where the current experience of the brand is not aligned with the brand positioning you've worked so hard to develop. This is normal. It is also where the mapping exercise becomes really valuable because it helps you identify where the brand promise of the positioning is out of alignment with the brand experience.

But you'll need to look at each connection point, not just the ones where you see obvious misalignment. Your goal should be to fix the connection points where there is a gap between the brand promise of the positioning and the current brand experience. But you'll also reveal opportunities to make the brand experience even better and more "on brand" in places where it is already strong.

Start by reviewing each interaction point and asking this simple question:

What could we do here to make the experience align even more closely with the positioning?

Asking this question forces you to begin thinking about the brand mantra, the points of parity, and the points of difference and how they might affect every interaction with your community. It is one of the most powerful tools you have for getting people to deeply explore the impact of the brand positioning on daily interactions.

INTERNAL ROLLOUT EXAMPLE #1: ENVICLEAN DRY CLEANERS

Your positioning project was a great success, involving many people both inside and outside the organization. Based on the input from this team, you've developed a brand mantra that is resonating well for EnviClean. It is three simple words: Everyday World Cleaning.

The word *everyday* helps highlight a point of parity around price and a point of difference around being approachable. The phrase *world cleaning* alludes to the "environmentally intelligent" point of difference and shows that EnviClean has a wider purpose than just cleaning clothes—instead it hopes to have an impact on the world. EnviClean is not just a dry cleaner; it is a world cleaner!

As part of your internal rollout, the employees on the original positioning team join up with some other enthusiastic employees from across the organization to begin mapping the brand community experience from the point of view of customers. The team maps every single place where customers come into contact with the EnviClean brand, from the drop-off experience to the pick-up experience, including phone calls, email updates, community event appearances, the recycling process, and more.

The team asks the question "How can we inject the ethos of *everyday world cleaning* into each of these experiences even more clearly than we do today?" Ideas start flowing, and before you realize it, the team has developed a set of recommendations for changes that will ensure that the experience of brand for the EnviClean community lives up to the promise of *everyday world cleaning.*

After you've mapped the brand experience for one community member type, expand the process to other groups and use this process to systematically design the brand experience to match the promise of the brand positioning.

You've probably noticed by now that the results of this project are designs for the *external* brand experience. Yet, I've included this project in the chapter on the *internal* brand rollout. Why?

Because specific projects like developing a brand story or designing a brand experience are the best ways to get people to deeply internalize the brand positioning. It is one thing for them to understand it in theory. It is quite another for them to attempt to put it into practice.

Projects that force people to put the brand positioning into practice are often the most effective internal rollout projects. These projects invite employees along on the creation journey, which will help ensure that they embrace the destination the brand is heading toward in the future. In addition, they create new shared experiences that bring your core internal brand community closer together.

> Projects that force people to put the brand positioning into practice are often the most effective internal rollout projects.

But the experience mapping process is good for more than just designing external brand experiences. You can also use this process to design the internal brand experience, and you'll see many examples of effective ways to do this through the rest of this chapter.

By designing brand experiences through an experience mapping project, you'll really begin to internalize the spirit of *esse quam videri*: To be rather than to seem to be. You'll find that people within your organization don't just talk about the brand or tell the brand story so much as they begin to *live* it in their daily interactions.

Democratizing Brand Experience Mapping

After your brand rollout team begins to implement the brand experience it has designed through the mapping process, you'll quickly see what a huge impact it can have in the relationships you are developing with members of your internal and external brand community. But chances are your small rollout group can only see a subset of the interaction points your brand community members have with your brand.

If you want to even more deeply instill the "to be rather than to seem to be" spirit within your organization, consider democratizing the brand experience mapping process by inviting groups all across the organization to participate in their own brand experience mapping projects. You'll be able to extend your reach and will uncover hidden parts of the experience that most people within your organization never see.

 Tip

> Consider democratizing the brand experience mapping process by inviting groups all across the organization to participate so you can uncover parts of the experience you might otherwise never see.

How do you do this? Ask to be invited to the team meetings of departments in different parts of the organization. Or even better, if you have put together a diverse group of people for your brand rollout team, ask team members to lead sessions in their own departments. Follow the same mapping process already discussed, but dive even more deeply into the specific community interactions that particular group experiences daily.

This process will work for any department within the organization. Perhaps you start by taking the experience mapping process to a group like your finance group. Attend their team meeting. Explain the role of brand positioning, and explain the brand positioning for your organization first (you can do this using many of the same introductory materials you used during the positioning workshop and for the rollout team kickoff).

Then brainstorm which brand community members the finance group interacts with most closely. Perhaps in your organization the finance group interacts mostly closely with customers and investors, so the group decides to focus on customers first.

Ask them how the brand positioning could be even more deeply embedded within their own interactions with customers in the finance department. Perhaps one of your organization's points of difference is "speed," but the time it takes to process payments and get the customer up and running on your product is measured in days. Your group might brainstorm ways to speed up the process of getting the customer running on the product to better live the "speed" part of your brand positioning.

Repeat this process everywhere you can within the organization. Attend team meetings, and even train people to run experience-mapping projects of their own. Eventually, you'll know you've been successful when you begin hearing the results of experience mapping projects happening across the organization that you didn't even plan yourself!

Hosting an Executive Brand Boot Camp

One great way to quickly internalize brand positioning in a meaningful way is to host a brand boot camp for executives. Your executive brand boot camp will be another opportunity for you to update the executive team on your team's progress developing the brand positioning, but it will also be an opportunity for the executives to begin using the positioning.

If you are not an executive yourself, consider either enlisting one of the members of your executive team to help co-host the session or bringing in a facilitator from the outside to run the session with you (so you aren't in the position of telling executives what to do). The session can be anywhere from an hour to a day long and can go as deep as your executive team is prepared to go. Here are some potential agenda items:

Positioning Update and Overview

Update the executives on brand positioning progress (include other members of your positioning/rollout team if possible so it is clear the project is a group effort involving folks from many parts of the organization). Share the brand story if you have created one. Get the executives' feedback.

Brand Story Practice Session

Facilitate a session in which executives practice telling the basic brand story, articulating key points of parity and points of difference along the way. If you've ever been a part of an executive communications or press training session, this practice session might remind you of a traditional "practice the elevator pitch" session.

Let the executives critique each others' telling of the story, and check after each one to ensure they hit each of the points of parity and points of difference along the way. Do the executives just capture the story, or do they capture the spirit of the brand as well? Are their stories passionately told? Discuss each approach and let the executives learn from each other.

Mini-Experience-Mapping Session

You want the executives to be able to go beyond telling the brand story and begin to see how to incorporate the positioning into the brand experience (live the brand). To do this, take the executive team through a mini experience-mapping session focusing on how people at their level interact with members of one or more brand communities. How could they align their interactions with the community better with the brand positioning?

During the brand boot camp session, executives will begin internalizing the brand positioning. They'll have the opportunity to practice their storytelling skills, and they can get feedback from colleagues on how well they communicate the story.

After you have the senior leadership of the organization communicating the story consistently and effectively (and you have all of them doing it together), it'll be much easier for others to follow.

Internal Positioning Rollout Ideation

Bring in the whole brand rollout team and spend some time sharing the team's rollout ideas. Share some of the ideas your team has already developed for implementing the brand positioning internally; then let the executives ideate further with you. It'll give the whole rollout team some face time with senior leaders (a great benefit for keeping people involved in the project), and it'll become a nice starting point for what might be an ongoing collaboration.

By the time you have completed the brand boot camp session, your executive team will probably have added many new rollout and experience design ideas and will be able to better articulate the brand story in their internal and external communications. Hopefully along the way, some of the excitement from you and the rollout team will have rubbed off—it is a huge asset to have members of the organizational leadership sharing and reinforcing the brand positioning in their daily work.

Hosting an Employee Brand Boot Camp

Why should executives have all the fun? Consider also hosting similar events for other employee groups, such as the sales, marketing, and services teams—any group that engages with individuals in the brand community (which usually includes about every employee, at least in my experience).

Perhaps the brand boot camp is a volunteer activity where anyone who wants to join can participate. Or you could host it offsite at a cool location as a reward reserved for people who've demonstrated brand leadership through their actions. Or you can run brand boot camps with different groups around the organization (or around the world) as extended team meetings, maybe covering the brand experience mapping and storytelling practice in the same event.

I've done these sorts of brand boot camp sessions across the United States and around the world. If your brand is global, you may find these boot camps to be a great opportunity to collect interesting examples of how your brand is expressed in different parts of the world. You'll also help ensure your brand speaks with one voice—even if it is using many languages.

Employee boot camps get people out of their normal day-to-day grind and allow them to think creatively, tell stories, and develop new ideas. Because of this, brand boot camps are not only great ways to deeply embed the brand positioning, but are also great ways to bring the organization together and reenergize people's spirit and passion for the brand.

INTERNAL ROLLOUT EXAMPLE #2: BUBBAPOP SODA COMPANY

Many of the people who flew in for your positioning workshop left so excited that they are eager to continue as part of the rollout team. So, you decide to put them to work. As part of your rollout plan, you gather the whole team via videoconference to build plans for a series of employee brand boot camps to be hosted at field offices across the company.

You've just completed an extremely successful executive brand boot camp at headquarters, and you take the team through the agenda you used for the executive session. You and others who participated share the lessons you learned.

Using the executive model as a starting point, the team collaboratively draws up plans to run five boot camps that will reach 75% of BubbaPop employees. Rather than host a separate session for the boot camp, you decide to tack it on as a half-day session to coincide with some training that the HR group already had planned. HR training will be in the morning, and then the brand boot camp will happen after lunch.

Over the course of a month, members of your rollout team host five brand boot camp sessions, and you have an opportunity to attend three of them in person. After a morning of traditional HR training, the employees really seem to enjoy the brand boot camp that your team has designed. You personally witness at least three or four stories told by employees that you'd like to ensure get captured on film at some point down the road. In addition, 20 more people are so interested in the project they ask if there are other ways they can get involved in helping make the brand positioning rollout more successful. You've just expanded your brand positioning rollout team.

Rethinking Your Interview, Hiring, and Orientation Process

One of the best, most effective ways of getting people to live the brand is to hire and train them to live the brand from the very beginning. This way, you ensure you only hire people who have the capacity to live the brand in everything they do and then communicate clear expectations to new employees at the beginning of their tenure.

Start with the careers or jobs section of your website. Are elements of the brand positioning clear in the descriptions of the organization's culture, values, and purpose? If not, consider rewriting this section of the website so that you will attract the type of people who will be able to help support and build on your brand's points of parity and points of difference (and maybe turn off those applicants you don't want, too). Also use this material to rewrite your job descriptions or create guidelines for how to write job descriptions that will attract the right people to support the brand.

Consider adding questions to your interview process that will help you determine which job candidates will easily live the brand. For instance, if you've decided that one of your points of difference is "radical sharing," you might want to ask some questions that test how likely a candidate is to share information with other employees rather than hoard it. How natural will it be for this candidate to share information with and work closely with members of the external brand community?

If you have a process the organization uses to evaluate candidates and compare them against each other before making a job offer, consider making one of the criteria you measure how well the candidate aligns with the brand positioning of the organization. Will the candidate easily become an "on brand" representative to your external brand communities?

Finally, after you've made the decision to hire someone, you'll need to ensure a proper introduction to the brand. At Red Hat, one of the first sessions in orientation was a storytelling session where we told the story of Red Hat, asked every new employee to share their own stories of how they first experienced the Red Hat brand, and then introduced the brand positioning and discussed it as a group. This positioning was then reinforced by the other orientation presentations throughout the day.

Even if you don't have a formal orientation process in your organization, put the brand positioning on the checklist of things you cover with a new employee. In an ad-free brand, this up-front training and information will be just as important as explaining where the bathrooms are and how the 401K matching works.

In my experience, it is much easier to teach a new employee about the brand than to teach an existing employee about the brand (unless you've involved him or her in the process). So, take advantage of the opportunity to tell new employees the brand story while they are excited and eager, and before they become overwhelmed and consumed by their new responsibilities.

> It is much easier to teach a new employee about the brand than to teach an existing employee about the brand.

Rethinking Your Review or Goal-Setting Process

I'm not a big fan of performance reviews, but if you have a performance review process in your organization, consider ensuring that people are measured on how well they are living the brand. Instruct people to provide examples of things they have done personally over the year to strengthen the points of difference and points of parity or reinforce the brand mantra.

If your organization sets high-level yearly or quarterly goals, consider aligning them with the brand positioning. Show how these goals will strengthen the brand's points of difference and points of parity. Measure pemployees on how well they do against these goals.

Rewarding Those Who Live the Brand Best

Each year, give public awards to the employees who best exemplify the brand in action, those who live the brand every day. Give these people organization-wide recognition, perhaps also including a physical award or trophy and a cash bonus. Invite them to have dinner with the board of directors, the executive team, or the founder. Add their names or pictures to a permanent display in your headquarters lobby.

This is a carrot instead of stick approach that I like a lot for reinforcing the positioning because it turns those who live the brand into heroes and encourages others to follow their lead.

At Red Hat, we celebrated those people who were the truest ambassadors of the brand in many ways, including an internal employee-to-employee awards process, a set of yearly Chairman's Awards, and regular stories about people who best exemplified Red Hat passed on through many internal communications channels.

Stopping Those Who *Don't* Live the Brand from Thriving

Every organization will have people who do things their own way. Often, if these people get the results (meaning they make their financial targets or otherwise achieve the goals that have been set for them), they are still praised and rewarded.

These off-brand people are a deadly disease for ad-free brands. Anyone who is rewarded for working in ways that are harmful to the brand experience the organization is trying to create will damage your ability to deliver on your positioning.

Although I love when people live the brand story their own way, I have little tolerance for people who insist on living a completely different brand story—especially if it counteracts the work others are doing to support the positioning. I work to remove these people from the organization as quickly as possible for two reasons.

First, they have a tendency to negatively impact those around them, perhaps even causing people who are positive, productive supporters of the brand to become demotivated or leave altogether. Second, they have a tendency to multiply like rabbits. If one person gets away with not living the brand, and they have the ability to hire new employees, they might hire more people in their mold. Or they might reinforce their own version of the brand with others and reward people who do things "their way."

My friend and former Fedora project leader Greg DeKoenigsberg explains this theory more frankly. He calls it his "Law of Institutional Idiocy."

GREG DEKOENIGSBERG'S LAW OF INSTITUTIONAL IDIOCY

Former Fedora project leader Greg Dekoenigsberg has developed something he calls the "Law of Institutional Idiocy." While it also applies at an even broader organizational level, it is one of the best ways I've seen of explaining how off-brand employee behavior can do an enormous amount of damage to a brand very quickly. Here is his explanation:

In the beginning, your organization has a tree full of healthy employees:

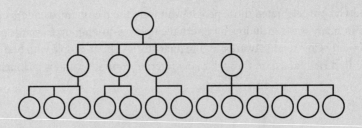

And then, an idiot sneaks into the company.

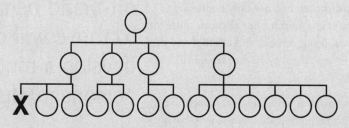

That idiot chases away people who don't like to deal with idiots and uses his or her influence to bring aboard more idiots:

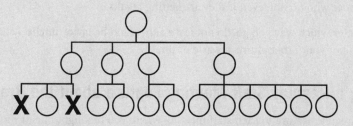

If you're not very wise and very careful, that idiot gets promoted because people tire of fighting with idiots, who also tend to be loud, ambitious, and politically savvy. And then he or she builds a whole team of idiots. Other idiots start popping up elsewhere in the organization:

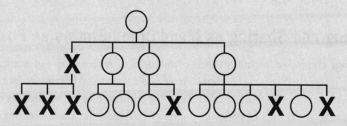

That is how you end up with an organization full of idiots.[3]

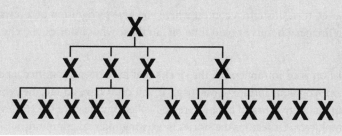

3. Source: Greg DeKoenigsberg, personal correspondence

Letting off-brand people continue unchecked is a quick path to a brand with a multiple personality disorder. It is not only confusing to your brand community, but also can cause lots of internal disagreement and conflict and generally just isn't the way ad-free brands like to operate.

Brands that allow off-brand behavior to thrive will quickly develop a multiple personality disorder.

How do you deal with those who don't live the brand? Some organizations have a no-tolerance rule and seek to quickly eliminate those who do not live the brand. Some instead just focus on the positive, rewarding those who live the brand while passing over those who do not, even if they are getting results.

No matter which way you go, do not leave anti-brand behavior unchecked. It could make all of your other efforts a waste of time.

Adding a Regular Staff Meeting Feature about the Brand

Add a regular feature to each staff meeting where you highlight one or more examples or stories in which a team member has gone above and beyond to live the brand either in her internal work or in interactions with the external brand community. Don't just talk about the brand positioning—show examples of people living it.

Collecting and Sharing as Many Brand Stories as Possible

Encourage employees to submit their own stories of where they—or another team member or group of team members—have gone above and beyond to live the brand. The best stories will articulate how the employee or group did work that strengthened the points of parity or points of difference for the brand or perfectly encapsulate the spirit of the brand mantra.

Perhaps even turn this into a contest where you give recognition or a reward (maybe a financial bonus or paid time off) to those whose stories you chose to feature.

Keep a list on your intranet of all the stories that have been submitted, and feature the best ones on your intranet homepage. If you don't have an intranet, consider setting up an internal brand blog where you collect and feature the stories submitted by employees. Or feature the stories in existing internal communications such as organization-wide email updates or newsletters.

Over time, this collection of stories will become a history of the brand in action that you'll be able to use for many purposes. Some of these stories might even become brand legends that are used to illustrate how to do things on-brand for years or decades to come.

Developing an Employee Deorientation Process

Instead of an employee orientation process, one of our New Kind clients has designed what they call a *deorientation process*. They use this process to help people unlearn the things they have learned in other organizations that might prove harmful to the effort to live the brand. For example, if salespeople have been taught (and rewarded) to hit their numbers at all costs, the deorientation process might show them that this organization values living the brand as much or more than getting the results.

Hosting an Internal Filmmaking Contest

Take a day and invite select employees (perhaps as part of a brand boot camp) to participate in an internal filmmaking contest. Split the employees into groups. Give each group a video camera, and let each group shoot and edit a short film telling a story that illustrates the brand positioning in action.

Groups might choose to tell their own versions of the brand story, act out an experience or interaction with a member of the brand community, or even re-create a brand legend. Every time I've tried this exercise, I've always been surprised and amazed by the creative results.

Watch all the final videos as a team. Put the best story or stories on the intranet or blog, or feature them in other internal communications and give the teams that created the best ones recognition or rewards. You may even find that some teams develop stories of a high enough quality that you'll want to use them externally as well (I've seen it happen!).

Adding a Standing Executive Meeting Agenda Item about the Brand

Have a standing agenda item at every executive meeting where executives update each other on what they've done within their groups to support the brand positioning. Consider using the time to brainstorm more ideas as a group, have one executive do an extended update on a project she is working on, or bring in a non-executive team member to present an idea that furthers the brand positioning.

Starting a Brand Book Club

Select a series of books that relate to your specific brand positioning or brand positioning in general (some of the books by the ad-free brand heroes I've highlighted in these pages or in the appendix might be great candidates). Although books can be related to brand or brand experience, they certainly don't have to be. Be as creative as you like with your suggestions.

Each quarter, assign a book for everyone to read and set up a discussion about the book and how it relates to the brand. Or assign many people different books, and have each do a presentation about the book, teaching others what they learned.

Making Brand Giveaways

In my experience, physical reminders and giveaways are where most groups go first when ideating potential rollout ideas. So, I mention this idea *last* because I'm very reluctant to encourage people to create these sorts of materials unless many of the projects like those previously mentioned that encourage people to live the brand are already underway or complete.

If you already have great internal rollout projects in progress, you might want to consider creating giveaways like t-shirts, hats, magnets, or posters that keep the brand positioning fresh in people's minds. These can be handed out at orientation, in team meetings, or in other places where you want to reinforce the brand positioning.

By themselves, brand giveaways epitomize *seeming* rather than *being*, and most employees will make fun of them (at best) or ignore them (at worst) if they aren't accompanied by clear, productive efforts to live the brand within the organization from the top down.

Even then, because these sorts of things are usually viewed as organizational propaganda, you may find that they actually hurt your effort rather than help. But in the hands of a talented creative designer or writer, you can create items that people are proud to wear or display at their desks.

Over the years at Red Hat, we were very careful not to create brand giveaways that were too directly "selling" the brand positioning to employees. Instead we created things that were more subtle, beautiful, or funny.

I still run into someone walking around town on occasion wearing a t-shirt or hat we'd designed years ago to help reinforce the brand (see Figure 5.5).

Figure 5.5   *Here's an example of a t-shirt we made at Red Hat that subtly reinforced the brand positioning while playing off Matthew Szulik's story about the "I'd rather be masturbating" t-shirt. It was a hit. (Photo by Jonathan Opp)*

The Launch (or Not)

Your team has put together an impressive internal rollout plan, and you are ready for the big internal positioning launch. Right?

Wrong.

There's no need for a big meeting where the CEO gets up and presents the new positioning to the whole organization, complete with balloons, a bowl of fruit punch, and a celebratory cake.

Just get to work. Ad-free brands shouldn't spend time congratulating themselves on their positioning or simply talking about it. They should spend their time embedding the positioning within the organization.

Don't get me wrong—it's great to have your top leadership publically supporting the positioning. But instead of having them talk about the positioning itself, have them tell stories about people who are living the brand or share examples of how they are applying the positioning to their work. Specific stories and examples trump theory and philosophy every time.

The first rule of launching brand positioning is that you do not talk about launching brand positioning. Don't make a big deal about getting started with the rollout—after all, you haven't actually changed anything yet.

🔍 *Tip*

The first rule of launching brand positioning is that you do not talk about launching brand positioning.

Instead, talk about the *results* of the rollout. When you have them.

Now It's Your Turn

I hope these ideas have shown you some of the many possibilities for how to embed the brand positioning deeply within your organization.

Do you think these techniques might work for your brand? I've seen many of these techniques used to get new brand positioning off to a good start inside an organization. But I've also tried many more, and in my experience, what works and what doesn't work often differs from place to place.

Your internal rollout group will come up with many ideas that will be more effective within the culture of your organization than those I've shared here. I encourage you to use my suggestions as starting points for your discussion, but let your team members' imaginations run wild. And if you come up with internal rollout projects that work well for you, please share them with me (you'll find my contact information in the back of the book). I'm always on the lookout for creative new ideas.

I'm sure it's clear by now. The goal of the internal rollout is to embed the brand positioning everywhere within the organization. It should eventually become part of the core DNA, the music that everyone inside the organization plays together.

Every time a new project begins in the organization the brand positioning should be considered. In fact, great brand positioning usually guides the projects that are chosen for the organization to complete. It can guide strategy for the brand, but it can also guide strategy for an entire organization when used effectively.

Building energy around your brand positioning internally takes time and patience, and it definitely won't happen overnight. Repeating these projects over a matter of years and continually inventing new ways to reinforce and update the brand positioning each year will provide the best results. So don't give up too soon because you might not see great results right away.

Eventually, your efforts will pay off. You'll notice the gravitational pull of the brand begin to have an effect without the rollout team's direct involvement. You'll start hearing people in the organization you've never even spoken to before effectively articulate the brand positioning without any assistance or leadership from the brand rollout team. You'll hear about projects that further the brand positioning where you had no direct involvement or knowledge. And you may even, from time to time, be lectured about the brand positioning (as I have been) by passionate new advocates who are simply excited about what they are working on.

The Outside World Awaits!

It's a wonderful feeling when you see the brand begin to emit its own energy and pull people in. And it is the perfect opportunity to start thinking about how to extend that gravitational pull beyond the organization to your external brand community.

6

The External Brand Positioning Rollout

During the internal brand positioning rollout, you began embedding the brand positioning deeply into the organization. Employees are starting to live the brand, and you've established a core group of people involved in the creation of the brand positioning who have become internal brand advocates.

With your brand effort gaining momentum, it's time to open up your brand effort to the outside world.

In Chapter 5, I used the metaphor of a thermonuclear reaction inside a star to describe how to build community around a brand. Our goal with the external brand positioning rollout is to bring even more people in, feeding our growing star. Nothing attracts a crowd like a crowd.

Tearing Down the Walls

The second I begin to discuss the external brand positioning rollout around traditional marketing folks, their wheels are already turning. I can almost hear them thinking to themselves, "Okay, I know how to do this part."

The daydreams begin. "If Nike's brand mantra was *Authentic Athletic Performance* and they externalized it by building a campaign around the *Just Do It* tagline, what can I do with my brand mantra? Who's my Michael Jordan? I need to call my agency...."

Before you know it, you're right back in the middle of advertising land. Telling people what your brand is about, writing press releases, hiring ad agencies, and so on.

Stop the madness before it starts.

Traditional brands would take the positioning they've put together and develop "messaging" for their target markets. They would then launch a campaign "targeting consumers" with "key messages." It's all *seeming* and no *being*.

Ad-free brands don't play that game. The goal of an ad-free brand positioning external rollout isn't to convince people to believe the brand positioning by beating them over the head with it. The goal of the ad-free brand external rollout is to tear down the walls separating the organization from the community of people around it.

Ad-free brands bring the community in and allow the brand out.

In the best ad-free brands, the hard walls of the organization disappear, replaced by a semipermeable membrane that allows ideas and benefits to flow freely between organization and community. It's not a campaign at all. It's an effort to open up and actually become a productive member of the communities that surround the brand.

> Ad-free brands bring the community in and allow the brand out. They open up and become productive members of the communities that surround the brand.

Wikipedia and the Future of Brands

There is no more extreme example of the power of a strong brand community than Wikipedia. In less than 10 years, this community has created the largest and most-used encyclopedia the world has ever known.

Over 400 million people visit Wikipedia every month. In most of the world, the encyclopedia is regularly used by between 20% and 50% of Internet users. More than 17 million articles have been created in 270 languages. Over the next five years, the Wikimedia Foundation—the nonprofit foundation that exists to serve the communities surrounding Wikipedia and related projects—hopes to have one billion users and 50 million articles.[1]

Wikipedia has almost 100,000 active editors who contribute content. But the Wikimedia Foundation has only about 50 paid employees.

A website used by 400 million users speaking 270 languages. Created by 100,000 volunteers with the help of only 50 paid employees. Wikipedia really highlights what a powerful brand community can create.

If you talk to folks at the Wikimedia Foundation, they'll quickly tell you that the only way such an effort was possible was by allowing the effort to be led by the community, with the Wikimedia Foundation playing a humble supporting role. In fact, later in this chapter, I discuss a strategic planning project undertaken by the Wikimedia Foundation illustrating just how much can be accomplished when an organization openly collaborates with a brand community.

I share this example here as an illustration of the future. Not every brand can cede the control (or reap the benefits) the Wikimedia Foundation has. But it dramatically illustrates what is possible when the walls between organization and community come down and the organization begins to operate as a productive member of the communities around it.

Community Versus Customer

You may have noticed that I have not talked about customers very much in this book. Yet in most of our organizations, we are attempting to sell something to make a profit. We need customers.

So why do I use the word *community* when most people would use the word *customer*? Am I just being naive about what pays the bills for our organizations to continue to thrive? Am I committing heresy?

I don't think so.

I believe that the dogged focus on marketing to customers alone has created a myopic view that makes us ignore many of the important people who interact with our brands.

 Note

> The dogged focus on marketing to customers alone has created a myopic view that makes us ignore many of the important people who interact with our brands.

---

1. This data is from the Wikimedia Strategic Plan available here:
   http://strategy.wikimedia.org/wiki/Main_Page

Customers are important; most organizations couldn't exist without them. So what is the issue?

Customers are not just listening to us anymore.

When organizations focus on just interacting with customers rather than taking a holistic view of the entire brand community, they forget that in the twenty-first century, the version of the brand represented by the organization might only be a small percentage of the brand the customer sees. Where is the rest of the story coming from?

Everyone else who interacts with the brand: the brand community.

WHOM DO YOU TRUST?

A few years ago if I were researching hotels to stay at, I had few options. I could go to a hotel's website, I could buy a travel guide, or I could look at advertisements. If I was lucky, I found a friend who had been where I was going before and stayed at an awesome hotel.

Then Trip Advisor (www.tripadvisor.com) came along. Now, any time I'm looking for a hotel, it is one of my first stops. Why? Because I can read the reviews real people posted of their visits to that hotel. I can hear the unvarnished truth, the positives and the negatives, the things the hotel itself is overselling and the hidden gems.

I don't always agree with the reviews I see on Trip Advisor. But I have found them a lot more reliable than anything I hear directly from the hotel itself and more timely than the information in travel guides.

Another example: When trying to decide whether to buy a book, I often consult the user-generated reviews on Amazon.com. Usually, they tell me whether I can trust the book jacket copy. A few years ago, a bad book review in a prominent newspaper could make or break a new title. For many books, Amazon's user reviews now play that role.

These are just two illustrations of the ways people have begun to make decisions to become a customer while barely consulting the brand that created the product directly. I'm sure you can think of many examples from your own life as well.

They illustrate why it is important to have a more holistic view of the communities surrounding your brand. With more people connecting in more ways due to the advent of social media tools on the Internet, it is increasingly difficult to control where people get their information about your brand.

But by engaging all of the communities that surround your brand with a consistent voice, you'll have more success ensuring your brand is clearly represented everywhere a customer might come into contact with it.

When rolling out brand positioning, ad-free brands understand that it matters what everyone thinks about the brand—not just the customers. By understanding and planning your interactions with all of the communities around your brand, you have a chance to impact the customers' views of who you are in a much deeper way than if you were just speaking to customers directly through marketing, advertising, and PR.

> "Ad-free brands understand that it matters what everyone thinks about the brand—not just the customers."

And that's just if you are only concerned with the success of your business itself. If you are a nonprofit or a member of the growing breed of socially responsible businesses interested in benefitting the communities they serve while remaining for-profit, you'll see even greater benefits from this approach.

When you focus your rollout on all the people around your brand and not just customers, you'll be on the path to much deeper, more fulfilling relationships with the communities surrounding your brand.

What Does Your Brand Community Look Like?

Now that we've begun to think about positioning beyond just customers, one of the most important early tasks of the external rollout is to map exactly what your brand community looks like.

In reality, it is not just one brand community, but a whole host of very different communities and subcommunities. The only thing these communities may share is that they are made up of individual human beings (well, unless you have a dog biscuit brand).

So, how do you determine exactly who is in your brand community? I recommend a simple exercise. Consider bringing together the team you convened for the internal rollout again and completing this exercise with them.

First, ask people to identify the communities surrounding your brand. Most groups will begin to throw out ideas like these:

- Customers
- Investors
- Donors
- Contributors

- Partners

- Press

- Employees

Most of these ideas will probably have one thing in common. They will be centered around your brand. Customers *of the brand*. Investors *in the company*. Partners *of the organization*. Press *covering the brand*.

Most people immediately think of communities by defining them with the brand at the center (see Figure 6.1).

Figure 6.1   *The typical way most organizations perceive the communities of people who surround their brand.*

But I bet most of the people in those communities don't orient themselves with your brand at the center of their universe. So you'll need to get your group to think about community in non-self-centered terms.

To do so, ask another question: to which communities does your brand (or, really, the people behind it) belong? What groups, organizations, affiliations, associations, or even loosely connected bands of like-minded people does your brand or the people close to it associate with? Consider things like industry associations, physical communities (like cities, states, or countries), universities or research institutions, political or lobbying groups, developer communities, civic organizations, governmental agencies, and whatever else you can imagine.

Now comes the hard part. Rather than framing these organizations in your context, try to imagine a map showing *how your brand fits into them*.

Remember Ptolemy from your history classes in high school? He was the guy who built a model with Earth at the center of the solar system, with the Sun and other planets orbiting us. Ad-free brands create gravity that pulls people closer, but they don't think of themselves as the center of the universe (see Figure 6.2). They avoid Ptolemaic thinking.

"Ad-free brands create gravity that pulls people closer, but they don't think of themselves at the center of the universe."

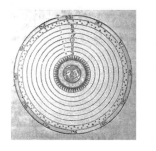

THIS...   NOT this...

Figure 6.2 *Although great brands create gravity that pulls others toward them, it doesn't mean they are at the center of the universe. Ad-free brands try to avoid envisioning themselves at the center of everything and instead understand that they are one gravitational force situated in a large context amongst many others.*

This is the key to really understanding how to interact with the communities surrounding your brand. Making this leap prepares you for the next one: ad-free brands must care not just about what is good for the brand, but also what is good for all the communities surrounding the brand.

 Note

> Ad-free brands must care not just about what is good for the brand, but what is good for all of the communities surrounding the brand.

Avoiding Tom Sawyer Thinking

One of the biggest mistakes I've seen organizations make when trying to understand how to interact with their brand community is that they think like Tom Sawyer.

Remember the story of Tom Sawyer and Aunt Polly's fence from *The Adventures of Tom Sawyer*? Here's how the basic story goes:

> After playing hooky from school and getting his clothes dirty in a fight, Tom gets in trouble with Aunt Polly. She orders him to whitewash her fence as punishment. At first, Tom is upset because Saturday is his day off, but he quickly develops a scheme to get his friends to actually trade him their stuff for the privilege of painting the fence for him. He gets out of doing the work and gets gifts from his friends who do everything for him.

I run into lots of people who approach their brand communities from the perspective of Tom Sawyer: what can I get the community to do for me? How can I get these people to paint my fence for free?

When organizations are thinking like Tom Sawyer, they are usually only engaging with the brand community as a means to getting people to do their work. These days, many organizations consider what they might call "crowdsourced" or even "open sourced" initiatives because they think a community of contributors is dying to help build their product for them. Then, with a Tom Sawyer-like gleam in their eyes, they envision being able to sell that product right back to them.

This attitude is at the heart of many failed community efforts I see.

Ad-free brands don't think like Tom Sawyer. Instead, they ask the question: *How can we ensure everyone's fence gets painted?*

They approach communities not from the point of view of just ensuring the brand wins, but from the point of view of figuring out ways to ensure *everyone* wins.

If you are a big, powerful brand like Apple or Google, you might find that there is a community of people out there eager to paint your fence for free. If people are breaking down your door to help your brand, you should consider yourself lucky.

All but the biggest, most powerful brands will see the greatest benefits not from trying to run communities with themselves at the center, but instead from becoming a productive, useful participant in the communities surrounding the brand.

✉ Note

All but the biggest, most powerful brands will see the greatest benefits not from trying to run communities with themselves at the center, but instead from becoming a productive, useful participant in the communities surrounding the brand.

Of the Community, Not Above the Community

Earlier I told the story of The Redwoods Group, an innovative B-Corporation (a for-profit company that also measures itself on the social good it creates) run by a visionary CEO named Kevin Trapani.

One day last year, my two business partners, Matt Muñoz and David Burney, were with Kevin discussing the unique relationship his organization has with its customers, employees, and other communities. The conversation turned to the ideas of service and humility, which are so often ignored by big organizations attempting to engage with communities.

Then Kevin encapsulated the entire conversation in a few short words:

"We should be *of* it, not *above* it," he said.

A beautiful, simple idea: of the community, not above the community.

So many organizations, intentionally or not, approach things as if they are above a community. Sometimes this means taking the Tom Sawyer approach of trying to get others to paint your fence for free. Sometimes this means creating a new community with your organization at the center rather than joining an existing community effort. Sometimes it simply means a lack of humility or selflessness shines through the organization's community interactions.

Ask Not What the Community Can Do for You...

A little humility can often go a long way in community interactions. Ad-free brands would do well to approach their community efforts by following these two simple tips:

- **Be selfless**—Spend more time figuring out what you can do for the community and less time thinking about what it can do for you. Think about the assets (funding, time, work, brainpower, brand power, relationships, and publicity) your organization could bring that might help the community effort. If you are creative, you'll figure out ways you can use these assets to help the community and your organization both at the same time.

- **Be present**—Develop ways for people close to the brand to personally interact with community members and participate directly in efforts that further the community's goals. Give people the tools (and permission) to be responsive, active, and involved without fear. Let multiple people represent the organization (and themselves individually) within the community rather than having one "official" voice that seems distant and slow to react.

I discuss these concepts and give you some concrete ways you can put them into practice later in this chapter.

Personally, I get excited when I see big brands focusing not just on what they take from the table, but also on what they bring to the table. I love to see brands that aren't afraid to be humble members of communities, rather than only building communities with themselves at the center.

Do not confuse this approach with organizational philanthropy. Although some of your efforts can have some of the benefits of philanthropy, being a productive member of the communities surrounding your brand is not just for good PR. Being a productive member of the communities surrounding the brand can be an extremely effective strategy for building a valuable, sustainable brand, especially when it is practiced over time.

What's Your Social Media Strategy? Wrong Question.

One of the most common questions I hear experts asking organizations these days is, "What's your social media strategy?"

I believe it is a bad question. Why? Because it encourages people to think of social media as an end rather than the means. Many believe having a presence in social media is a strategy by itself. It's not.

If you completed some of the activities in the last chapter, you might have developed a brand story. You might be designing experiences that will help people live the brand positioning. And you might be having an impact on what your brand actually is, rather than what it seems to be.

Many organizations immediately jump to "we have to be on Twitter and Facebook" without spending enough time thinking about the meaning or purpose behind how you will use the tools. I refer to this as the *tool trap*.

The tool trap is the mistake of focusing your energy on figuring out which tools to use and how, before you understand the impact you are trying to achieve by using them.

 Note

> The tool trap is the mistake of focusing your energy on figuring out which tools to use and how, before you understand the impact you are trying to achieve by using them.

Please don't misunderstand me: I'm an enormous believer in the power of social media. I'm a big user of Twitter, and I blog enough that my own mother doesn't have time to read everything I write. I'm just tired of seeing brands with nothing to say and nothing to accomplish putting up Facebook pages, creating Twitter accounts, and writing "blogs" that are really just press releases with a new veneer. Often, they end up using social media tools as simply new avenues for old advertising.

Social media tools will become effective only when the stories you want to tell, the experiences you want to create, and the relationships you want to nurture are already clear.

I go into more detail on how ad-free brands should use social media tools in service of the brand positioning later in this chapter.

Activating the Core External Brand Community

In Chapter 5, I discussed how to activate the core within an organization. The same lessons apply when attempting to extend that core into the external brand communities. It is still important to channel the orchestra conductor mindset, although when you start working with the external brand community you will have an even wider array of instruments to explore.

If you already began involving people outside the organization during your positioning work, you have a big head start. If not? It's time to get going.

The Internal Rollout Team Goes External

The first step to activate the core brand community externally is to go back to your internal rollout team. Many of the people on this team will want to continue to help with the external rollout, and in fact many of the projects already underway—like the brand story and experience design projects—will also be useful during the external rollout.

Consider inviting some additional people into the process at this point. In addition to involving people who have communications or marketing roles, consider inviting people who have extensive contact with external brand communities as part of their jobs. A few examples include people in these roles:

- Sales
- User support
- Community relations
- Investor relations

- Business development
- Receptionists

By this point in your positioning project, you've probably begun to have some of your original team members move on, and it never hurts to bring in some fresh blood anyway. Be sure to bring any new team members up to speed on the brand positioning and everything the team has accomplished to date (maybe even in the form of an informal new member orientation if enough new members are joining the group).

It is very important not to stop your internal rollout activities just because you are expanding to the external rollout. Remember that when building a brand from the inside out, the biggest impact you can have on the external world starts with the brand story being lived by those within the organization. So, view the external rollout as an extension of what you are already doing instead of a completely separate activity.

You might choose to have one team handling both the internal and external rollout, or you may choose to split them into two separate groups. But for the purposes of this chapter, I refer to this team as the *external rollout group*.

Identifying Key Brand Communities

If you've already completed the activity I described earlier in this chapter and mapped the communities surrounding the brand, use the map you created to begin a discussion with your rollout group. If you haven't yet completed this activity, this is a great first step for the external rollout team.

Once you have all the communities surrounding the brand mapped where everyone can see them, ask the group to think about which of these communities have the biggest impact on how the brand is perceived. Take a Post-it vote. Give everyone three Post-its and let people vote for the three communities they feel have the biggest impact on the brand (or they can put all their votes toward one community if they like, of course).

Encourage people to not just vote for communities framed with your organization at the center (such as customers, partners, etc.), but also for communities where the brand or the people behind it are a member. No matter how much you stress this, if you are a for-profit company, customers will inevitably end up on the list. If you are a nonprofit, donors will probably end up on the list.

This is a good thing—as I said earlier, the goal is not to ignore the customers and donors who sustain an organization. The goal is to put them in a larger community context, preferably one that does not assume the brand is at the center.

How to Help the Brand Communities

After you have the top three to five community groups identified through the Post-it vote, ask the rollout team to do a deep dive into each community. Ask the following questions:

- What is the shared purpose or goal of this community?

- What aspects of our brand positioning will resonate most with this community?

- What aspects will resonate least?

Discuss for 10–15 minutes, capturing ideas on a whiteboard or having someone take good notes along the way. At the end of the discussion, you should have a good sense for the points of connection and divergence between your brand and this community.

Now throw in the kickers, the questions crucial to building an ad-free brand relationship with an external community:

- Which resources can our brand bring to bear that might help this community achieve its goals or purpose?

- What could we do with this community that would help it achieve its goals and help us further embed the positioning at the same time?

In other words, how can we ensure that everyone's fence gets painted?

The dream of every business is that when customers buy its products, the customer will have all his or her needs fulfilled. But the reality is that organizations have a lot more to offer the communities around them than the products they sell. When they unselfishly offer assistance to the communities around them, they can build powerful relationships based on trust and shared value.

Sure, building this foundation will often mean that people in these communities would be more likely to consider buying products or services from you down the road (in case your marketing types ask). But if that is central to your thinking, community members will smell a rat. It is not enough to simply *seem* selfless while remaining selfishly motivated by your own bottom line.

You must actually care what happens to these communities. You must want to help them be more successful at achieving their own goals.

> ✉ *Note*
>
> Ad-free brands must actually care what happens to the communities around them and want to help them be more successful at achieving their goals.

Although this approach seems so obvious, my experience of working in the business world for the last 20 years indicates that it's not. If you need help shifting your thinking, consider the following types of things your organization might do to help the communities around your brand:

- **Funding**—Consider investing money in projects that help the community achieve its goals. Bonus points if the investment will also help your organization achieve its goals or further the brand positioning. Red Hat and other open source software companies have done this extremely well, investing in projects that later become the heart of products they sell while also creating value for community members at the same time.

- **Gifts**—Many communities are in need of assets that individuals can't buy on their own. Are there assets you already own or could buy and then give to the community as a gift? Red Hat bought many companies over the years with useful proprietary source code and then gave away the code for free. The community was able to innovate more quickly, and everyone—including Red Hat—reaped the benefits. Your organization might have other assets that would be of value, such as a conference facility that could be used or land you haven't developed. You could donate your products, services, web server space, or other supplies and materials that might otherwise go to waste. All of these things could be useful to your brand community.

- **Time**—Your organization probably has knowledgeable people who might have a lot to offer. Consider allowing employees to spend on-the-clock time helping on projects that further community goals and support the brand positioning.

- **Connections**—Who do you and others in your organization know, and how might these relationships be of value to others in the brand community? Perhaps you can make connections that not only help the brand community, but also help your organization at the same time.

- **Brand power**—Could you use the power of your brand to shine the light on important community efforts, drawing more attention and help to the cause?

I'm sure your rollout group will come up with even more ideas to help these communities. Spend some time discussing all the potential ways your organization could help this brand community. Then repeat this exercise with each of the important brand communities you've identified.

Connecting to Key Brand Communities via Brand Ambassadors

After you've identified the key communities you'd like to engage with and developed a set of meaningful ways you could help them, it's time to decide who will represent the brand within these communities. By now, you should have a good understanding of what the purposes of those communities are and what they will be predisposed to like and dislike about your brand.

Next, identify the people inside your organization who have the best relationships with each community. These people are the best candidates to become your brand ambassadors to that community.

The ideal brand ambassador is already an actual community member, actively participating in conversations and projects with other community members. While an employee of your organization, this person shares common values, interests, and experiences with other community members. It is less important what position they hold within your organization and, more important, how they are viewed by the community itself.

> ✉ *Note*
>
> A brand ambassador is someone within your organization who is already an active member of an important brand community and is willing to represent both the organization and themselves in interactions with that community.

After you've identified possible brand ambassadors, reach out to them to see if they are willing and interested in expanding their personal roles in the community to include being representatives of your brand as well. Some might already be playing this role, others might be playing this role and not realizing it. Don't force or pressure people. The ideal candidate will be excited to be considered and will be passionate about the opportunity, so if your best candidate doesn't seem interested, try to find someone else who is.

If you don't have anyone in your organization who is already a member of the community, you'll need to have someone join. With your external rollout group, choose someone who understands the positioning well and already shares interests, values, and experiences with the community in question. Have this person attend meetings, join mailing lists, participate on forums, and otherwise begin to contribute to the community first as an individual. It will take a little longer to get started, but it will be worth it if your brand ambassador has a deep contextual understanding of the community before they dive right in representing your organization.

You should ensure that your brand ambassadors deeply understand the brand positioning, so they can live it (not just speak to it) in their activities within these external communities. If they haven't already been part of the positioning project to this point, consider hosting a brand ambassador bootcamp (using many of the same boot camp ideas from Chapter 5) where you'll give them an overview of the positioning and the reasons why it is important and explain their key roles in helping it become an authentic part of the brand experience.

You may also have some communities where there is a whole team of ambassadors, not just one. For example, at Red Hat, a large team of developers represented Red Hat (and themselves) in the Fedora community. Invest as many ambassadors as you need in order to provide the best possible support for and adequately communicate with the community.

> "As you recruit brand ambassadors, you extend the internal core of the brand."

As you recruit brand ambassadors, you extend the internal core of the brand. Although it is wonderful to see your core group getting bigger, extending the reach of the brand positioning beyond your internal and external rollout teams is also an important time to ensure consistency. Be very careful to take the time to educate all brand ambassadors well so the entire brand orchestra stays in key.

The Brand Ambassador Philosophy

Wikipedia defines an ambassador as "the highest ranking diplomat who represents a nation and is usually accredited to a foreign sovereign or government, or to an international organization."[2]

Usually an ambassador lives and operates within the country or organization where he is assigned. Your brand ambassadors should channel the same philosophy. While they are members of your organization, they should "live" within the communities they are assigned to as much as possible while representing your organization within that community.

Great brand ambassadors are loyal to the organization and to the community at the same time. They develop relationships of respect, honesty, and trust within the community, which allows them to clearly, openly, and transparently communicate the priorities, desires, and needs of both sides.

---

2. http://en.wikipedia.org/wiki/Ambassador

✉ *Note*

Great brand ambassadors are loyal to the organization and the community at the same time and communicate transparently and openly with the community in order to develop relationships of respect, honesty, and trust.

Brand ambassadors are not just mouthpieces for the organization, but should also maintain their own personality, interests, and opinions in the community—often distinct from those of the organization. In places where they are representing their own opinions and ideas, they should provide the proper disclaimers. With a little practice, this is not nearly as difficult as it might sound. The key is maintaining an authentic personal voice while being open, transparent, and human in their communications.

Don't think someone in your organization has the right makeup to be a good ambassador based on what you see here, even if he or she has good relationships within the community? Don't make him or her an ambassador. The brand ambassador is a representative of your brand to the outside world, and the job carries a lot of responsibility and requires a high emotional intelligence and diplomatic sensibility to do well.

The Walls Come Down

Your brand ambassadors are in place and trained on the brand positioning, your external rollout team is engaged and ready for rollout, and your internal rollout projects are well underway. You are now ready to open up and begin building a deeper relationship with the communities around the brand, creating value for the brand and the brand communities at the same time.

A List of Great External Rollout Projects to Consider

You'll need to build an external rollout plan in much the same way you built the internal rollout plan in the last chapter. In fact, you'll be building upon many of the projects you began during the internal rollout and using them for external rollout as well.

Convene your external rollout team to come up with a set of external rollout projects for your brand. The following list will give you a lot of great ideas for places you might consider starting, but as always, many of the best ideas will come from people in your own team.

The low-cost, high-value rule still comes into play here. Here, I share ideas that require little work while creating great value, while also sharing others that can require more time or money from the organization to implement. Consider bringing in an external agency to help if you are short on time but have money to spend.

As in Chapter 5, I begin with the ideas I believe are most important for you to consider.

Externalizing the Brand Story

As part of your internal rollout plan, you began to develop a brand story that is authentic to both the past and future of the brand. It encapsulates the core purpose, values, context, and legends surrounding the organization while clearly articulating the brand positioning you've developed.

You might have created a simple book that tells this story, a short film, or a presentation. Once you have a great story, it is time to share it with the world.

Ensure everyone on the rollout team and all of your brand ambassadors are familiar with the story. Consider hosting a workshop with them where everyone practices telling their own version of the story.

Remember to think like a conductor. Don't try to force everyone to share the story the same way. Instead, encourage people to use their own personal stories and examples to color their own version. Remember, you want everyone playing in the same key, not simply playing the exact same notes.

You might be wondering how and when exactly to tell the brand story. The short answer? Use it everywhere you can, but don't force it where it doesn't belong. If people begin just reciting the story everywhere, forcing it down people's throats, it won't be much more effective than advertising.

Remember that ad-free brands try to show, not tell, whenever possible, so be aware of your community's receptivity to the brand story. The real purpose of the brand story is to create a shared context for the brand. If you are telling the story just to tell it and the people on the other end aren't interested, it won't be effective. But if it provides history, helps illuminate a larger brand purpose, is told in a way that resonates with the people you are communicating with, and creates common ground upon which connections can be made, it will be a very effective tool for an ad-free brand.

Here are some examples of a few places where you might be able to use the brand story without having to force it:

- When someone asks you about where you work and what your organization does

- When you are giving a presentation at a conference and need to introduce the organization

- In the "About Us" section of your organization's website

- When you are introducing yourself or the organization in an online community

You'll want to practice enough that you can communicate the whole story in a compelling way, but there will also be plenty of opportunities where a shorter version of the story makes more sense. Encourage your ambassadors and rollout team to practice using shorter and shorter versions of the story until they have figured out how to capture it in one or two sentences.

In some cases, you won't have the time or opportunity to share the story yourself; this is where the book, presentation, and film will all play starring roles. Consider pointing people to the online version of the book or presentation, or put the film on YouTube and link to it from your emails. If you are attending a live event, bring a stack of copies of the printed book with you and hand them out to people you believe will enjoy the story.

With your external rollout team, brainstorm as many possible avenues for sharing the story as you can. The wider and more consistently a great story is shared, the more it will begin to remain in the consciousness of people in your brand communities.

Sharing the Brand Story

When everyone in your organization is comfortable with the story and you've begun sharing it with the outside world, you may see something amazing happen. People in the brand community may begin sharing the story on their own.

If your brand story speaks on behalf of a movement and resonates at a wider level than just with employees of the organization, people might begin to see themselves in it and take ownership of it as "their" story, too.

THE "TRUTH HAPPENS" STORY

Back in 2003, Red Hat CEO Matthew Szulik asked us to create a short film to help introduce a keynote he was going to give at a major conference. At the time, our team at Red Hat was very small—about five people—and we didn't know anything about how to make films. We told Matthew we would do it anyway.

Our first conversation was with David Burney (who is now my business partner at New Kind). David ran a creative agency that my company had worked with in the past, and he had just hired a young digital media genius named Tim Kiernan right out of design school.

We collaboratively wrote a story and gathered some interesting clips to illustrate it, and in a few weeks, we had pieced together a short 3 1/2-minute piece called "Truth Happens."[3]

We thought "Truth Happens" would be shown only once and then we would move on to other projects. We were wrong.

Right after the keynote, people who had seen it immediately began asking us for copies (this was before YouTube, of course). I began to receive requests from folks who wanted to translate it into other languages or who wanted permission to show it at their event.

I even had a Fortune 500 company contact me and ask if we minded if they used it for their marketing. I personally showed "Truth Happens" on four continents. To our amazement, it resonated with people around the world and has been viewed millions of times on the Red Hat website, on YouTube, at events, and in many other places as well.

Eventually, we lost count of the times people came to us asking if we could do "another 'Truth Happens'" for them. Today, the film is part of Red Hat lore. It was the first film we did, the first great story we told.

There are no guarantees this will happen, but if it does, you should be prepared. Ensure the story is readily available and easy to share online. If it is a film, ensure it is up on YouTube and other media-sharing sites. If it is a book, consider printing extra copies of the book to give away, or make it available at-cost on a site like Lulu.com or Blurb.

Aligning the Brand Experience

In Chapter 5, you worked with the internal rollout team to map the brand experience. Now that you have a deeper understanding of the most important communities around the brand, you can take this work even further.

---

3. http://www.redhat.com/videos/truth_happens.html

If you started a brand experience mapping project during the internal rollout, you've probably begun to eliminate many of the gaps between the brand promise and the experience for your brand community. Now, with a deeper understanding of the elements of the positioning that will resonate with a particular part of the brand community and your brand ambassadors to help you, you can make the experience even more relevant or resonant. Understanding the purpose and values of this community might give you the opportunity to make the experience even more aligned.

Ask What You Can Do for the Community

After your brand ambassadors are in place as active members of the communities surrounding your brand, your organization can actually begin to play a productive role, helping these communities using ideas your external rollout team has developed.

But rather than assuming your team has come up with all the best ideas for how you could help the community, consider involving the community in the process of deciding how your organization can help it most.

Each brand ambassador should be in charge of hosting these conversations with the community she belongs to, although she might invite others from inside the organization to participate. By this time, the brand ambassador should have developed a good sense of the right way for the organization to engage. The ambassador might consider asking individuals within the community for personal advice on what the organization could do to help the community the most or reach out to a broader group.

If members of the community helped you with your positioning as part of an open community approach, this is a good time for you to return the favor. These people will be perfect entry points from which to begin a conversation about how your brand can help. Start by asking them, and perhaps they'd even be willing to help you host a larger community conversation about how the organization could help.

> ✉ *Note*
>
> If members of the community helped you with your positioning as part of an open community approach, this is a good time for you to return the favor.

Perhaps your external rollout group's ideas form the starting point for this conversation, and you handle it informally. If the community is large, consider using an online survey tool like Survey Monkey (www.surveymonkey.com) to ask people what they think. But keep the interaction somewhat personal and don't make it seem like a focus group. Remember, part of the point is to begin to develop personal relationships with people in your brand community.

The most important rule to follow is this one: do not ask community members how your brand can help them unless you are prepared to follow through on their ideas.

The worst mistake you can make is to ask people for their ideas and then not do anything with them. You'll immediately destroy any trust you've built in the community.

Of course you won't be able to do everything the community asks you to do, and you should set that expectation up front. For example, you might try setting up the conversation like this:

> "Do not ask community members how your brand can help them unless you are prepared to follow through on their ideas. The worst mistake you can make is to ask people for their ideas and then not do anything with them."

"We are eager to hear your ideas for how [our brand] could do more. Of course, we can't promise we'll be able to do everything. Some of your ideas may be out of our reach financially or logistically, while others might not work for other reasons. But we want to hear *all* of your suggestions. We promise we'll carefully consider every idea. If there are things we simply can't do, we'll provide transparent explanations as to why. Ask as many questions as you like, and we'll do our best to answer them."

This positioning sets the tone for the dialogue that will follow. It will be open, honest, and practical. If you set this tone up front, you'll not only receive more reasonable requests, but community members will more readily accept when you can't help. Be sure to put this introduction in your own words and write in a way that will resonate with the community you are addressing.

After you commit to providing help to the community, whether it is through funding, gifts, time, connections, brand power, or something else entirely, you must follow through on that commitment. Set a reasonable timeframe you know you can meet. If you don't meet your commitments, you might as well write any relationship with that brand community off. It will be almost impossible to recover.

But if you meet your commitments and provide help in whatever ways you promised, you will be well on the way to a deeper, more sustainable relationship with members of the brand community.

Convening a Community Council

If you involved members of the external community in creating your brand positioning, you might already have the raw materials of a community council.

A community council is a group of interested community members (often representing many parts of the brand community) who come together on a regular basis either in person or via mailing list or other collaboration platform to share opinions, ideas, and information.

Think of members of the community council as the "foreign" counterparts to your brand ambassadors. You'll want to make them comfortable operating within your walls to the point where they almost feel like they are part of your organization even as they are representing their community's point of view in your discussions.

While your brand ambassadors will already be having regular conversations within individual communities, the community council is an opportunity to cross-pollinate ideas across related brand communities.

The best community councils will have two key characteristics:

- **They spend as much (or more) time discussing how the brand can help the communities as they do giving the organization advice on how to improve the brand**—This is different from a typical "customer advisory council" you see in many corporations today, which concerns itself almost exclusively with focus-group-like thinking: giving the organization advice on what it can improve. Although this feedback is valuable, organizing the entire council around it would be more of that Ptolemaic thinking we are trying to avoid.

- **There is value for community members in their interactions with each other in addition to their interactions with the organization**—The community council is also a way to convene a group of people who might be able to form valuable, useful relationships with each other at the same time. Probably one of the best examples of this practice today is in the advisory boards of local community banks, which serve as connecting points for citizens as well being valuable input points for the bank. In an ad-free brand community council, everyone's fence gets painted, not just the sponsoring organization.

Consider convening your community council in person once a year if you can. This way, people get a chance to meet each other, eat together, and form relationships above and beyond the brand. This session is the perfect chance to address problems or opportunities using a design thinking approach like the one I outlined in Chapter 4 and get group members working together collaboratively.

The problems or opportunities don't have to be related directly to the brand. Consider exploring things that affect the future of the industry or community and focus on areas where either the community members or the organization can take concrete actions based on the outcome of the session.

You can also consider holding regular meetings with the council, perhaps one per quarter via phone or webcast. Also consider connecting the group on an ongoing basis either via a mailing list or a collaborative platform like Basecamp (www.basecamphq.com). This way, you can have ongoing conversations and even discuss multiple topics at one time.

Think of the community council as a garden needing regular care. Rotate people off the council who either don't contribute or are not positive contributors to the community. Plant new seeds by inviting new contributors into the community on a regular basis. Consider making changes to the council at least once a year.

If there are certain people who have become valuable, helpful members of the council, keep them as long as you can. These people are extending the core of the brand outside the organization and can become one of the most valuable brand assets you have. Treat them well.

Convening the Community

One of the most powerful things you can do to develop deeper, more meaningful relationships with members of your brand community (and help them develop deeper relationships with each other) is to give them opportunities to get together.

Humans are social creatures. Every opportunity we create for community members to meet each other, share ideas, form relationships, and explore new business or social opportunities—not just with the organization but with each other—adds to the strength of the brand community.

Convening opportunities come in many forms. You might consider hosting in-person events, online meetings, traveling road shows, or webcasts, or even creating ways for community members to organize their own events with your support.

Perhaps the current master of the "convening the community" strategy is TED (www.ted.com) the small organization responsible for the TED conference and online TED Talks. The positioning of TED is "Ideas Worth Spreading," and the organization has come up with some incredible strategies to ensure it does just that. In the process of sharing ideas, many community members have developed deep, lasting relationships with others they've discovered through TED who share their ideas.

TED: CONVENING A COMMUNITY ON A MASSIVE SCALE

TED is a nonprofit devoted to spreading great ideas. Although TED doesn't necessarily refer to it as their brand mantra, it has a great, simple one: "Ideas Worth Spreading." The organization began in 1984 with a conference convening people interested in technology, entertainment, and design (TED). Invitations to the conference were hard to come by, and the talks (given by some of the world's most interesting and compelling people) were only seen by attendees. When TED began posting these TED Talks on its website and on YouTube, the community began to grow quickly.

In June 2009, TED announced a new program called TEDx that would allow anyone to organize his or her own TED conference anywhere on the planet. In short order, hundreds of people and groups all around the world did exactly that.

By the end of 2009, almost 300 TEDx events had been held around the world. By September of 2010, another 500 events had taken place and almost 750 more were being planned.[4]

TED went from one event per year with a small number of people attending at a very high cost to *almost two TED events per day*, held around the world, in a little over a year.

Along the way, hundreds of thousands of new people were made aware of TED and became part of the TED community. By democratizing the process of convening TED events, the organization was able to exponentially scale the value of the TED brand and the impact of the TED community.

Remember that the events you create should bring as much value to those who attend as they do to your organization. While it is okay to discuss your products and services, try to make the events about much more than what you have to sell. If the events are extended sales pitches, they won't help you build your brand or your community relationships. And people probably won't come back next time you hold them.

Although there are all sorts of ways you might choose to convene members of your brand community, the key is to do so in a way that is memorable and makes people want to join you again and again. The people who come back year after year might become some of your most important external extensions of the brand.

---

4. These stats are from an article in the *New York Times* that appeared in September 2010. You can find the story here: http://www.nytimes.com/2010/09/26/fashion/26TEDX.html

The Red Hat Road Tour and World Tour

One of the convening strategies we used at Red Hat with great success was the brand tour. In Chapter 5, I mentioned the Red Hat Road Tour 2002 and Red Hat World Tour 2004. In the former, we packed four brand ambassadors and a driver into an RV and drove across the country in search of open source adventure (see Figure 6.3).

We planned events with all types of community members, including Linux user groups, partners, and customers, and blogged along the way. In the process we learned what people were thinking about Red Hat in particular and about open source in general. We also created an opportunity for community members to meet each other, and some people drove from hundreds of miles away to be a part of Road Tour events.

Figure 6.3   *The RV from the Red Hat Road Tour, right near the beginning of the tour, taken while the roll-up awning was still intact (photo courtesy Jonathan Opp).*

While we did talk about Red Hat products at some of the events, the primary purpose of the tour was not to sell. It was to meet people, to solve their problems, to hear their opinions, and to introduce them to each other. In other words, the purpose was to build community.

In 2004, we extended the idea to reach a worldwide community with Red Hat World Tour 2004 and added a filmmaker to the entourage. I went on this trip myself. We visited four continents in two and a half weeks; slept on planes; and hosted events in Japan, Australia, Canada, the United States, and across Europe.

Each of the brand ambassadors blogged along the way and we captured the whole trip with a video camera (see Figure 6.4).

Figure 6.4   *Some of the more conservative people within Red Hat worried that the tone of the original Red Hat Road Tour was too casual and fun for an enterprise software company. So for the Red Hat World Tour, as a joke we posted both "enterprise" and normal versions of our bios and took pictures to match.[5]*

What was interesting about these tours is that they were stories themselves, with drama, action, crisis, and happy endings. On the Road Tour, the awning blew off the RV in heavy winds on an interstate while crossing the Rocky Mountains. When the team stopped in Lawrence, Kansas, they met two system administrators who had driven 5 1/2 hours from Iowa just to have a beer with the Road Tour team.

On the World Tour, we sung karaoke until three in the morning with new friends in Tokyo. We met Antonio, who lived in Spain and actually travelled to Germany and the United Kingdom to meet us at two European events. But we also lost Alphonse, our cameraman, who missed his flight from London to Boston after a late night on the town, only to have him actually beat us to Boston by being rebooked on a direct flight that arrived an hour earlier.

In both cases, we captured these stories via regular blog entries and, in the case of the World Tour, on film. On the World Tour, we each blogged from a different perspective, with some of us covering technical subjects and others covering the adventure itself.

---

5. As of this writing, the full World Tour bios (both versions) are still up on the Web at https://www.red-hat.com/worldtour/travelers/index-b.html

A TASTE OF RED HAT ROAD TOUR 2002

Here's a blog post written by Jonathan Opp while on the Road Tour that gives a taste for the tone and perspective of the trip.

Wednesday, Nov. 7

Day 8 | Mile 2345 | Oakley, Kansas

In the morning we cross the Mississippi River. The West is waiting on the other side.

Pennsylvania just lost the distinction of having the worst road of the tour. Congratulations, Missouri. You're the reason they make Dramamine.

We drive all morning to Lawrence, Kansas, on the other side of Kansas City. Lawrence is the home of the University of Kansas and has all the trappings of a college town: Bookstores, coffee shops, breweries.

The event is in the back room of the Free State Brewery. We walk in and the room is absolutely full, around 100 people crowd onto the main floor and the balcony above. Jeremy has to stand on a chair to speak to everyone and answer questions.

One of the first people we meet is Mark. Mark built a Star Trek fan site back in the days of Red Hat Linux 4.2 and is still running it today. He says it's still rock solid. It's been running continuously for 700 days. He averages 50,000 hits per day on a Pentium 75Mhz processor.

A new record has been set tonight. Dan and David drove *five and a half hours* to be here—from Iowa City, Iowa. We learn that Dan was also a graduate in Red Hat's first class of RHCE, Red Hat Certified Engineer, certification. He said it has paid for itself many times over. David is studying for his first try at RHCE certification in just a few months.

We also meet Dan, Rhonda, and their son Austen, who's hanging out in his stroller. Dan runs 8.0 on his home desktop computer. Austen likes to play with the mouse.

The local Linux user group is the KCLUG. We meet Al who is the LUG's webmaster. You can check out their site at http//:www.kclug.org.

We can't stay in Lawrence for long. It's 560 miles to Denver and our first event is at noon tomorrow. We volunteer Dave for the first shift of Cookie's shoulder rubs.

Unlike Missouri roads, the road in Kansas is fantastic. Unfortunately gale-force crosswinds are making it hard to actually stay on it. We share another round of Dramamine, and Cookie has us pile up on one side of the RV to keep it from tipping over.

At around 1 a.m. we give up for the night and pull off the interstate at a small town called Oakley, as in Old West legend Annie Oakley. The chain motel is full, so we check into the one down the street.

James had been asleep on the RV for about two hours, so he was at least 65% more frightening looking than he normally is—hair everywhere and blurry eyed. He opens the door to his room, and let's just say it was already occupied. Ahem…. OK, there were naked people in it.

Just picture this for a moment. You're at a motel with a friend. It's 1 a.m. You're all snuggled up in bed when somebody puts a key in the lock, the door swings open, and there's a guy that looks like an angry lumberjack standing in the doorway.

Chain your doors, people.[6]

We witnessed an interesting effect as the tours went on: the stops became more crowded and we often had folks come up to us to ask us about our adventures along the way. I believe people had been following the story online and wanted to be a part of it, too.

Over the years, we continued to hear from many of the people we had met on these tours. Antonio, our friend from Europe, flew to the United States multiple times to attend the Red Hat Summit, our yearly community event. I still occasionally meet people at events who've looked me up online and stumbled across the World Tour blog.

Completing a Project

Through this chapter I hope you have noticed a theme. I encourage organizations to communicate positioning through *action* rather than using the traditional language of marketing, PR, and advertising to tell people who you are.

Creating opportunities for people to see you live the brand (and to live it with you) will be an ultimately more effective way to create community around your brand than advertising ever will. Perhaps the most effective way to build a sense of community around the brand is to work on a project collaboratively with the people who care about the brand.

 Tip

Perhaps the most effective way to build a sense of community around the brand is to work on a project collaboratively with the people who care about the brand.

---

6. Source: Jonathan Opp, personal correspondence.

Imagine working in the same office with someone for years, but never having done anything with him or her outside of work. Then you both end up going on a work trip, eating meals together, going out drinking until 2 a.m., and flying back home with hangovers. Afterward, you are much closer than you ever were before and maybe even become friends outside of work.

The shared experience of the trip brought you together. It allowed you to be yourself completely, not just the side of yourself you show on the job. While convening members of the brand community with events like those mentioned here are a great way to create shared brand experiences, an even more interesting—and ultimately rewarding—way to create these relationships is by starting a project that can be collaboratively worked on by people in your brand community.

These projects create a sense of belonging while giving people concrete ways they can get involved with the community with a clear and desirable end goal.

EXTERNAL ROLLOUT EXAMPLE #1: ENVICLEAN DRY CLEANERS

During your positioning project, you worked with some of your best customers to develop brand positioning, epitomized by your new brand mantra Everyday World Cleaning. During the process, your customers also had the idea to create a community council with the goal of living up to that brand mantra.

You kick off an EnviClean community council meeting by taking the group through a design thinking process to identify the most important communities EnviClean can impact. Although customers are clearly important, you've also learned that a disproportionate number of your customers are young professionals. In the region where EnviClean shops are located, there is an active community of young professionals who run together (you know this because several members of the community council and many of your student employees are part of it). You decide this group will be one interesting community that not only shares a lot in common with the EnviClean "Everyday World Cleaning" mantra, but is also filled with customers and potential customers for the business.

This running community has led efforts to ensure the outdoor running trails in the area are kept clean and well-maintained by starting a trail maintenance program. EnviClean decides to reach out to the running community (through someone who is both a runner and a EnviClean employee) to ask how EnviClean might help their efforts.

As it turns out, the group is desperately in need of funds to repair a series of bridges that were damaged in a recent flood. In addition, the flood left debris all along many of the trails.

After asking members of the running community to share ideas for ways EnviClean can help raise the funds, the group agrees on the following strategy. First, for an entire month, EnviClean will put donation boxes in every store where customers can donate money to the cleanup effort. Second, EnviClean declares one day during that month "Everyday Trail Cleaning Day" and pledges half of the day's profits to the cleanup effort.

At month's end, the EnviClean effort has raised almost $5,000 to help with bridge repair and debris cleanup, well more than the group has ever raised before. Over the next month, you allow every EnviClean employee who'd like to join the effort to take a paid day off to help with the cleanup work. Over 200 of your employees join in.

For a long time afterward, your employees tell stories of customers coming in expressing appreciation for EnviClean's efforts on Everyday Trail Cleaning Day. In fact, you begin to notice more and more people in running gear in your shops dropping off their dry cleaning.

The open door brand positioning project described in Chapter 4 is one example of a project that can be undertaken collaboratively with community members. If you chose this model for your brand positioning project, you might have noticed that some members of your brand community formed relationships with each other as well as with your organization during the process. This is a very good thing.

But as you think about potential projects for your community to work on with you, consider projects that don't just benefit the brand itself. There is a risk of appearing like Tom Sawyer—only interested in getting others to paint your fence for free—if your projects are always self-serving.

When choosing potential projects, ask yourself the following questions:

- Would this project help to achieve the goal or purpose of the community (or multiple communities)?

- Would it provide as much or more benefit to these communities as it does to the brand?

- Does it have a clear objective or outcome?

- Is it easy for community members to understand how they could participate or bring value?

- Would it also inspire your employees and would they be proud to be represented or participate?

Consider convening your external rollout team for an ideation session about potential projects. Use the previous questions to steer the conversation, and use a Post-it vote to select the best candidates.

If you already completed one of the earlier exercises, either asking the community what you can do to help it or convening a community council, you might have plenty of ideas already. You may also have a group of trusted external brand advocates you can ask for advice and opinions.

Running a Collaborative Community Project

Once you have chosen a project you think will provide benefits for the brand and the community, help bring it closer to meeting its goals, has clear objectives and outcomes, and makes it easy for people to understand how they can contribute, you are ready to begin.

A collaborative community project is best run by a great facilitator. While the lead for the project should be one or more of your internal brand ambassadors, if none of them are trained facilitators with a good understanding of how to run a design thinking project, consider bringing in a professional facilitator familiar with design thinking.

If you've never run a project like this before, start small, probably with no more than 10–20 outside contributors. Make sure you involve people from inside the organization as well, but not so many that you overwhelm the external contributors.

Although it is best to start small, some revolutionary organizations are now running collaborative projects with hundreds or thousands of contributors. I've included one example, the Wikimedia strategic planning project, here.

WIKIMEDIA: HOW A THOUSAND VOLUNTEERS BUILT A STRATEGIC PLAN

All too often, strategic planning is an activity reserved for the organizational elite—executives aided by consultants. The term *strategic planning* conjures up images of suits in conference rooms diagramming the path to world domination on whiteboards. The generals think up all the big ideas, and the "troops" execute the plan.

Not so for one organization.

In 2010, the Wikimedia Foundation, the 50-person nonprofit supporting Wikipedia and related projects, turned the conventional approach to setting strategy on its head. Against a backdrop of slowing Wikipedia contributions and a declining number of active editors, the foundation went where it has always gone for answers: to its worldwide community of volunteer "Wikimedians."

The entire community was concerned with the slowing growth, and this project gave community members an opportunity to help by sharing their ideas and insights and working as a part of the planning team.

In total, more than 1,000 people contributed to the Wikimedia strategic planning project, writing nearly that many proposals for ways to meet the community's challenges and priorities. These volunteers created over 1,500 pages of new content in 50 languages.

Since a strategic planning project with just a normal-sized team is often a challenge, I wanted to find out more about how this project was run. So I called Philippe Beaudette, head of reader relations for Wikimedia. According to Philippe, the idea for collaborating with the Wikimedia community on strategic planning was originally the idea of Sue Gardner, the executive director of the Wikimedia Foundation. Although it might be considered an innovative approach for other organizations, this type of collaboration was par for the course here.

"The Wikimedia community would have hung us by our toenails if we tried to develop a strategic plan any other way," Philippe said.

They began the project by openly soliciting ideas from community members and were quickly overwhelmed with proposals. Some were big, bold strategic ideas, while others were small and tactical. According to Philippe, soliciting ideas from the community up front was the smartest thing they did during the project. "This was the thing that got people involved and into the concept, and at the same time it gave us a solid sense for what the community was thinking," he said.

It would have been impossible for such a small team to figure out how to use all these ideas. So the team didn't try. Instead, it was left up to the community to make sense of those proposals. The community came through, as it would many times, categorizing and discussing the many proposals.

The team organized a series of task forces centered around important subjects of study such as community health, international expansion, and technology strategy. True to the Wikipedia model, all the work of these task forces was completed transparently—in the open, on the wiki. In addition, each of the task forces was led and staffed almost entirely by volunteers who did nearly all the work analyzing the proposals.

The organizing team helped identify the core contributors for each task force, but anyone could volunteer for any project that interested him or her. While they were supported by professional facilitation, the community members themselves were accountable for the success or failure of their task forces. Not every task force was a success. In the end, each task force analyzed all the proposals relevant to its area and presented a set of recommendations summarizing the findings.

Synthesizing these recommendations into one strategic plan was the hardest part, Philippe said. "We had to take all of these great ideas and figure out which of them were actually feasible for us."

During synthesis, most strategic planning projects tend to go dark, emerging only when the final plan is ready for the light of day. Not this one. Even the synthesis was a transparent process—everything was available on the wiki, including early drafts.

Finally, the plan was completed in late 2010, and the finished strategic plan is now available on the Wikimedia website.[7,8]

Here are a few key lessons to keep in mind while planning your collaborative community project:

- **Return to Linus's Law, "Given enough eyeballs, all bugs are shallow"**—This adage holds true for collaborative community projects. The more people you can effectively involve, the more great ideas you'll collect.

- **The journey is as important as the destination**—Remember, the product isn't just the goal the group achieves or the thing it creates; it's also the sense of community and relationships that come out of the project.

- **Clearly define the process up front**—Plan out your project as a series of manageable phases, each with a clear end point and output, and communicate that plan. Contributors will be eager to know where and when they can contribute best. By clearly defining the process, you'll be more organized and show respect for their time and effort.

- **The more deeply you involve people, the more accountable they'll feel for the end result**—By asking people for their ideas and involving them in the process, you encourage them to have a stake in the result. When people see their own ideas and work reflected in the project, they'll be more apt to take ownership and ensure it is executed well. Rather than implementing someone else's plan, they'll be implementing their own.

---

7. The Wikimedia Strategic Plan is available at http://strategy.wikimedia.org/wiki/Main_Page

8. This case study is adapted from an article I wrote for the *Management Innovation Exchange* in March, 2011.

- **Let the community lead**—Don't stop at just getting ideas from the community. By giving your contributors key leadership roles in executing the project itself, you'll show them trust and respect and receive it in return. On its strategic planning project, the Wikimedia Foundation put volunteer contributors in lead roles, and many of these people continue to run a valuable follow-on project with very little involvement from the Wikimedia Foundation itself.

- **Leave room to explore uncharted territory**—Don't be too rigid. Sometimes great ideas for how to move forward with the project will emerge from the community itself. By being flexible and incorporating contributors' ideas not just to the work but to the process itself, you'll improve things as well as ensure that people stay engaged and interested along the way.

- **Make heroes out of contributors**—One mistake I see many brands make is that they involve their community in projects and then have the brand take all the credit for the community's hard work. There is no better opportunity to bring value to members of your brand community than by giving them public recognition for their work on the project. Sometimes this means just simply saying thank you, but in many cases, you can leverage you brand's reach and power to help people use their project work to build their own personal brands as well. I explore this concept more deeply in the next section.

I love working on collaborative community projects. They are a perfect way for the brand positioning to come alive through actions and not just words, and there are few better ways to begin working side-by-side with members of your brand community as peers rather than customers, investors, donors, or whatever other label you might have stuck on them before.

And let's not forget, the collaborative community projects can actually do real good. Not only will your relationship with the brand community strengthen, but you might create lasting value for the brand, the community itself, or some other cause or effort important to you and the community.

Today, many brands are using collaborative community projects to deliver redeeming social value, and I expect this will only increase in the coming years.

Forming Relationships via Social Media

As I've already stated, I very much dislike the idea of social media for the sake of social media. But now that I've established some of the basic elements of an external brand positioning rollout strategy, we are finally ready to talk about social media.

In Chapter 1, I referred to the rise of social media, including tools like blogs, Twitter, YouTube, and Facebook, as the second Internet revolution and one of the most important factors that has caused organizations to have less and less control over their brands.

In her book, *Social Media Marketing:Strategies for Engaging in Facebook, Twitter and Other Social Media*, Liana Evans[9] breaks down social media into the following types:

- **Social news sites**—Websites where users can submit news, articles, videos, blog posts, and photos and other users can rate them. The most popular examples of this are Digg (www.digg.com) and Reddit (www.reddit.com), but almost every news-related site has embraced the trend.

- **Social networking**—Websites where community members can connect to friends or colleagues, post comments and photos, join events, and identify themselves as "fans" of things they like, among other things. Facebook (www.facebook.com) and LinkedIn (www.linkedin.com) are two great examples of very different types of social networking sites.

- **Social bookmarking**—Websites where you can bookmark your favorite websites and then share them with others. The most popular example is Delicious (www.delicious.com).

- **Social sharing**—Websites that allow you to share your own photos and videos with others. The most popular examples by far are YouTube (www.youtube.com) and Flickr (www.flickr.com).

- **Social events**—Websites you can use to plan events and find out who is planning to attend. Evite (www.evite.com) and Meetup (www.meetup.com) are very popular, although the Facebook event-planning tool might now be the most widely used.

- **Blogs**—Websites where people can express themselves to the entire Internet quickly and easily. While anyone can now set up his or her own blog in a few minutes, the most popular blogging platforms are WordPress (www.wordpress.com) and Blogger (www.blogger.com).

- **Microblogging**—Blogs distilled down to very short messages. Twitter (www.twitter.com) is by far the most popular microblogging platform.

- **Wikis**—Websites where people can work together to collaboratively create content. Wikipedia (www.wikipedia.com) is the most famous example.

- **Forums and message boards**—Perhaps the oldest form of social media on the Internet, forums and message boards are still one of the most

---

9. *Social Media Marketing* by Liana Evans, Chapter 2, "Understanding Social Media Strategies"

popular. They make it easy to quickly share opinions and information with like-minded people. I would also add mailing lists to this category—one more old-school social media tool that is still used by a great number of people and organizations.

A complete discussion of how to use all these social media types is beyond the scope of this book, but if you take a trip to your local bookstore, you'll find that more words have been written about social media over the past few years than one person could probably read in a lifetime.

I'm not a big fan of most social media books (because they tend to lure people into the tool trap), but here are a few that stand out for me as providing a good foundation of knowledge on the topic:

- *Trust Agents* **by Chris Brogan and Julien Smith**—Perhaps the godfather of social media, Chris Brogan started blogging way before the rest of us and has now become a leader on Twitter (where he has almost 200,000 followers) and Facebook as well. This book is required reading for anyone exploring using social media personally or within his or her organization; this book will save you from making a lot of common mistakes.

- *Groundswell* **by Charlene Li and Josh Bernoff**—Probably one of the most popular books on social media among executives, written by two of Forrester Research's top analysts. Read it because your executives probably have and it will help you speak their language.

- *The Dragonfly Effect* **by Jennifer Aaker and Andy Smith**—Based on a class taught by Dr. Aaker at Stanford University, this book is one of the best at explaining the psychological underpinnings of social behavior on the Internet. Unlike many social media "strategies," this book provides a model for how to achieve very concrete goals using social media.

The Ad-Free Brand Perspective on Social Media

Although most social media books concern themselves with how to promote your brand or cause using social media tools, ad-free brands approach social media from a fundamentally different perspective that should be familiar to you by now.

Ad-free brands use social media to help members of their brand communities as much or more than they use it to help themselves.

> "Ad-free brands use social media to help members of their brand communities as much or more than they use it to help themselves."

Again, a simple concept. But one that most brands (and people, for that matter) ignore entirely.

EXTERNAL ROLLOUT EXAMPLE #2: YOUR BEST FRIEND CHAUNCEY

Now that you've completed the mini-positioning project and Chauncey has a much stronger, clearer idea how to present himself to potential employers, he gets to the hard work of finding a job.

In a crowded job market where there are hundreds of applicants for every open position, Chauncey needs an advantage. He starts researching many of the leading people in the telecommunications industry who are active on Twitter and who blog regularly. He follows almost 100 people on Twitter and starts reading about 30 telecommunications blogs. Chauncey also sets up a listening post made up of a Twitter search for anything related to telecommunications, creates a column in TweetDeck where he can see the posts of all 100 telecommunications Twitterers, and uses Google to collect the RSS feeds of all the telecommunications bloggers so he can read them easily.

A few days later, one prominent blogger writes about a problem he is having trouble solving at work. As it turns out, this problem is one Chauncey already solved at his previous company. Chauncey reaches out via Twitter, helping solve the problem in just under 140 characters. A few weeks later, the blogger reaches out to Chauncey via Twitter with a similar issue, and again Chauncey is able to quickly help. Impressed, the blogger asks Chauncey who he works for. When Chauncey replies that he is in the market for a new job, the blogger refers him to a colleague who has a few open positions.

One of these positions ends up being a good fit. By this time, Chauncey is adept at positioning himself and communicating his story. He does well in the interview, and he gets a job offer. Unfortunately for you, the position itself is in San Diego, so Chauncey will have to move. While you are sad to have a good friend moving away, you are happy his unemployment was mercifully short and glad you could help him.

If you want to see what I mean, try this simple exercise. Go to any big brand-related Facebook page or Twitter feed. Calculate the percentage of posts or tweets written to promote the brand or related products. For most brands, their use of social media is entirely self-serving.

These brands are essentially applying the rules of advertising, marketing, and PR to social media. What a shame. And—in many cases—what a complete waste of time and energy.

How can you help the members of your brand community using social media? Here are a few examples:

- **Use your organization's blog to make heroes out of community members or highlight the projects important to them**—Rather than using your organization's blog just to talk about your own products and projects, consider using it to tell the story of someone in your brand community doing something amazing. Perhaps it is a customer who has started an innovative charity. You can use the convening power of your brand to bring more attention to his or her effort and make a hero out of him or her in the process. Bonus points if can you tell the story in such a way that it highlights how this person is living one aspect of the brand's positioning.

- **Create short documentary films showing people in the brand community living the brand**—At Red Hat we created many films that achieved this effect. We filmed musicians, philosophers, and others with dreams, goals, or successes we believed would inspire the rest of our community members. These documentaries would highlight people or efforts we believed aligned closely with our brand.

  For example, in one film we introduced Dr. Vandana Shiva, a scientist and activist leading an effort to ensure that the DNA of seeds for planting crops could not be owned by corporations, but instead could be openly accessed by anyone needing to grow food. Though very different from making open source software, we felt this effort not only related to what we were doing at Red Hat in terms of protecting freedom and choice, but would also provide inspiration to our brand community and give community members a sense for how their work fit into a larger context of doing good for society.

  We had so much success with the documentary format at Red Hat that we ended up building out a digital media team within the company. One of the primary responsibilities of this group was to tell the stories of people inside and outside the organization who were, knowingly or not, living the Red Hat brand in some meaningful way. Some of these were highlighted via a regular internal documentary feature we called "The Show." Others were posted directly to the Red Hat website[10] or to YouTube.[11]

  You can do this with your brand as well. Post the stories you create to YouTube, put them on your website and blog, show them at events, share them internally, and share them with the outside world any way you can.

---

10. You can see some of these stories here: http://www.redhat.com/videos/

11. The Red Hat channel on YouTube is located here: http://www.youtube.com/user/RedHatVideos

- **Use your official Twitter feed or Facebook page to highlight your followers and friends as much or more than you use it to promote the brand**—I learned this simple advice from Chris Brogan, author of *Trust Agents*, and it has served me very well. Rather than always posting tweets or updates about what is important to your brand, use Twitter and Facebook to acknowledge and shine a light on the thoughts and ideas of your followers. This is especially useful on Twitter, where the majority of people only have a few hundred followers, while if you have a popular brand, you might have thousands or more. One simple tweet from the official brand account can bring one of your followers more attention than she ordinarily receives in a year.

In late 2009, my blog Dark Matter Matters (www.darkmattermatters.com) had been up for just under a year when I spoke on a panel with Chris Brogan at a small event in New York. Chris and I talked before and after the panel, and that night I wrote my first post about Tom Sawyer thinking.[12]

I tweeted the post to Chris that night right after I published it, and imagine my surprise when the next morning I saw that he had written a whole article on his blog about me and our conversation, titled "Small Powerful Words."[13] In it he linked to my blog post.

To that point, my little blog was getting about 20–50 visitors a day. The attention from Chris Brogan drove traffic to my blog to a traffic level I'd never seen before and gained me a large number of new followers on Twitter as well.

A small favor from Chris ended up being a huge favor for me and really was one of the turning points that convinced me to keep blogging. I'm now a very loyal member of the Chris Brogan brand community.

> "I try to follow a general rule of having at least half of my tweets and blog posts highlighting the ideas and projects of someone other than myself."

Today, my blog posts continue to have a pretty decent regular readership, and I've continued to try to pay Chris Brogan's favor forward, regularly highlighting people or organizations whose ideas I respect greatly. I try to follow a general rule of having at least half of my tweets and blog posts highlighting the ideas and projects of someone other than myself.

---

12. You can read the original post here: http://darkmattermatters.com/2009/09/09/tom-sawyer-white-washing-fences-and-building-communities-online/

13. Chris's post is available here: http://www.chrisbrogan.com/small-powerful-words/

EXTERNAL ROLLOUT EXAMPLE #3: BUBBAPOP SODA COMPANY

During your internal brand positioning rollout, you hosted a series of brand boot camps where you heard stories of employees who were living the brand in unique and interesting ways. You captured these stories as mini documentary films and have begun to share them internally by showing them at company meetings and on the corporate intranet.

One of these short films somehow snuck outside the company walls and ended up on YouTube, where it received over 15,000 views in less than a week. At many companies, management would be furious that the story leaked. But the fact is, the story paints BubbaPop in a great light. Instead of getting angry, you wonder if the other stories might be interesting to people outside the company as well.

You create an official YouTube channel for BubbaPop and begin posting videos of the people behind the brand. Many of these short documentaries show that BubbaPop is not just an organization looking to maximize profits, but also does plenty of good stuff, too.

You decide to extend the program beyond just employees because you know there are great stories of partners and customers out there as well. You set up a program where any customer, partner, or employee can submit a story of the interesting, compelling, or valuable work he or she is doing. You capture the best stories as short documentaries (which you dub BubbaFilms) and publish them via the BubbaPop YouTube channel, via Twitter, and on a new BubbaFilms blog. Many of these stories highlight angles that support the BubbaPop brand positioning, so the organization benefits as well.

Through this program, many in the BubbaPop community receive additional attention, support, and even funding for their work and become grateful supporters of BubbaPop for life.

- **Highlight collaborative projects with the brand community**—Twitter, Facebook, blogs, and documentaries are great ways to draw attention to the collaborative projects you undertake with your brand community.

  Use these tools to draw attention to the heroic work of community members and individuals inside the organization while downplaying the brand itself. The brand should take a humble storyteller role and let the project participants be the stars.

Your external rollout group and community council may have even more ideas for how you can highlight the thinking, work, and successes of members of your brand community. Consider hosting a session or series of sessions to get their ideas above and beyond those I've listed here.

Empowering the Entire Organization to Be the Eyes, Ears, and Mouth of the Brand

In Chapter 1, I asserted that the people interested in the brand now have as much control or influence over the future direction of the brand as any brand expert within the organization.

You can guide and influence the direction of the brand by developing strong positioning and rolling it out internally and externally in the ways I've described in the last two chapters. But the reality is that the types of social media and the avenues for members of your brand community to make their ideas and opinions known are so numerous that it is almost impossible for you to watch for brand activity everywhere by yourself.

So why try?

Today, many organizations are beginning to develop a much more liberal approach to the use of social media by individuals within the organization to cover more ground more quickly. The results are powerful.

Ad-free brands eschew the old policy of having one official voice for the brand through which all messages are emitted and one set of eyes and ears registering all complaints, ideas, and information. Instead, they empower as many people as possible to listen and speak on behalf of the brand.

> "Ad-free brands empower as many people as possible to listen and speak on behalf of the brand."

This is another place where having strong positioning embedded internally is incredibly important. When you free up every employee to speak on behalf of the brand, you'll need to ensure that they are staying on brand, both in what they say and how they act.

By now, you've probably recruited a set of brand ambassadors who have been through a boot camp and are prepared to speak and listen effectively on behalf of the brand. But if you'd like to extend this group even further, or perhaps extend it to the entire organization, you'll need to send more people to boot camp. Use the internal positioning boot camp process I covered in Chapter 5 to ensure everyone has a good grasp of the positioning and a deep understanding of the story behind the brand.

Once people are properly trained on the brand positioning and understand the basic rules of the road for using social media safely and effectively (again, you'll find many books that cover the subject, but start with the three I've listed previously), channel your inner conductor again and lead the orchestra.

How do you lead? Provide people with the information they need to listen and communicate effectively. Here are a few ideas:

- **Show employees how to set up an online listening post**—In Chapter 3, I introduced the idea of an online listening post as a way to easily do research about your brand online. *Listening post* is a fancy term for describing a set of tools, like Google Alerts, TweetDeck, Social Mention, Radian6, and others, that you can use to hear what people are currently saying about your brand on Twitter, on Facebook, via blogs, in forums, and anywhere else people can comment or hold conversations online. Refer to Chapter 3 for more details on how to set up a listening post for yourself. The more people within your organization who have brand listening posts covering the areas they care most about, the more you will (collectively) hear.

- **Empower people to use social media to communicate on behalf of the organization**—After people have their ears attenuated to the conversations happening online about the brand, the next step is for them to get involved in these conversations. You'll have to decide how to do this in a way that makes the most sense for your brand. Some brands will limit permission to communicate officially to a group that might just include the brand ambassadors. Others might let only certain people communicate on some subjects while allowing almost anyone in the organization to communicate on others.

  For example, it probably isn't a good idea for everyone to feel empowered to discuss the organization's financial prospects. There can be strong legal or investor-related reasons this is a bad idea. But if a customer is asking for help on Twitter with an issue, perhaps you empower anyone to be able to help him or her.

  Probably one of the strongest examples of this in action is Twelpforce, an often-cited (for good reason) example of how big-box retailer Best Buy is using Twitter. Twelpforce is a large group of volunteer Best Buy employees using the Twitter handle @twelpforce to answer customers' questions. Any Best Buy employee can volunteer to help customers via Twelpforce, and almost 35,000 people are following its Twitter feed.

Even though this group will probably not tell you whether you should buy or sell Best Buy stock, it can probably help you understand the differences between LED, LCD, and plasma televisions.

- **Encourage both official and personal interactions using social media tools**—Many brands communicate with their brand communities using only their official Twitter channel, official blog, or official Facebook page and avoid having employees interact from their personal accounts and blogs. I think this is a mistake.

Your official channels are great venues for turning members of your brand community into heroes in the ways I've outlined here, but they are not as good for having personal dialogue unless it is very clear that there is one human being behind the account.

I believe that using a thoughtful combination of personal and official social media accounts is the best approach for most brands. Ad-free brands aren't just faceless logos, they are communities made up of individuals, each with a distinct personality and ideas.

Ad-free brands will accentuate the people behind the brand by encouraging (not forcing) people to communicate as themselves, as well as on behalf of the brand. Some people won't be comfortable with this. Either they like to use their personal social media accounts just for personal stuff or they don't feel confident enough with their own voice or command of the story to communicate as themselves in a brand context. That's okay.

📩 *Note*

Ad-free brands will accentuate the people behind the brand by encouraging (not forcing) people to communicate as themselves, as well as on behalf of the brand.

Let people represent the brand and themselves in whatever ways they feel comfortable. Eventually some stars will emerge who want to represent the brand with their personal voice and who are also really good at it. These people are great candidates for becoming brand ambassadors.

Can Ad-Free Brands Advertise?

In the previous chapter, I left brand giveaways for last because I feel like, without implementing many of the other internal rollout ideas, they are naked tools of *telling* the brand positioning rather than *living* it.

In this chapter, I leave advertising last on the list of things ad-free brands should consider as part of their rollout for exactly the same reason. Without implementing many of the other external rollout strategies covered in this chapter, I do not believe advertising is a good investment for ad-free brands.

But can ad-free brands advertise? Yes.

In the same way brand giveaways can be reminders of the brand positioning, advertising can be a reminder of the brand positioning with external communities—but only after many of the activities to help people live the brand both inside and outside the organization are already in place. Just remember that advertising is a high-cost and (if you are lucky) high-value strategy, so it won't be the first choice for an ad-free brand if other options to achieve great impact are available.

If you choose to use advertising as part of your external positioning rollout, use it to enhance the brand-building work you are already doing, not as a strategy on its own. At Red Hat, we would run the occasional *Wall Street Journal* advertisement, appear in trade magazines, or sponsor signage at tradeshows or other events, but usually just as an way to draw additional attention to a major event, issue, or opportunity.

Advertising was not a core part of our brand-building strategy. We realized that, other than in these rare situations, we could create more brand value in other—ad-free—ways.

The Core Brand Community Grows Larger

In this chapter, I've covered many ways to roll out your brand positioning externally by giving people inside and outside the organization opportunities to live it and learn about it rather than just talking about it in advertising, marketing, and press releases.

By implementing these strategies, you should be able to quickly extend your brand community outside your organizational walls. This community can become a powerful amplification system for your brand positioning and can create broad-reaching benefits for your organization, which I cover in more detail in the next chapter.

7

Continuing Engagement

In Chapter 2, I outlined four phases of a brand positioning project: research, positioning, initial rollout, and the
phase I cover in this chapter: continuing engagement. In
the two previous chapters, I highlighted many ideas for
how to roll out your brand positioning while deeply
embedding it internally and externally. But your positioning work isn't done just because you've completed an initial set of rollout projects. We've only just begun.

Jeff Bezos, chairman and CEO of Amazon.com, has a
famous quote about building brands:

"A brand for a company is like a reputation for a person.
You earn reputation by trying to do hard things well.
People notice that over time. I don't think there are any
shortcuts."[1]

The best-designed, most creatively rolled-out brand positioning effort will still fail if it is not sustained over time.
There are, as Bezos says, no shortcuts.

---

1. http://www.businessweek.com/magazine/content/04_31/b3894101.htm

In this chapter, I share some ideas for how you can continue to engage both your internal and external communities beyond the initial rollout. Ultimately, you'll find that this sustained focus is key to brand-building success.

The Most Boring Person in the Organization

At Red Hat, I was lucky enough to have an opportunity to work with one brand exclusively for a decade—an experience I might never have again.

Sometimes, I would say that my value to Red Hat was that I would repeat the same things over and over, year after year. Every two weeks, I'd show up at orientation and tell the same stories, show the same videos, preach the same values and mission, and ask the same questions. I'd return to the same themes—freedom, choice, openness, among others—in my work, and I'd encourage others to explore these concepts as well.

Sometimes I felt like the most boring person in the organization.

When someone on my team would tell me something like, "We are thinking about giving away black hats to people who attend our events this year because we're getting tired of the red ones," you could count on me to respond, "But we are *Red Hat…*".

I've always believed the old adage that just about the time you get bored with saying or doing something, it is probably beginning to sink in with everyone else. So, despite often feeling like a broken record, we kept on hitting the same themes, year after year.

That's not to say we didn't innovate. There are a million different ways to tell a story, and we tried many of them. Our goal was to approach the same themes from as many angles as we could.

So, how do you ensure your brand positioning isn't just a flavor of the month? How do you ensure positioning becomes so deeply ingrained in the DNA of the organization that it has the capacity to actually increase the value of the organization itself? Read on!

Continue Reinforcing the Brand Positioning Internally

In Chapter 5, I showed you many examples of ways you could embed the brand positioning deeply within the culture of the organization. You might already be working on your brand story or have made changes to the brand experience. You may even be integrating the positioning into organizational processes like performance reviews, team meetings, and hiring practices.

How do you reinforce the brand positioning even beyond these first rollout steps? Simple. You stick with it. Year after year.

Don't just write the brand story and consider yourself finished as soon as you've put a version of it on your intranet. Tell the story every chance you get, everywhere you can. Make improvements along the way. The more you and others begin to share the story, the better you'll get at doing so.

The same thing goes with the other internal rollout projects. Keep with them. Don't try to complete every single project on the list during your initial rollout. Save some for year two and year three. Continue to meet with your internal rollout group on a regular basis (although it doesn't have to be every week) to brainstorm new ideas, and check in with each other to see how the ideas you've already implemented are doing. Consider working with the internal rollout group to choose a few new ideas to focus on each quarter of the year while continuing to improve the old ones.

By continually improving your rollout techniques using the "release early, release often" and rapid prototyping mentality, you ensure they always remain relevant and effective. So if some of your rollout projects start feeling tired or bureaucratic (or the people who run them are no longer as passionate), reinvent them or replace them with strategies you believe will work better.

Remember that while the positioning itself should stay relatively consistent over time, the tools you use to embed it and roll it out can change and often do.

 Tip

> Remember that while the positioning itself should stay relatively consistent over time, the tools you use to embed it and roll it out can change and often do.

Continue Reinforcing the Positioning Externally

The same advice applies to reinforcing the positioning externally. If you've already begun to implement some of the concepts you learned in Chapter 6, stick with them.

View your positioning work externally as an ongoing conversation rather than a campaign with a beginning and end. Just like servicing customers or making products, you have to continue to do it if you want to remain successful.

Some external activities—like community councils, for example—will be ongoing, and you'll need to ensure that someone is in charge of them who is accountable for their continued success. Other activities can be opportunistic—

a chance to bring people together to discuss and solve a crisis that affects members of your community, for example.

Be sure to keep the momentum going with a mix of new and old ideas, keeping roll-out techniques fresh but themes and stories consistent.

Measuring Your Progress

Probably one of the toughest aspects of managing an ad-free brand is measuring how you are doing. Often, you will have an intuitive sense and will see passion and energy growing in the internal and external brand communities; you'll have examples that showcase the progress you've made.

For traditional, metrics-driven organizations, the ad-free brand approach can pose some unfamiliar measurement challenges. In this section, I share some ideas that will help you prove the impact of what you are doing in a language that resonates within the typical organization.

Dark Matter Matters

I hope you'll humor one final story if I promise that this is the last astronomy- or physics-related reference in this book. In late 2008, I was struggling mightily with the question of how you measure and quantify the value of brand-related activities like those we have discussed here.

As someone whose father is an amateur astronomer, I'd long been intrigued by the concepts of dark matter and dark energy in the universe. If the concept of dark matter is new to you, Wikipedia describes it as:

"…matter that is inferred to exist from gravitational effects on visible matter and background radiation, but is undetectable by emitted or scattered electromagnetic radiation."[2]

In other words, it is matter out there in the universe that is incredibly difficult to see, basically invisible, but that has a large gravitational effect. What's particularly interesting about dark matter is that, apparently, there is a lot of it. In fact, scientists hypothesize that about 95% of the mass of the universe is made up of dark matter and its counterpart, dark energy. Only about 5% of the mass of the universe is made up of the type of matter you can actually see.

I find this fascinating.

And dark matter is still a theoretical concept. Again from the Wikipedia entry:

"As important as dark matter is believed to be in the cosmos, direct evidence of its existence and a concrete understanding of its nature have remained elusive."

---

2. http://en.wikipedia.org/wiki/Dark_matter

But it was actually reading about all the problems with the Large Hadron Collider in 2008 (at the very same time I was having my own problems figuring out how to measure the value of brand-related work) that helped me make the connection between what I do for a living and this concept of dark matter.

The Large Hadron Collider is the world's largest particle accelerator. It was built on the border of France and Switzerland and is about 17 miles wide. One of the things that particle physicists hope to prove with this enormous project is the existence of dark matter.

I'm no physicist, but as I understand it, the accelerator shoots protons at super-high speeds around the collider, and, if these scientists are lucky, the collisions eventually *might* produce a few particles that will exist for only a few milliseconds and then disappear again. And these particles *might* prove that dark matter isn't just a theory.

Might being the key word. In fact, Stephen Hawking has bet $100 that they won't find anything.[3]

The cost of building a collider to *maybe* prove the existence of dark matter? Between $4-8 billion dollars.

Another attempt to prove the existence of dark matter used the Hubble Space Telescope. Figure 7.1 was taken by Hubble and first shown by NASA in May 2007.[4]

Figure 7.1   *This image from the Hubble Space telescope shows evidence of gravitational distortion that might prove the existence of dark matter.*

---

3. http://www.breitbart.com/article.php?id=080909150154.yzfml9cn

4. http://www.space.com/3806-hubble-reveals-ghostly-ring-dark-matter.htm

In this picture, you are looking at many galaxies a really, really long way away. But you can also see fuzzy gray areas all over that look like clouds. When the astronomers first looked at this photo, they thought the fuzzy areas were a problem with the image. But after analyzing it for over a year, they realized that the fuzziness might actually be evidence of dark matter.

Their reasoning? The fuzziness is actually a gravitational distortion of the light rays from distant galaxies that are being bent by dark matter on their way to Earth. The effect you see is kind of like looking at the bottom of a pond that is being distorted by ripples on the surface.

So finally, scientists had discovered some real visual evidence of dark matter.

I believe the type of activities we talk about in this book—those related to building brand, culture, and community—are the dark matter within organizations. Often brand, culture, and community are extremely difficult to measure well, and sometimes accurate measurement is simply impossible.

 Note

Brand, community, and culture are extremely difficult to measure well and sometimes accurate measurement is simply impossible. They are the dark matter of organizations.

That's not to say we don't try anyway. I've seen and even tried many formulas, processes, and products that attempt to measure the value of brand, community, and culture-related efforts. Some of them (like the brand tracking study and other types of research I highlighted in Chapter 2) can provide valuable information. Others, not so much.

Yet here's the kicker: brand, community, and culture are having a huge impact on your organization, whether you can effectively and cost-effectively measure that impact or not.

Just as dark matter is a strong gravitational force within the universe even though it is notoriously hard to see and measure, so are many of the things that will lead to the long-term success of ad-free brands.

Brand, community, and culture are having a huge impact on your organization, whether you can effectively and cost-effectively measure that impact or not.

A Low-Cost, High-Value Approach to Measurement

So, what is my point? We've spent billions of dollars trying to measure dark matter with minimal success, while it continues to have a huge gravitational impact on the universe. We can likewise spend a large percentage of our time and budget measuring the success of our brand-building efforts. Or, instead, we can spend more of that time and money building the brand.

I prefer a low-cost, high-value approach to measurement. Measure the things you can easily and inexpensively measure, just enough to give you the information you need to ensure you are headed in the right direction, and focus your efforts on actually moving the needle.

Don't feel like every measurement or data point has to fit into a spreadsheet to be a meaningful sign of progress. Sometimes stories and experiences might be the most useful data you'll collect. And don't think data always needs to be used as proof of positive or negative progress. Sometimes it's just not that black and white. Data can just be data.

> ... don't think data always needs to be used as proof of positive or negative progress. Sometimes it's just not that black and white.

Some Examples of How to Measure Your Progress

In Chapter 3, I shared many examples of places where you could collect information about your brand. Many of these same places are great sources for ongoing data about the impact of your brand efforts. What's more, because the positioning process is a continuing cycle, you might uncover information during your analysis that makes you want to revisit your brand positioning, starting the cycle over again.

Here are some examples of places where you can get ongoing information about the success of your positioning efforts.

Web Analytics

While data about what people are doing on your website won't necessarily tell you if your brand efforts are successful, there is some information you can collect that might inform an overall view. For example, if more people are coming to your website more often than before you began your brand positioning work, this *might* be a sign that you've built some additional momentum around the brand (but isn't always).

If you see a trend like increased web traffic in combination with some of the other measures listed here, this can be a sign of meaningful progress. But resist the urge to assume that simply because your website traffic goes down in a month that your brand efforts were less successful that month. Too many other factors, including product promotions, links from other websites, and news events, come into effect to make short-term trends meaningful. Usually brand measurements are best viewed through a wider lens.

In addition to simple traffic measurements, some other things to look at include visit length (are people spending more time on your website), demographic and geographic information (who are they, where are they coming from, and how did they get there), and where the visitors go on the site (which can help you get a sense for areas of the brand positioning that are resonating more than others).

Media Coverage

Media coverage is another indirect place to look for data on your progress. Sometimes doing a regular analysis of media sentiment is helpful, but just as important is getting a sense for the sentiment of the people reporters cover in their stories. Often you'll see direct quotes from members of your brand community giving you proof that your positioning rollout efforts are or are not working. Given enough data points, you might be able to spot a trend.

Listening Post

Probably the source of data I rely on more heavily than any other for tracking progress on brand positioning efforts is the online listening post I discussed in Chapters 3 and 6. By setting up an online listening post tracking mentions of your brand across social media such as blogs, Twitter, and Facebook, you'll have access to a real-time feed of information about your brand.

When I find particularly telling examples (interesting tweets, posts, or other community opinions or thoughts about the brand), I collect them in the hope of being able to see trends over time.

Internal and External Surveys and Interviews

Consider running surveys and interviews like the ones I highlighted in Chapter 3 internally and externally on a regular basis. During your brand positioning research phase, you probably conducted some of these surveys and interviews and have already established a baseline. If you continue to do these surveys regularly—perhaps once per year—you might see trends emerge over time.

Brand Tracking Study

Those working with larger budgets or larger brands with more at stake might consider investing in a formal brand tracking study to be conducted once or twice per year. Refer to Chapter 3 for more information on how to run a brand tracking study.

The Brand Report Card

Many organizations should create a simple brand report card they can use to track their observations over time. These report cards can be fairly simple or be complex and data rich.

On one end of the spectrum, I had an agreement with one of our first community managers at Red Hat that his success would be measured on his and my combined view of whether community karma was "mostly positive." That was the report card, "mostly positive": yes or no.

Once each year, we'd evaluate the data we were seeing from many different sources on how our community work was progressing, and, if karma was mostly positive, we were happy.

But I've also created complex brand report cards measuring a variety of factors and even assigning them brand health values.

For me, the most meaningful brand report cards are documents created on a regular basis, perhaps once per week, month, or quarter, highlighting specific examples of the impact of the brand positioning in action while tracking ongoing metrics like web analytics, media sentiment, and survey results as data becomes available. I've included a sample template for what a brand report card might look like in the appendix.

🔍 Tip

You'll find an example of a brand report card template you might use for reporting your progress in Appendix A.

Think of these report cards as an ongoing dialogue about the brand. Consider actually discussing your findings in ongoing internal and external rollout meetings or in regular meetings with the executive team. But remember: this is not just a report for the executives; it's for you and your team as well.

Looking back at your old report cards will be like looking at baby pictures or yearbooks from times past. By examining the information you collected earlier, you'll not only begin to clearly see your progress, but you'll also be amazed by how far you've come.

But whatever you do, don't turn the brand report card into a burden. If it becomes more work than the value it brings (high cost, low value), consider slimming it down or doing it less often. Or, if you feel really good about your own instincts for analyzing the success of your team's brand efforts and don't need to report results to others in the organization, consider moving to a slimmer "karma: mostly positive"-style measurement.

One other idea to consider is creating an internal blog (or external if you want to be a *really* open brand) where you track ongoing progress on the brand positioning rollout. Share what you learn and what you experience along the way. Over time, this narrative of the growth and journey of the brand will become a priceless resource you can refer to for reminders, examples, stories, and data about your progress.

Revising Your Positioning Over Time

The brand is a work in progress. As you conduct more and more of the rollout activities from Chapters 5 and 6 over a period measured in years, you'll learn a lot about what resonates with your brand community and what efforts result in the greatest success.

At the same time, the world around you is changing. Your competitors will come and go. Your own products and services can change or become more or less desirable to your brand community because of things outside of your control.

Your brand universe is a dynamic, rapidly changing place. While you want your brand positioning to remain relatively rooted over a long period, to remain relevant you might have to correct your course from time to time.

Because of this, I recommend thinking of the four phases of brand positioning as a continuous process. Research, positioning, rollout, continuing engagement, leading back to more research, subtly revised positioning, new rollout, and continuing engagement tactics. Your brand positioning must remain vigorous, alive, and relevant. Never stagnant or dated.

Here are a few tips for how to make changes to your brand positioning over time without damaging the impact.

> While you want your brand positioning to remain relatively rooted over a long period, to remain relevant you might have to correct your course from time to time.

- **Make no sudden moves**—If you have spent years establishing your brand positioning, don't suddenly drop the old positioning and move to something completely different, even if the need for change is urgent. Because building a brand takes time, sudden moves (especially when there are multiple sudden moves in a short time frame) will quickly lead a brand to meaninglessness. How many times have you witnessed organizations chasing brand opportunities, jumping from one theme to another without giving any positioning strategy a chance to take hold? To me, sudden positioning changes show a lack of confidence in the strategy. I often see them as a sign of a dying brand.

> Sudden positioning moves will quickly lead a brand to meaninglessness.

- **Build peninsulas, not islands**—I refer to making sudden positioning moves as *island hopping*. Meaning that a brand jumps from position to position, leaving old positioning completely behind and the brand community confused. Instead, I recommend that brands build peninsulas connecting old positions to new ones. Brands following a peninsula-building strategy already know their destination and have plotted a path to get there, perhaps in multiple stages. If you are forced to make an extreme change to your brand positioning, consider trying to make the move over a period of years—rather than making the move overnight—with a few interim steps in between.

- **Never leave a man behind**—When moving toward new positioning, some brands have a tendency to turn their backs on the people in the brand community who are its most passionate supporters. Even if you don't think your old community members will fit well into your new world, don't abandon them. Bring them along to pass on some of their energy to the new community members and, if at some point along the way, they decide the brand no long resonates with them, let that decision be theirs, not yours. Who knows? You might find that some members of the brand community love what you stand for so much that *they* are willing to change to remain a valuable member of the brand community. And, if you take the time to involve them, they might even have great ideas for what your new brand positioning could be. The same rule applies for members of your internal brand community as well. Long-time employees who've been passionate advocates of the brand for years and know it inside and out often feel alienated if they aren't made a part of the change process. Consider asking them to help develop the new positioning using an open positioning approach like those I described in Chapter 4.

Ad-Free Brands in Crisis

Just like any relationship has its ups and downs, the relationship an ad-free brand has with its brand community will be better at some times than at others. If you think of your goal as keeping your community karma "mostly positive," you'll leave room for the occasional problems that occur from time to time. No relationship with a brand community will be perfect every day.

How Good Relationships Go Bad

How can things go bad? A number of things can cause a crisis in a brand community. Some common issues:

- **The organization makes a decision adversely affecting members of the brand community**—Intentionally or not, organizations often have to make decisions having negative consequences for members of the brand community. A company might raise the price of its products, for example, putting them out of the range of some members of the community. Another common example is when an organization makes a decision to focus more resources on providing services that benefit one part of the community while reducing the services they provide to another. It isn't easy (nor particularly good business) to try to make everyone happy all of the time. Remember that while you want to have a dialogue with your brand community, you don't want to take orders from it. Make the decisions that are best for the long-term health of the organization. Although the reaction you'll get from the brand community will obviously be one factor to weigh in these decisions, it is not the only one.

> While you want to have a dialogue with your brand community, you don't want to take orders from it.

- **The organization doesn't act on feedback it has received**—The most common mistake I've seen organizations make in attempting to develop deeper relationships with members of their brand community? Asking for feedback and ideas from the community and then doing nothing with them. When people invest their time and energy in your brand, they will expect a return on that investment. If they don't see a return, they will be less likely to invest their time in the brand in the future. So be careful when asking for help; make sure you plan to actually do something with the suggested ideas from your brand community and that you communicate that plan clearly, updating community members often on your progress. Set expectations up front and don't promise to act on every piece of feedback. Instead show that you have considered every piece of feedback and are willing to communicate transparently about why you do or do not plan to act on it.

Tip

Be careful when asking for help; make sure you plan to actually do something with the suggested ideas from your brand community and that you communicate that plan clearly, updating community members often on your progress.

- **The organization doesn't follow through on a promise made to the brand community**—One of the worst mistakes an organization can make is to renege on a promise made to the brand community. The loss of trust caused by a broken promise is almost impossible to repair. It is better to not make a promise at all if there is any threat that the organization will not be able to follow through.

> If you aren't confident the brand can follow through on a promise, don't make it at all.

- **The organization communicates poorly or inconsistently with the brand community**—One of the reasons recruiting brand ambassadors to join individual groups within the brand community is so important is because of the necessity of not just communicating well, but communicating often. Organizations with just a few solitary points of official communication (like the CEO, PR team, and a handful of executives) will be unlikely to be able to communicate regularly enough to satisfy members of all but the most passive brand communities. Lack of consistent communication leads to even larger issues. Community members might begin to misinterpret the organization's motives or interpret silence as apathy or arrogance. The quality of the communication is as crucial as the quantity. This is why it is especially important to recruit brand ambassadors who understand the communities they are working with well, have built deep relationships based on trust, and communicate honestly and openly. Maintaining the right tone is also critical. Brand ambassadors often need high emotional intelligence to be successful.

- **The organization hides crucial information from the brand community**—Another way trust between an organization and the brand community can be damaged is when the organization hides important information. If this information impacts the brand community in a negative way, community members will want to know why they were not informed earlier. In the worst cases, community members might even feel betrayed by the organization.

- **A larger change or crisis impacts the organization, the brand community, or both**—Sometimes, through no fault of the organization, its ambassadors, or the brand community, a crisis emerges that throws everything into chaos. This can be caused by the emergence of a new disruptive force or organization that changes everything. It can be caused by a social or political impact beyond the organization's control (like a new law or a war); it might even be caused by a natural disaster (like a hurricane or an earthquake). When a crisis emerges that impacts both the organization and the brand community, great communication is more important than ever. Often, these crises end up being extremely positive galvanizing events for the brand community and can be opportunities for you to work closely with members of the internal and external brand community to bring the crisis to closure, combining their ideas and your own.

- **There is intense disagreement within the brand community**—Sometimes relationships within the brand community become strained based on disagreements over priorities, competing interests, or other outside forces. Often, the organization has little control over these disagreements, but it can sometimes play a positive peacemaker role and help bring competing groups closer together.

> A crisis can be an extremely positive galvanizing event for a brand community if it is handled well.

- **A competitor develops a more compelling or interesting story that members of the brand community find attractive**—Sometimes a disruptive new player emerges with a value proposition that is even more appealing. This is one of the places where having a strong relationship with your brand community can help. Often a passionate brand community will stick with a brand and might even help the organization create a more compelling and competitive value proposition.

HANDLING A CRISIS EXAMPLE #1:
ENVICLEAN DRY CLEANERS

One day you receive a call you hoped you'd never get. One of your dry cleaning shops has just been robbed. During the robbery, one employee and two customers were shot. The store manager who calls you to break the news is inconsolable, and you turn on the television to find new crews are already on the scene, reporting on the tragedy.

Fortunately, all three victims end up recovering, but the mental toll on your organization, your customers, and the community is high. You organize an emergency meeting of your EnviClean community council, bringing together people from inside and outside your organization to come up with ideas for how to help the healing process.

During this meeting, one of your employees suggests that the brand mantra Everyday World Cleaning shouldn't just apply to keeping the environment clean, but to keeping the *social* environment clean as well. The group begins to brainstorm ways that EnviClean can help "clean up" crime in the communities in which the shops are located. It quickly becomes apparent that fighting crime is well beyond the scope and resources of what the group can do alone.

Eventually one customer tells a story of how he formed a neighborhood watch group in his community and wonders if there are similar groups in many other communities near EnviClean shops. After some investigation, you find that there are already active neighborhood watch programs near about half of your shops. Your team decides that at least one employee from each of your shops will join the neighborhood watch team nearest them, attending regular meetings and occasionally offering up small donations and meeting space to aid neighborhood watch organizing efforts.

But a regular customer of the shop where the robbery took place has perhaps the best idea of all. The neighborhood in which that shop is located had no neighborhood watch program at all. This customer asks if EnviClean would be willing to help start a new watch program from scratch for this shell-shocked community. You reply that there is nothing EnviClean would rather do.

The healing process has begun.

Recovering from Crisis

When any of the previous situations occur, it is important for an ad-free brand to move quickly to minimize the damage. Any of these crises can quickly escalate and turn into much more complex, hard-to-solve problems.

Following these tips should help you rebound quickly and maybe even emerge from crisis with a brand stronger than it was before:

- **Communicate early and often**—When a crisis happens, ad-free brands should attempt to alert their brand communities as quickly as possible. If, for example, the organization makes a decision to raise prices, it is better to let community members hear directly from you rather than discovering the higher prices on their own. The advantage of proactively communicating bad news directly is that it allows you to fully explain the reason for the change rather than have community members begin to form their own (sometimes erroneous) stories about why a change was made. Remember the John Lilly quote: "Surprise is the opposite of engagement."

> It is better to let community members hear negative news directly from you than to let them hear it elsewhere.

- **Engage in dialog**—But it is not enough to simply broadcast information about an emerging crisis. Ad-free brands should engage in dialogue with community members. Social media tools like those discussed in the previous chapter are great ways to conduct ongoing dialogue with community members. Being responsive on Twitter and Facebook and replying to comments on blog posts are all great ways to engage.

- **Default to open**—A relationship built on trust requires openness. Where most traditional organizations keep information hidden by default and choose what information to share, ad-free brands are as transparent as possible, making decisions about what information they cannot share. They are open by default, rather than closed.

- **Apologize or admit fault when necessary**—When they've made a mistake or done something that negatively affects the brand community, ad-free brands say they are sorry. Community members will often respect and accept a decision that they don't like upon receiving a simple acknowledgement of their pain. This doesn't mean you have to change the decision; you just need to acknowledge or apologize for its consequences.

- **Ask for help and ideas**—Ad-free brands in crisis don't try to solve their problems in isolation. In fact, they openly request help and ideas from members of the brand community. In the case of a crisis affecting both the organization and the community, the crisis might end up being a galvanizing event that brings the brand community closer together.

- **Report progress**—When good things begin to happen, when progress in resolving the crisis is made, shout it from the rooftops. It is important that the entire brand community quickly sees signs of positive progress. This can create momentum that will help resolve the problem even more quickly.

The Bounce-Back Effect

In my view, one of the most important measurements of how successful you've been at creating a strong brand community is how quickly the brand can bounce back from a crisis.

If your relationships with members of the brand community are based on trust and respect developed over a long period of time, you'll be able to bounce back quickly. The very strongest brand communities might be able to avoid crisis entirely if trust is so deep that community members begin by assuming the best rather than the worst.

Measuring the amount of time your brand takes to recover from crisis and the depth of anger or resentment caused by it are two good ways to test the health of your brand community.

HANDLING A CRISIS EXAMPLE #2: BUBBAPOP SODA COMPANY

The numbers are clear. Even though you know there is a small, vocal group of people who absolutely love grape-flavored BubbaPop, you just can't seem to sell it in large enough quantities to make a profit. Your CFO is telling you that production of Grape BubbaPop will stop at the end of the year.

Believe it or not, a group of Grape BubbaPop aficionados have their own website. Members have posted videos extolling their love of BubbaPop. They have conversations on the online forum. In one recent post, a fan posted a hilarious story about a BubbaPop "bender" from which he'd recently recovered.

You know these passionate folks are going to be upset when they hear the news. Fortunately, one of your brand ambassadors is keeping tabs on the fan website—in fact, he recently posted a video of his own. You ask him to gently break the news about the demise of Grape BubbaPop, but not to stop there.

Basically, your brand ambassador lays out the honest truth. He explains to the community members that the current sales numbers can't sustain production of Grape BubbaPop beyond the end of the year. But, he promises, if the group has ideas that can help get sales up by the end of October, BubbaPop management will keep production going while the long-term prospects are analyzed.

The community members are devastated by the news. But they don't take it lying down. Soon, the online forum is flooded with ideas on how to improve sales. The ideas are fantastic and creative.

Ultimately, one fan creates his own "Save Grape BubbaPop" video and posts it on YouTube. The piece is over the top and is watched by 100,000 people during the first week alone. You begin to promote this fan's video through your own social media channels, and before long, the video has received almost one million pageviews. Meanwhile, on Facebook, a group of Grape BubbaPop aficionados who saw the video have created a "Save Grape BubbaPop" fan page, which is quickly joined by 10,000 people.

You see comments on the fan page from people who'd never tried Grape BubbaPop before but are now extolling its virtues. You personally thank each person who makes a positive comment. One of your team members suggests that perhaps you begin to capture the stories of some of the people who've joined what has now become the "Save Grape BubbaPop" movement. The team produces some inexpensive videos highlighting these people and the great ideas they've come up with under the title "Heroes of BubbaPop." This exposure encourages even more people to share their stories.

By the time the end of October rolls around, not only has the CFO made the decision to save Grape BubbaPop, it has become the star of his next investor call. And the community wins, too because their Grape BubbaPop lifeline remains open.

That's a Wrap

You now have all the basic tools and information you need to create an ad-free brand of your own. In the final chapter, I try to answer some remaining questions and offer some of my ideas on where ad-free brands should go next.

8

Some Final Thoughts

I hope I have given you a clear sense of how to build a healthy ad-free brand by combining simple, timeless brand positioning principles with new ways of engaging with communities born out of the open source movement.

You've probably seen many familiar ideas within these pages, including uses of social media and other digital strategies that you might already be testing in your own organization. But perhaps you can now organize and think about them in a new way.

In 2010, I left Red Hat after spending a full decade building an ad-free brand from scratch. I love Red Hat and still consider myself a loyal member of the Red Hat brand community. But, along with some of my best friends in the world, I saw an opportunity to apply many of the brand, culture, and community-building principles I learned from the open source movement. We believed strongly that these principles could help organizations of any size in any industry become better, faster.

Our company, New Kind, was born.

Over the past two years, I've been hard at work at New Kind applying these principles in organizations well beyond the technology industry, from banks to governments, nonprofits to accounting firms. Based on my New Kind experience, I'm very optimistic about the potential for the ad-free brand philosophy to help organizations in a wide array of settings.

While I've narrowed the aperture here to looking at strategy through just a brand lens, some of these ad-free concepts can be extended more broadly in the organization as well. Over these final pages, I'd like to answer some questions and share ideas on where you might consider taking your ad-free approach even further.

Can Traditional Marketing Co-Exist with an Ad-Free Brand Approach?

I have not spent much time discussing the nuts and bolts of traditional marketing. But does that mean you should immediately cease all your current marketing activities and replace them with those you see in these pages?

Absolutely not.

While you are in the process of building a strong ad-free brand community, you'll need to continue many of the traditional activities that drive leads, sales, or donors to your cause. Keep the cash register ringing while you simultaneously invest for the future.

> ✉ *Note*
>
> While building a strong ad-free brand community, you'll need to continue many of the traditional activities that drive leads, sales, or donors to your cause.

I suggest you begin to change the way you operate using a "build peninsulas, not islands" approach like the one I described in Chapter 7. Start by taking a small percentage of the highest-cost, lowest-value segment of your marketing budget (perhaps including traditional advertising) and use it instead to test some of these ad-free brand concepts. If you see success, try a little bit more.

Over time, you might be able to eliminate some of these traditional expenses altogether. Some marketing programs you'll choose to continue, but maybe the thinking behind them and the way they're executed will change.

For example, you might want to continue spending money attending trade shows because you are confident that these are great places for you to get new customer leads. But your interactions with people at these events may completely change because of your new ad-free thinking.

Rather than simply hosting talks where you try to pitch your products, perhaps you use your booth space to host a meet-up for people interested in solving a problem shared by many in your brand community. Or you could offer slots on the presentation calendar to some of your customers or partners who are doing interesting things you think others will want to hear about. Or, rather than giving away t-shirts to people who swipe their badges, you might offer to make a small donation in the name of each person to a cause that's important to the brand community.

I believe brand-building and traditional marketing efforts must be tightly integrated. If the official stories from the public relations and product marketing folks don't match the stories being told by your ad-free brand advocates, your brand community won't hear an orchestra; they'll just hear noise. And probably tune it out.

At its best, the ad-free approach becomes a philosophical point of view that permeates marketing, PR, and advertising efforts and results in an open culture inside and around the organization built on trust and respect—of the community, not above the community.

How Do Organizations Need to Change to Support an Ad-Free Approach?

I believe we are still at the very beginning of a fundamental shift in how our organizations operate. Perhaps no one has done a better job articulating this coming shift than management guru Gary Hamel.

In his book *The Future of Management*, Hamel makes the case that *management* is the technology of human accomplishment. Further, he says that management as a technology was created to help make organizations work better. Yet the technology of management was developed during the late nineteenth and early twentieth centuries and has changed little since that time. Meanwhile, our organizations operate in a social and political landscape very different from the ones innovators were faced with during the Industrial Age.

His theory? The technology of management needs to be reinvented for the modern world.

In *The Future of Management*, Hamel shares a few case studies of companies that have already made fundamental shifts to their management models and, because of these changes, are better equipped to compete.

Many of the strategies used by the organizations featured in Hamel's book are similar to strategies I've seen employed with effective results in the open source world. Hamel also covers the importance of having a purpose beyond making money, strategies for enabling communities of passion, natural and flexible organizational hierarchies, meritocracy, and rapid prototyping—all characteristics of open source communities.

AD-FREE BRAND HEROES PART 7: GARY HAMEL

Gary Hamel, who was named by the *Wall Street Journal* as the world's most innovative business thinker, is the author of some of my favorite management books and articles, including his most recent book *The Future of Management*, which I recommend highly.

But if you really want to learn more about the future of management, including ways you can change your own organization to better position it for ad-free brand success, consider joining his online community, the Management Innovation Exchange (MIX), at www.hackmanagement.com, where some of the world's leading management thinkers gather with folks like you and me who are trying new and innovative ideas within their organizations.

I joined the MIX community in 2010 and now contribute as the MIX Community Guide, where I have the opportunity to work closely with a group of very smart theorists and practitioners who are passionate about reinventing management.

Here's an example: during my time at Red Hat, we tried one management experiment I believe is an interesting one for ad-free brands to consider. We merged the brand and human resources functions together into a new group called People & Brand.

This change made it much easier to be successful with some of the internal rollout techniques I described in Chapter 5, including modifying the hiring, orientation, and performance review process and making internal communications a more strategic role within the organization. Although this combination of human resources and brand might not make sense for every organization, I have no doubt that a closer connection between the functions impacting organizational culture can make an enormous difference quickly.

You might want to consider other organizational changes that make it easier for employees to work closely with members of the external brand community. Perhaps consider organizing all your internal brand ambassadors so they are communicating with each other on a regular basis.

If you are hesitant to make permanent changes, consider creating organizational "speed dating" activities where parts of the organization that rarely collaborate begin working closely together for a week or even a month. This can be a great way to build more collaborative cross-functional relationships within the organization.

Or consider deploying an internal collaboration platform that reduces the importance of the org chart and increases employees' ability to reorganize themselves quickly to tackle opportunities or issues. There is a fascinating array of emerging technologies and strategies for connecting and managing people within organizations. So many in fact that this could be the subject of another book altogether. Stay tuned.

Does your organizational structure need to change in order to see ad-free brand success? No. But making some cultural changes can often help.

What Is the Role of Core Ideology?

I've hinted at the importance of core ideology—the purpose and values of an organization—as a key driver in the success of an ad-free brand approach. The most successful ad-free brands are backed by a deeply held purpose or mission.

> The most successful ad-free brands are backed by a deeply held purpose or mission.

Many of you who work with larger brands might not have the opportunity to develop and articulate the core ideology of your organization. In some cases you must do your best to align the brand to the core ideology that already exists, or, in rarer cases, you might have opportunities to impact the expression of the core ideology.

Those of you who are in leadership roles or are otherwise well positioned to explore opportunities to uncover, modify, or simply improve the articulation of the core ideology of the organization will have a huge advantage in building an ad-free brand.

If you plan to run a project to define or improve the core ideology of your organization, I recommend reading *Built to Last* by Jim Collins and Jerry Porras and *Good to Great* by Jim Collins and employing the strategies they suggest (we did this with great success at Red Hat).

But even if you don't have those opportunities, you'll likely find the more closely your brand positioning is aligned with the organization's core ideology and the more this core ideology is aligned with the worldview of members of your brand community, the more successful you will be with your ad-free brand.

Why Your Human Resources Folks Will Love the Ad-Free Brand Approach

In my experience, ad-free brands have an advantage when it comes to recruiting and retaining employees. Because your organization embraces a more open, collaborative culture and because the inner workings of the organization are thus more visible to the outside world, it is often easier for people to see what it is like to work there.

This open, collaborative organizational approach is also more appealing to a young generation of new employees who have grown up in an atmosphere of greater openness and collaboration thanks to the impact of the Internet and social media. Given the choice between staying with an open, collaborative organizational culture and moving into a more traditional, hierarchical command and control culture, in my experience most young folks seem to vastly prefer the former.

In addition, because most ad-free brands have a deeply held mission or purpose, if that mission is one that many people are passionate about, the opportunity to help achieve that mission can be even more important than other organizational incentives like high salary, stock options, and benefits.

Finally, every rollout project you work on with members of your external brand community is an opportunity for you to meet and work with a group of potential new employees. These projects give community members a chance to test-drive working with your organization, while also giving you a chance to evaluate and get to know the skills and talents of members of the brand community.

At Red Hat, our engineering group was often able to identify the best candidates for full-time positions by looking at the work of people who were already contributing code as members of the open source community. In many cases the best and brightest leaders in the open source communities with which Red Hat worked eventually were able to parlay this work into full-time positions with Red Hat.

In this exchange, everyone would win. The company took a much smaller risk because it already knew well the work of the engineers and knew they had good real-world experience and training from their community work. For the employees, they came to Red Hat well prepared to understand their role and they had pre-existing relationships with those with whom they'd be working.

How Do You Measure the Value of an Ad-Free Brand?

For some reason, when people ask me questions about return on investment (ROI) of ad-free brand efforts, it makes me cringe. It's not that asking about ROI is necessarily a bad question; it's that most traditional measurements of ROI are incapable of accurately assessing the value of ad-free brand investments. Dark matter matters, even if it doesn't show up in a spreadsheet.

At Red Hat, I spent quite a bit of time thinking about ways to measure or prove the impact of our work building the brand and brand community, even as the company was growing quickly and seeing great success.

Even though the company didn't get to be its size because of brand alone—great products and great timing had a lot to do with it—I believe the consistent way we built the brand using many of the techniques I covered in this book over a period of years had an impact.

A few years ago, an analyst at Piper Jaffray named Mark Murphy wrote a research report about Red Hat in which he raised his price target for the company. Of the reasons he gave, three stood out for me: superior brand recognition, unique vision and culture, and ability to hire superior employee talent.[1]

I believe these three things—brand recognition, unique vision and culture, and our ability to attract great talent—were all directly related to the strategy we used to build the brand and the consistency with which we applied it over a long period of time.

My point? Brand measurements tend to be most meaningful when viewed at the broadest levels over the longest timeframes, and they become less accurate in deeper dives and shorter timeframes. I've sometimes struggled to give meaningful measurements of brand, culture, and community over weeks and months, but progress could easily be seen in years.

In the case of Red Hat, our most accurate metric of brand success was growing a small company with one office in Durham, North Carolina, into a global company with almost $1 billion in annual revenues. Mark Murphy's report said it all: the value of the company had risen significantly, in his mind due in no small part to the relatively intangible dark matter of brand, community, and culture.

And that is a pretty good way to make the intangible, well, tangible.

The lesson here is to try to help your organization relax a bit when it comes to short-term, detailed ROI measurements of brand, culture, and community-related efforts. Rely on both hard and soft data and, above all, just because you can't prove success with hard data, don't assume you haven't been successful until you take a step back and inspect your work from the broadest possible view.

---

1. While Murphy's report is not publicly available, you can learn more about his work here:
   http://www.piperjaffray.com/1col.aspx?id=7&analystid=516&title=Analyst%20Information%20for%2
   0Mark%20Murphy

Your broadest view might look something like this:

- Has shareholder value improved significantly since our ad-free brand efforts began?

- Have we created value for the communities we serve?

- Are we closer to achieving our core mission or purpose?

As your perspective widens, the answers might look much better than you thought.

What Are Some of Today's Most Successful Ad-Free Brands?

A look at the 2010 Interbrand list of the best global brands[2] reveals only a few I would classify as having strong ad-free brand DNA. Number 4 on the list is Google, which ironically enough, is probably an ad-free brand itself, although almost all of its revenues are derived from selling online advertising.

Even though they each occasionally advertise, other organizations on the list showing many ad-free brand traits include Amazon.com, eBay, Harley-Davidson, and Starbucks. The first two are organizations that have grown up in a digital world and have strong relationships and ongoing dialogue with their brand communities. The last two understood the power of a mission-based, community-driven branding strategy before Red Hat was a glimmer in co-founder Bob Young's eye.

Beyond that, the Interbrand list includes a host of traditional brands executing community-based brand strategies while still investing heavily in advertising. Some notable examples include IBM, GE, Coca-Cola, Nike, Apple, Cisco, and Pepsi.

But there is a new class of twenty-first-century brands emerging. They are the future denizens of top global brands lists, many of which were founded by people who barely remember a world without the Internet. Facebook, Twitter, Wikipedia, TED, Mozilla/Firefox, and Craigslist are just a few community-centered brands that have radically changed the world as we know it.

The non-corporate world has seen its share of organizations that have embraced many of these ad-free brand concepts. The Democratic Party in the United States won the 2008 presidential election on the back of simple, solid positioning and a community-based approach. Its success set the standard for how almost every successful political campaign has been run since.

And perhaps no type of organization has seen greater success moving from advertising to ad-free strategies than nonprofits. During the recent downturn, community-based fundraising efforts have provided a much-needed lifeline.

---

2. http://www.interbrand.com/en/best-global-brands/best-global-brands-2008/best-global-brands-2010.asp

But the biggest area of growth in ad-free brands over the next 10–15 years will likely come from small- and medium-sized organizations for which advertising-based strategies are not a cost-effective option. An ad-free brand approach will help these organizations save money and innovate faster, all while helping them become good citizens within their brand communities.

How Do You Sell the Ad-Free Brand Approach to Your Executive Team?

In summary, let me offer some ideas on how you might sell the ad-free brand approach to your executive team. In the simplest possible terms, why should they consider this approach? Here are five key benefits:

1. **Save money**—Over time, ad-free brands can eliminate many expenses related to traditional advertising and PR. In addition, many ad-free brands can save money on research and development and avoid making costly mistakes by working closely with an external community of people passionate about the brand.

2. **Improve resilience**—Ad-free brands having deep, trusting relationships with their brand communities can often weather crises that would devastate other brands. Because members of these brand communities often care deeply about the brand, they may even offer to help solve problems or recover from the crisis.

3. **Increase preference**—Members of passionate, trusting brand communities are often more likely to consider new offerings from your organization over those of your competitors. They often participate in projects or activities where they put some skin in the game, making them less likely to defect to a competitor.

4. **Innovate faster**—Because new ideas can come from anywhere, inside and around the organization, ad-free brands are often able to innovate smarter and more quickly.

5. **Recruit and retain top talent**—Ad-free brands can, in many cases, be more interesting and meaningful places to work, especially for a younger generation of workers that has grown up with the Internet and social media.

The bottom line of all these benefits I've listed? If you are a for-profit company, this might mean that your products and services can command a premium in the marketplace. If you are a non-corporate entity, the increased value of the brand may mean that you can have a greater impact or attract more volunteers, partners, or donors to your cause.

Ultimately, your brand will be worth more.

Let's Make This a Conversation

I really appreciate the time you have taken to read what I have written here.

Thank you.

If I have sparked any ideas, or if you'd like to ask any further questions about the ideas I've shared within these pages, I'd love to connect with you.

You can find me in any number of ways:

My email address is chris@newkind.com, and you can visit my company's website at www.newkind.com. Yes, we are available to help.

I spend a lot of time on Twitter. Please reach out to me anytime: @cdgrams

I blog regularly. You can find my posts on my own blog by visiting www.darkmattermatters.com.

I also blog regularly for the business channel of opensource.com: www.opensource.com/business.

I spend a lot of time hanging out at the Management Innovation Exchange (www.hackmanagement.com) where I am the MIX Community Guide.

But I don't expect people to always come to me. I have ideas, will travel.

As a naturally curious person, I love stumbling upon new communities of folks with whom I share common interests or experiences. So, if you see conversations happening anywhere on the Internet or in person around the world that you think I'd be interested in joining, it'd be an honor if you'd point me to them.

I'm always looking for new ideas, new stories, and new friends.

Again, thank you for investing your time in this book. It means a lot to me.

Acknowledgments

One day last September, I received an interesting email out of the blue from someone named Lisa who had stumbled across a blog post of mine. She asked me whether I had ever lived in Indiana as a child.

I was born in West Lafayette, Indiana.

As it turns out, Lisa was my neighbor and childhood best friend. I moved to Kansas City, Missouri, at age 5 and had lost touch with her until I received this email, almost 35 years later.

As Lisa and I caught up, we learned we each had book publishing in the blood. Lisa is a senior publicist at Pearson in Indianapolis. I spent the first five years of my career as a literary agent and editor.

In one email to her, I mentioned that I had been thinking of going back to my publishing roots and actually writing a book of my own. Lisa introduced me to Rick Kughen, an executive editor at Pearson. One thing led to another, and before I knew it, I was writing.

So I'd like to thank my childhood friend and current publicist, Lisa Jacobson-Brown, without whom this book would probably still be something I was thinking about doing... eventually. I'd also to thank Rick Kughen, a true writer's editor—responsive, thoughtful, and with a hint of poetry to his own words.

I've benefitted from the wisdom and friendship of many wonderful people along the journey.

Thanks first to Maggie, my source of energy. This book would have never been possible without you.

Thanks to my mother and father, who I hope see parts of themselves in me and in this book.

Thanks to my sister, Erika, who has been a great friend and confidant ever since she quit telling on me.

To Matthew Szulik, my mentor and friend, for letting the best ideas win. To Jonathan Opp for helping me find a voice. To David Burney, for opening my eyes and making me a designer. To Matt Muñoz, for always bringing optimism and passion.

To Jeff Mackanic, for your friendship and for quietly, consistently making everything happen. To Rebecca Fernandez, for bringing value before words. To DeLisa Alexander, for your faith and friendship.

To Tom Rabon and Elizabeth Hipps, for making each day at New Kind better than the last.

To all of my friends from the Red Hat nation, past and present, around the world. Special thanks to the Red Hat Brand Communications + Design team, a group of the most talented folks I've had the opportunity to work alongside.

To Kevin Keller, for your wise advice, guidance, and contributions.

To Michele Zanini, Polly LaBarre, Gary Hamel, and the team at the Management

Innovation Exchange for introducing me to a new set of friends.

To Bob Young, Lisa Sullivan, Michael Tiemann, and Donnie Barnes, who were open when open wasn't cool. To Greg DeKoenigsberg, Jeremy Hogan, Chris Blizzard, Paul Frields, and Max Spevack, who know more about inspiring communities than I ever will.

To Kevin Trapani and Dan Moore, for inspiring us to consider a better way.

To Alina Wheeler, Philippe Beaudette, and Jelly Helm, for perspective, at the right time.

To the rest of the Pearson team, especially Seth Kerney, Megan Wade, and Bill Camarda, for all of your hard work bringing this book to life.

And finally, thanks to my other friends who don't give a crap about brands, ad-free or not. You know who you are, and I appreciate everything you do.

Chris Grams

July 15, 2011

A

Sample Documents

Throughout this book, I've referred to sample materials such as surveys and discussion questions that you'd find in the appendix. Well, here they are!

Over the following pages you'll find a set of resources that should help you research, build, and roll out your organization's brand positioning.

Chapter 3: Sample Email Survey

When designing a brand survey for the external world, you'll need to keep things simple. There is a delicate balance here. Ask too many questions, and people will be less likely to finish the survey. But don't ask enough questions, and you can leave a gaping hole in your research that you regret later.

Remember that the purpose of the survey is to get data that helps you answer the following four questions:

1. What does your brand community currently believe about or value in the brand?

2. What might your brand community believe or value about the brand in the future?

3. What does your organization currently claim about the brand?

4. What would your organization like the brand to become down the road?

You'll be able to get information from an external email survey that directly informs the answers to the first two questions, and you'll even be able to collect data that tells you how your answers to the last two questions are resonating or might resonate in the future.

Introduction: Making the Pitch

Start your email with a direct, to-the-point subject line and a clear ask. Here is a sample you can use as a starting point.

> Subject: We'd like to hear what you think about [brand].

> Over the past few months, we've been thinking about the future of [brand] and would love to incorporate your feedback and ideas.

If you have the information, consider also adding a sentence here that acknowledges their relationship with the brand—for example, customer, partner, and so on.

> The link below leads to a short survey that will take no more than five minutes of your time. We look forward to hearing what you think.

> [insert survey link here]

The Survey

In designing your survey, you'll need to keep it as short as possible. I recommend 8–10 questions as a good target length. Under each subject area, I've listed a few sample questions that can help you get the information you need.

Who is this person, and what is his or her relationship with the brand?

Sample questions:

1. Have you purchased a product from [brand] in the past year?

   ❑ Yes

   ❑ No

This question informs whether this is an actual customer, which can be an important distinction for commercial brands.

2. What is the most recent time you shopped in a [brand] store?

   ❑ This week

   ❑ This month

   ❑ This year

   ❑ Longer than this year

   ❑ Never

This question informs whether this person has had a first-person brand experience prior to filling out the survey.

3.   What is your current occupation?

[choose list relevant to your community]

This question gives you demographic information about the person filling out the survey.

Other common demographic questions include organization type, industry, age, sex, and income. But you might choose to explore very different demographics, depending on the competitive frame of reference in which your brand competes. Choose your demographic questions carefully because these often provide a strong basis for profiling your brand community.

What is the depth of this person's relationship with the brand?

Sample questions:

1.   On a scale of 1–10, how likely would you be to recommend [brand] to a friend (10 meaning "extremely likely" and 1 meaning "extremely unlikely")?

This is probably the best question I've encountered for determining how strongly someone feels about a brand. Often this question is used as the basis of a Net Promoter score.[1]

2.   On a scale of 1–5 with 5 meaning "extremely close" and 1 meaning "not at all close", how close do you feel like the [worldview] of [brand] is to your own?

You can replace *worldview* with a number of other words and phrases here (for example, you might consider *spirit, mission,* and *values* as replacements). This question can reveal some interesting data showing how well the brand resonates with the brand community.

What is this person's current perception of the brand?

Sample questions:

1.   [Brand] = _____ .

The "blank line" question is probably my overall favorite question because it makes people immediately think of the first thing that comes to mind when they think of the brand. This question is especially useful for finding key points of difference.

---

1. To learn more about the Net Promoter metric, start at the Net Promoter Wikipedia page here: http://en.wikipedia.org/wiki/Net_Promoter

It is similar to the approach used by the Brand Tags website (www.brandtags.net) to build a tag cloud of all the concepts people associate with a brand. Consider developing a tag cloud with the answers you get to this question, and you'll be able to quickly visualize what the brand community thinks your brand stands for.

2. Which of the following [concepts/products/services] do you associate most closely with [brand]?

    [choose list relevant for your community]

This is another valuable question, although I like it less than the previous one because the list can influence people's thinking and may cause respondents to read something into your line of questioning and tell you what they think you want to hear.

You might want to ask a few different questions like this to test the strength of different pieces of your current positioning and your competitive frame of reference. For example, you might want to test product categories (for example, cleaning products, soap products, and dishwashing products), service categories (for example, restaurants, Mexican restaurants, and taco stands), or even broader concepts people might associate with your brand (for example, freedom, trust, and reliability).

What does this person currently value about the brand, and what might he value in the future?

Sample questions:

1. What [is/are] the most [valuable/useful] thing[s] about [brand]?

This can be asked as an open-ended question, a drop-down list, or a series of check boxes. As an open-ended question, you'll get the broadest range of answers and might uncover something you had not considered before. You'll be able to analyze the data better if you have a predetermined list from which to choose, but you'll lose some of the richness of the ideas.

Also, with an open-ended question or a drop-down list, people will only be able to choose their top answer. If you'd like to see multiple characteristics from each person, you might want to use a series of check boxes instead.

If your survey is small, I'd lean toward to the open-ended option, but if you expect hundreds or thousands of responses, the other two options can give you more flexibility in analyzing the data.

2. <u>What do you think is the biggest [opportunity/threat] [for/to] [brand]
   in [timeframe]?</u>

This question will give you some data showing what people might value in the
brand in the future. If you choose the "threat" option, you might also get some good
ideas for aspirational points of parity to consider.

Again, you can consider whether to make this an open-ended question, a drop-
down list, or a series of check boxes.

Call to Further Engagement

Don't forget that an email survey is a perfect place to recruit people who might be
interested in playing a deeper ongoing role in the development of the brand. I suggest ending your survey with a question like this one:

1. <u>Would you be interested in participating in future conversations about
   [brand] with us?</u>

End by thanking people for their time. Don't forget to include a way for people to
opt out of future emails.

Chapter 3: Sample Employee Survey

The same rules apply for surveying your own employees that apply to an external survey—the simpler the survey is, the more responses you'll likely get. If you want to collect the most honest, accurate information, you might need to give people the option to make their answers confidential.

But don't make the survey totally anonymous by default—if you do, you'll lose the opportunity to connect with people who might make great candidates for your internal and external rollout teams.

You might also want to consider combining your internal employee brand survey with other employee engagement surveys already being run within your organization, so they become regular annual or biannual activities giving you ongoing data points you can use to measure progress over time. Combining multiple internal surveys into one can often reduce survey fatigue and increase response rates in organizations that survey employees regularly fill out.

Demographic Questions

Just as in the external survey, you should begin with some demographic questions that help you determine who is filling out the survey. Common demographic questions include

- Length of tenure with organization
- Geographic location
- Department, division, or group within organization
- Job level (for example, associate, manager, senior manager, or executive)

Repeat External Survey Questions

If you have done an external survey like the one here in the appendix, you'll need to repeat many of the same questions, asked the same way, for the internal audience.

Asking the same questions the same way will allow you to test the differences between how your organization views itself and how it is viewed by the community. I've found these differences to be some of the most enlightening, often illuminating organizational blind spots.

If you have not already designed an external survey, develop your questions using the hints provided in the Sample Email Survey section of the appendix.

Additional Employee Questions

You might want to ask one or two additional questions to get a sense for how passionate employees are about the brand. In their surveys of employee engagement, Gallup has found that perhaps one of the strongest indicators of engagement is found in whether people report that they have a best friend at work.[2]

There are many other questions to consider that can help you better understand how passionate employees are about the organization. Some examples include

1. On a scale of 1–5, where 5 means "clearly understand" and 1 means "don't understand at all," how well do you understand the [mission/purpose] of [organization]?

2. On a scale of 1–5, where 5 means "fully support" and 1 means "don't support at all," how much do you support the [mission/purpose] of [organization]?

3. On a scale of 1–5, where 5 means "contribute regularly" and 1 means "don't contribute at all," how much do you feel that you contribute to the [mission/purpose] of [organization]?

4. On a scale of 1–10, where 10 means "extremely likely" and 1 means "extremely unlikely," how likely would you be to recommend working at [organization] to a friend?

Some of these questions might already be asked on existing employee engagement surveys. If so, consider using the data from those surveys rather than asking again to avoid overlap and confusion among employees.

Call to Further Engagement

End your employee survey by explaining how you plan to use the information (perhaps even going into some detail about the brand positioning project itself), and be sure to ask whether the employee would like to get more involved in the positioning project. This is one of the best ways to recruit a diverse group of people to the internal and external rollout teams.

---

2. Learn more about this question and Gallup's Q[12] approach here: http://www.gallup.com/consulting/52/Employee-Engagement.asp

Chapter 3: Internal Brand Conversation Discussion Questions

Often, many of the questions you are asking in internal and external surveys provide a good starting point for an internal discussion about the brand. But the discussion gives you the opportunity to go much deeper and understand some of the thoughts, data, and experiences behind these answers.

If you have already done an internal or external survey, consider starting (or ending) the discussion with a brief overview of the results. Make sure to write down everyone's ideas, ideally on a whiteboard or computer screen that everyone can see.

Here are 10 sample questions you can consider to get the conversation going:

1. [Brand] = _____. (or When you think of [brand] what is the first thing that comes to your mind?)

2. What do you think [brand] stands for?

3. What do you believe [brand community members] think the brand stands for?

4. What do you think represents the biggest opportunity for [brand]?

5. How do you think [brand community members] would answer the question above?

6. Who are the most passionate members of the brand community? What are they passionate about?

7. Who are our most passionate employees? What are they passionate about?

8. What do you believe is the biggest threat to [brand]?

9. How do you think [brand community members] would answer the question above?

10. Where are the biggest gaps between what we say about [brand] and the experience [brand community members] have with the brand today?

Chapter 3: External Conversation Discussion Questions

If you choose to host external brand conversations in addition to internal brand conversations, consider asking similar questions so you can quickly see differences between how the brand is viewed inside and outside the organization.

Also, consider coming out from behind the curtain and showing the results of surveys you've conducted to this external audience as well. By revealing this data (again either before or after the discussion), you'll not only give your brand community members information that will empower them to help you more effectively, but will also be showing them signs of trust and respect.

Here are 10 sample questions:

1. [Brand] = _____. Discuss. (or When you think of [brand] what is the first thing that comes to your mind?)

2. What do you think [brand] stands for?

3. What do you think represents the biggest opportunity for [brand]?

4. Are there things that matter a lot to you that you also believe matter to [brand]? If so, what are they?

5. What do you believe is the biggest threat to [brand]?

6. Do you perceive any gaps between what we say about [brand] and the experience you have today? If so, what are they?

7. What is your favorite thing about [brand]?

8. What do you like least about [brand]?

9. What would you change if you were running [brand]?

10. What would you keep the same if you were running [brand]?

Chapter 3: Checklist of Research Options

Basic Research Options

❑ Website content

_____

_____

❑ Web analytics

_____

_____

❑ Public relations materials

_____

_____

❑ Marketing materials

_____

_____

❑ Corporate online footprint

_____

_____

❑ Brand elements

_____

_____

❑ Existing brand community research

_____

_____

❑ Existing employee research

_____

_____

❑   Executive communications

_____

_____

❑   Media coverage

_____

_____

❑   Customer references

_____

_____

❑   Brand footprint on Web and social media

_____

_____

❑   Existing core ideology

_____

_____

❑   My other basic research

_____

_____

Advanced Research Options

❑   Brand inventory

_____

_____

❑   Email survey

_____

_____

❑   Web survey

_____

_____

❏   Employee survey

_____

_____

❏   External interviews

_____

_____

❏   Internal interviews

_____

_____

❏   Executive conversation

_____

_____

❏   Employee conversation

_____

_____

❏   External conversation

_____

_____

❏   Brand tracking study

_____

_____

❏   New core ideology

_____

_____

Chapter 3: Research Test

Based on their analysis of the research, have each person fill out this survey independently and then come together to compare and discuss your answers.

1. What does your brand community currently believe about or value in the brand?

   _____

   _____

   _____

1a. Now summarize that answer in one concise sentence.

   _____

   _____

1b. What are the five most important words you would associate with this answer?

   _____

   _____

   _____

   _____

   _____

2. What might your brand community believe or value about the brand in the future?

   _____

   _____

   _____

   _____

2a. Now summarize that answer in one concise sentence.

   _____

   _____

2b. What are the five most important words you would associate with this answer?

_____

_____

_____

_____

_____

3. What does your organization currently claim about the brand?

_____

_____

_____

_____

3a. Now summarize that answer in one concise sentence.

_____

_____

3b. What are the five most important words you would associate with this answer?

_____

_____

_____

_____

_____

4. What would your organization like the brand to become down the road?

_____

_____

_____

_____

4a.   Now summarize that answer in one concise sentence.

_____

_____

4b.   What are the five most important words you would associate with this answer?

_____

_____

_____

_____

_____

Chapter 3: Blank Version of Four-Question Chart

Here is a blank version of the four-question chart you can copy and use.

	PRESENT	**FUTURE**
COMMUNITY	What do they believe or value?	What would they believe or value?
ORGANIZATION	What do you currrently claim?	What would you like to become?

Chapter 4: Sample Questionnaire for Testing Brand Positioning

The following sample questionnaire is designed as something you could send via email with a link to a survey. But with a few modifications, you should also be able to use this as the script for a phone or in-person interview as well.

Introduction:

We have been working on a project to better understand what people like about [brand], and we know you answered a survey we sent out recently. We'd like to share some ideas we are considering based on information we learned from this survey and other research.

Would you be willing to help us further by telling us if these ideas resonate with you, or if you have additional thoughts that might help us improve [brand]?"

__ Yes

__ No

If the respondent selects no, thank her for her time and end the survey. If she selects yes, move on to the following questions.

1. In our research, we've found many people like you view [brand's] primary competition as [brands] like [competitor 1], [competitor 2], and [competitor 3]. We view all of these together as [competitive frame of reference]. Does this sound right to you?

__ Yes

__ No

If the respondent selects no, ask this follow-up question. If the respondent selects yes, move on to question 2.

1a. Is there another way you would group these [brands] together instead? What term would you use?

_____

2. Are there any other thoughts or comments you'd like to add?

_____

_____

_____

Next, move on from competitive frame of reference to points of difference.

3. We've learned that one of the things other people like you believe sepa-
    rates [brand] from our competitors is [point of difference]. Do you
    agree with this assessment?

    __ Yes

    __ No

Repeat this question for each point of difference you'd like to test. When you've
asked about each point of difference, ask this follow-up question.

4. Are there any other things I didn't mention that you believe separate
    [brand] from our competitors?

    _____

5. Are there any other thoughts or comments you'd like to add?

    _____

    _____

    _____

Next, move on to points of parity.

6. If you were to consider other [brands] like [brand], would [point of
    parity] be a primary reason?

    Repeat this question for each point of parity you'd like to test. When you've
    asked about each point of parity, ask this follow-up question.

7. Are there any other things I didn't mention that might cause you to
    consider competitors over [brand]?

    _____

8. Are there any other thoughts or comments you'd like to add?

    _____

    _____

    _____

9. Thank you for taking the time to offer your thoughts. Please share any
    final ideas or opinions in the space below. We appreciate your willing-
    ness to help us continue to improve [brand].

    _____

    _____

    _____

Chapter 7: Brand Report Card Template

[Brand] Brand Report Card

Date: _____

Prepared by: _____

Overview

This should be a paragraph highlighting the key brand-related news since the last report card. This paragraph might include some of the most interesting pieces of data collected, important news, changes, or crises occurring since the last report. It might even provide a taste of some of the best information, examples, and stories that will be found in the report. Think of this paragraph as the executive summary.

Highlights and Analysis

- This section should be a set of bullets that go into more detail on some of the things from the overview.

- You might also include key quotes from people inside the organization or in the brand community that really highlight the points you are making.

- Sometimes this is a place to feature current news articles or blog posts that either support the brand positioning or run counter to it.

- It is also a good place to feature members of the brand community or employees who are doing work that supports the positioning.

- You might even try to answer the question "What does it all mean?" in this section.

- By the time a reader finishes this section, he should have a good sense for the current state of the brand, even without reading further detail.

Key Stats

If you have determined a set of data points that you'll be reporting consistently in each report, include them in this section. Some examples of things to include might be important website data, social media activity, results from a brand tracking study, press and blog mentions/sentiment, and so on.

Consider putting these stats in a table that makes them easy to glance at or import charts that show fluctuations over time. Remember the data is not meaningful in a vacuum. Always answer the question "As compared to what?" by showing the stats in the context of data points from previous months, years, or averages.

Stories and Projects

In this section, include a series of short illustrations, stories, or examples of progress toward the positioning since the last report.

You might report on the progress of internal or external rollout projects.

Be sure to always mention the names of the key brand ambassadors, employees, and community members who are helping make these projects successful.

I'm a big fan of putting lots of quotes that illustrate progress directly from emails, blog posts, news articles, Twitter, Facebook, or other places where people discuss the brand. If the comments were made to you in private communications, be sure to ask for permission before including them in the report card.

You might even have visual examples you can show.

If the story, illustration, or example you are highlighting is on the Web, be sure to include a URL.

Social Media Listening Post Data

Consider a deeper dive into social media data. Some items to consider include

- Number of Twitter followers (total followers, increase since last report)
- Number of Twitter mentions (as compared to...)
- Number of Twitter retweets of brand account (as compared to...)
- Top retweets (as compared to...)
- Top followers on Twitter (in terms of their reach or influence)
- Number of fans on Facebook (total fans, increase since last report)
- Number of wall posts on Facebook (number posted, total "likes", total comments)
- Number of LinkedIn followers (total followers, increase since last report)
- Number of discussion comments on LinkedIn (as compared to...)

Other Data

This is where you can take a more extensive look at other data you might be collecting. This section can be very short, or it can be a much deeper look into some of the data from the key stats section.

Recommendations and Actions

I like to end with a set of key recommendations and actions based on everything that has happened since the last report. You can also include the most important recommendations in the overview or highlights section.

B

Bibliography

I've benefitted from the ideas of many great people during the making of this book. Writing is hard work, and it makes you appreciate the hard work of others who have written before you. This text would not be complete without highlighting a few of the books and authors that have provided inspiration to me.

Thank you, thank you, thank you.

Aaker, Jennifer Lynn, Andy Smith, and Carlye Adler. *The Dragonfly Effect: Quick, Effective, and Powerful Ways to Use Social Media to Drive Social Change.* San Francisco: Jossey-Bass, 2010.

Argenti, Paul A. *Digital Strategies for Powerful Corporate Communications.* New York: McGraw-Hill, 2009.

Bacon, Jono. *The Art of Community.* Sebastopol, CA: O'Reilly, 2009.

Bedbury, Scott, and Stephen Fenichell. *A New Brand World: 8 Principles for Achieving Brand Leadership in the 21st Century.* New York: Viking, 2002.

Bennis, Warren G. *On Becoming a Leader.* Reading, MA: Addison-Wesley Publishing Co., 1989.

Brafman, Ori, and Rod A. Beckstrom. *The Starfish and the Spider: The Unstoppable Power of Leaderless Organizations.* New York: Portfolio, 2006.

Brogan, Chris, and Julien Smith. *Trust Agents: Using the Web to Build Influence, Improve Reputation, and Earn Trust.* Hoboken, NJ: John Wiley & Sons, 2009.

Brown, Tim, and Barry Katz. *Change by Design: How Design Thinking Transforms Organizations and Inspires Innovation.* New York: Harper Business, 2009.

Cesvet, Bertrand, Tony Babinski, and Eric Alper. *Conversational Capital: How to Create Stuff People Love to Talk About.* Upper Saddle River, NJ: Financial Times Press, 2009.

Collins, James C. *Good to Great: Why Some Companies Make the Leap—and Others Don't.* Boston: HarperBusiness, 2001.

Collins, James C. *How the Mighty Fall: And Why Some Companies Never Give In.* New York: Jim Collins, 2009.

Collins, James C., and Jerry I. Porras. *Built to Last: Successful Habits of Visionary Companies.* New York: HarperBusiness, 1994.

Duarte, Nancy. *Resonate: Present Visual Stories that Transform Audiences.* Hoboken, NJ: Wiley, 2010.

Earls, Mark. *Herd.* West Sussex, UK: John Wiley & Sons, 2007.

Evans, Liana. *Social Media Marketing: Strategies for Engaging in Facebook, Twitter and Other Social Media.* Indianapolis: Que, 2010.

Fried, Jason, and David Heinemeier Hansson. *Rework.* New York: Crown Business, 2010.

Gilmore, James H., and B. Joseph Pine. *Authenticity: What Consumers Really Want.* Boston: Harvard Business School Press, 2007.

Gladwell, Malcolm. *Blink: The Power of Thinking Without Thinking*. New York: Little, Brown and Co., 2005.

Gladwell, Malcolm. *The Tipping Point: How Little Things Can Make a Big Difference*. Boston: Little, Brown and Co., 2000.

Hamel, Gary. *The Future of Management*. Boston: Harvard Business School Press, 2007.

Haque, Umair. *The New Capitalist Manifesto: Building a Disruptively Better Business*. Boston: Harvard Business Press, 2011.

Heath, Chip, and Dan Heath. *Made to Stick: Why Some Ideas Survive and Others Die*. New York: Random House, 2007.

Heath, Chip, and Dan Heath. *Switch: How to Change Things When Change Is Hard*. New York: Broadway Books, 2010.

Keller, Kevin Lane. *Strategic Brand Management: Building, Measuring, and Managing Brand Equity*. Upper Saddle River, NJ: Pearson/Prentice Hall, 2008.

Kelley, Tom, and Jonathan Littman. *The Ten Faces of Innovation: IDEO's Strategies for Beating the Devil's Advocate and Driving Creativity Throughout Your Organization*. New York: Currency/Doubleday, 2005.

Lencioni, Patrick. *The Five Dysfunctions of a Team: A Leadership Fable*. San Francisco: Jossey-Bass, 2002.

Levine, Rick. *The Cluetrain Manifesto: The End of Business as Usual*. Cambridge: Perseus Books, 2000.

Li, Charlene, and Josh Bernoff. *Groundswell: Winning in a World Transformed by Social Technologies*. Boston: Harvard Business Press, 2008.

Lockwood, Thomas. *Design Thinking: Integrating Innovation, Customer Experience and Brand Value*. New York: Allworth Press, 2010.

Martin, Roger L. *The Design of Business: Why Design Thinking Is the Next Competitive Advantage*. Boston: Harvard Business Press, 2009.

Martin, Roger L. *The Responsibility Virus: How Control Freaks, Shrinking Violets-and the Rest of Us Can Harness the Power of True Partnership*. New York: Basic Books, 2002.

Mooney, Kelly, and Nita Rollins. *The Open Brand: When Push Comes to Pull in a Web-made World*. Berkley, CA: New Riders, 2008.

Neumeier, Marty. *The Brand Gap*. Berkley, CA: New Riders, 2006.

Neumeier, Marty. *The Designful Company: How to Build a Culture of Nonstop Innovation*. Berkley, CA: New Riders, 2009.

Neumeier, Marty. *Zag: The Number-one Strategy of High-performance Brands : A Whiteboard Overview.* Berkley, CA: AIGA, 2007.

Patterson, Kerry. *Influencer: The Power to Change Anything.* New York: McGraw-Hill, 2007.

Peters, Thomas J. *Re-imagine!: Business Excellence in a Disruptive Age.* London: Dorling Kindersley, 2003.

Pink, Daniel H. *Drive: The Surprising Truth About What Motivates Us.* New York: Riverhead Books, 2009.

Pink, Daniel H. *A Whole New Mind: Moving from the Information Age to the Conceptual Age.* New York: Riverhead Books, 2005.

Raymond, Eric S. *The Cathedral and the Bazaar: Musings on Linux and Open Source by an Accidental Revolutionary.* Sebastopol, CA: O'Reilly, 2001.

Ries, Al, and Jack Trout. *The 22 Immutable Laws of Marketing: Violate Them at Your Own Risk.* New York: HarperBusiness, 1993.

Ries, Al, and Jack Trout. *Marketing Warfare.* New York: McGraw-Hill, 1986.

Ries, Al, and Jack Trout. *Positioning the Battle for Your Mind.* New York: McGraw-Hill, 2001.

Roam, Dan. *The Back of the Napkin: Solving Problems and Selling Ideas with Pictures.* New York: Portfolio, 2008.

Scott, David Meerman, Brian Halligan, and Jay Blakesberg. *Marketing Lessons from the Grateful Dead: What Every Business Can Learn from the Most Iconic Band in History.* Hoboken, NJ: Wiley, 2010.

Surowiecki, James. *The Wisdom of Crowds.* New York: Anchor Books, 2005.

Sutton, Robert I. *The No Asshole Rule: Building a Civilized Workplace and Surviving One That Isn't.* New York: Warner Business Books, 2007.

Tapscott, Don, and Anthony D. Williams. *Wikinomics: How Mass Collaboration Changes Everything.* New York: Portfolio, 2006.

Trout, Jack, and Steve Rivkin. *Differentiate or Die: Survival in Our Era of Killer Competition.* New York: Wiley, 2000.

Trout, Jack, and Steve Rivkin. *Repositioning: Marketing in an Era of Competition, Change and Crisis.* New York: McGraw-Hill, 2010.

Twain, Mark. *The Adventures of Tom Sawyer.* London: Chatto & Windus, 1876.

Ury, William. *Getting Past No: Negotiating with Difficult People.* New York: Bantam Books, 1991.

Wheeler, Alina. *Brand Atlas: Branding Intelligence Made Visible.* Hoboken, NJ: Wiley, 2011.

Wheeler, Alina. *Designing Brand Identity: An Essential Guide for the Entire Branding Team.* Hoboken, NJ: John Wiley & Sons, 2009.

Zinni, Anthony C., and Tony Koltz. *Leading the Charge: Leadership Lessons from the Battlefield to the Boardroom.* New York: Palgrave Macmillan, 2009.

Index

C

D

S